D1766709

6/2209314

ALL IN THE COOKING

ALL IN THE COOKING

COLÁISTE MHUIRE BOOK
of
HOUSEHOLD COOKERY

Compiled by
JOSEPHINE B. MARNELL,
NORA M. BREATHNACH,
ANNE A. MARTIN
Diplomées of Irish Training School of Domestic Science ;

MOR MURNAGHAN,
*Diplomée of St. Catherine's Training School of
Domestic Science*

(Staff Teachers, Coláiste Mhuire, Cathal Brugha St., Dublin)

PREFACE BY
KATHLEEN M. O'SULLIVAN, D.I.T.S.
Former Principal of the College

THE O'BRIEN PRESS
DUBLIN

The Educational Company of Ireland

The City of Dublin Vocational
Education Committee have approved
the use of this book, entitled *All in the
Cooking*, as an official Text-book for
all their Schools.

This facsimile edition first published 2015 by
The O'Brien Press Ltd.
12 Terenure Road East, Rathgar, Dublin 6, Ireland.
Tel: +353 1 4923333; Fax: +353 1 4922777
E-mail: books@obrien.ie; Website: www.obrien.ie
and
The Educational Company of Ireland
Ballymount Road, Walkinstown, Dublin 12, Ireland.
Tel: +353 1 4500611; Fax: +353 1 4500993
E-mail: info@edco.ie; Website: www.edco.ie
First published 1946 by Longman, Browne & Nolan.

ISBN: 978-1-84717-787-2

1 3 5 7 9 10 8 6 4 2

15 17 19 20 18 16

Printed and bound in Poland by Białostockie Zakłady Graficzne S.A.

FOREWORD

ALL IN THE COOKING was first published in 1946 as the official textbook of Coláiste Mhuire Cookery School, Cathal Brugha Street, Dublin. It remained in use in schools and colleges throughout Ireland until the 1970s. It was updated and revised regularly, and a second volume, ALL IN THE COOKING BOOK TWO, was released in the 1960s.

We have chosen to reprint the third edition of Book One, which contained updates and additional recipes.

The endurance and widespread popularity of the ALL IN THE COOKING books were always of enormous joy to me and my fellow authors. The Irish diaspora has ensured that they can be found all over the world.

In my 97th year, I, together with my family, am delighted to see ALL IN THE COOKING in print again. I am so pleased to know that traditional Irish preparation and cooking of good food are enjoying renewed admiration, and I hope this book will also be appreciated by a new generation.

Is mise le meas,
ANNE A. BROWNE (NÉE MARTIN),
Co-author of ALL IN THE COOKING,
JUNE 2015

On the following page is ALL IN THE COOKING's original Preface, written by Kathleen M. O'Sullivan, the erstwhile principal of Coláiste Mhuire. Continued happy cooking!

PREFACE

THE primary aim of the compilers of this the first volume of ALL IN THE COOKING is to provide the students of Coláiste Mhuire, in the first instance, and the students of other colleges, schools and classes of Domestic Science, with a book giving a clear explanation of the fundamental principles of cookery. The book is also intended for the busy housewife or the family cook who needs a reliable reference book in which the information she seeks will be readily accessible.

Neither time nor labour was spared in the compilation of the work. The various recipes and explanations contained in it are the result of varied and scientific experience, and have been compiled with minute care and detail. It provides Irish students with a modern text-book and one which will save them the trouble of writing lengthy class notes ; and it will be for the Irish housewife a handy reference book for cookery recipes suited to our own conditions. The public have the further assurance that every recipe has been carefully tested and tried before it was included in the book.

So far the only Cookery Books available to students and to the public in Ireland were, with one or two exceptions, compiled abroad, and while these were quite suitable to the needs of the people for whom they were specially written, they could not be regarded as meeting fully the requirements and tastes of the Irish student or housewife. ALL IN THE COOKING does. It is to be noted that, in addition to recipes, and theory, original charts have been provided to show the practice generally followed in this country in the method of cutting up meat.

The compilers of ALL IN THE COOKING are to be congratulated on making this admirable text-book available for the students not only of this college but for all students of Domestic Economy throughout the country, and for the housewife seeking guidance in matters of modern cookery. They have placed us all under a debt of gratitude.

K. M. O'SULLIVAN, *Former Principal,*

COLÁISTE MHUIRE LE TIGHEAS,

DUBLIN.

CONTENTS

The Kitchen

Much thought should be given to the planning of the kitchen. It is probably the room in which the housewife spends most of her time, yet often it is poorly laid out with a bad arrangement of the various items of equipment. Work tops should be at a comfortable height to suit the housewife — 2 ft. 10 ins. is considered average, but if the housewife is tall 3 ft. would probably be less fatiguing. Constant bending to low tables causes backache and unnecessary fatigue. A kitchen stool of a suitable height is a necessity and the housewife should utilize it as much as possible when working.

Lighting is very important. Good lighting, both natural and artificial, should be available at the stove, sink and work area. When using fluorescent lighting a soft tone is preferable to avoid distortion of colour. Food prepared under harsh light can appear to be a different colour when under the soft light of the dining-room.

Surfaces should be such that they can be cleaned easily; stainless steel and plastic laminated tops are most satisfactory, but the former is noisy. Washable adhesive paper may also be used for covering shelves, etc., and makes for easy cleaning. When planning the general lay-out of the kitchen a sequence pattern should be followed, one process following another in the working area, e.g., work table, sink, work space, cooker, serving top to dining-room.

Adequate power points should be available for the use of an electric kettle, toaster, refrigerator, mixer, blender, coffee grinder, etc. These appliances may not all be available to the young housewife at first, but in later years they will not only be available but will be considered essential.

Storage space for cutlery, equipment and food is required. Drawers are most suitable for the cutlery, and cupboards with shelves for the other equipment. A large house may have a special food pantry which is a great convenience. In a small house a built-in food cupboard with a window or ventilator may be provided but, if not, a food cupboard for dry goods is necessary, and a refrigerator or meat safe for perishables, such as meat, fish, butter, etc. A rack should be provided for vegetables and fruit.

BASIC KITCHEN EQUIPMENT

The following is a list of the equipment which will be required for the average home. It is an economy in the long run to buy good equipment if it can be afforded, and to care it well. Before buying any gadget it is well to ask oneself does it work and do I really need it ?

1–1½ pint saucepan with lid.
2½–3 pint saucepan with lid.
6–8 pint saucepan with lid.
Frying pan approximately 9 inches in diameter.
Kettle.
Steamer with lid — to fit various sizes of saucepans.
Deep-fat frying pan and basket.
Baking tin to fit oven.
Roasting tin to fit oven.
Tray of patty tins (12 in set).
Pair of sandwich tins, 7″ in diameter.
Cake tin, 6″ in diameter.
Cake tin, 8″ in diameter.
Tart plate.
Swiss roll tin.
Bread knife.
Chopping knife, 7″–8″ blade.
Vegetable knife 3″–3½″ blade
Palette knife 7″–8″ blade.
Steel or knife sharpener.
Vegetable peeler.
Tablespoons.
Dessertspoons.
Teaspoons.
Large basting spoon.
Ladle.
Wooden spoons of different sizes.
Fish slice.
Corkscrew.
Egg Beater.
Cook's fork.
Cook's tongs.
Set of skewers.
Scissors.
Apple Corer.
Pastry brush.
Rubber spatula.

Potato masher.
Piping bag.
Eclair and Rose pipes.
One icing set.
Scales.
Tin opener.
Refuse bin.
Storage jars for flour, sugar, cereals, etc.
Bread bin.
Graduated measure.
Colander.
Strainers.
Tea Caddy.
Flour dredger.
Wire cake cooler.
Chopping board.
Pastry board.
Bread board.
Set of Cutters.
Lemon squeezer.
Rolling pin.
Grater.
Sink basket.
Casseroles, 2 or 3 of different sizes.
Pie dishes of various sizes.
Pudding-bowls of various sizes.
Mixing bowls.
Mouli sieve.
Mincer.
Vegetable rack.
Vegetable brush.
Scrubbing brush.
Dish drainer.
Dish cloth.
Wash up mop.
Drying cloths or tea cloths.
Oven cloths.

COOKER—This may be electric, gas, oil or solid fuel. There is a wide range of choice in each. An essential point is to ensure that there is adequate top space and that the oven is large enough to take an average sized joint or turkey.

SINK—Stainless steel is probably the best buy because it is hard-wearing and easy to clean. The draining space should be on the side that is most convenient to allow for easy handling of draining and drying. A level work top should be fitted at the other side of the sink for dirty dishes, vegetable preparation, etc.

Sinks may be bought in single or double units, and if there is adequate space and the cost is not prohibitive, it is a decided advantage to have the second sink for rinsing, washing of vegetables, etc.

A waste disposal unit may be fitted into one sink if desired or, better still, fitted into a small space between two sinks. The sink should not be too large because this is extravagant on water.

REFRIGERATOR—The refrigerator is becoming a household necessity. It can be a great asset in the kitchen. Buy a size adequate for your present and future requirements ; the frozen food section should be large enough to hold a small supply of frozen foods for short periods.

Points to observe in using the Refrigerator.

1. The manufacturer's instructions should be read and carried out.

2. Correct loading is most important to allow for the circulation of air. Food which requires a low temperature, e.g., fish or raw meat, should be placed near the ice-box. Milk and milk products should be placed in compartments on the refrigerator door where the temperature is not so low.

3. Plastic covered containers or polythene bags should be used for foods in the refrigerator to prevent drying.

4. Food which is already prepared and stored in the refrigerator, should be removed a short time before use, otherwise it will have little flavour.

5. Excessive frosting and a rise in temperature is caused by putting hot food into the refrigerator, therefore all food should be cooled beforehand.

6. Frozen foods should be placed in the freezing compartment, and should not be kept for more than a couple of days unless a guaranteed temperature of —6°C. is maintained, then they will keep for one week. Frozen food must never be re-frozen after it has thawed, because re-frozen food is dangerous.

7. The ice containers should be refilled with cold water after use.

8. The refrigerator should be defrosted regularly, i.e., when frost on the ice-box is about ⅓-inch thick. Excessive frost prevents the refrigerating unit from working efficiently. After defrosting the cabinet should be washed, rinsed and dried both inside and outside. A strong-smelling detergent should not be used.

DEEP-FREEZE CABINET—The temperature of this cabinet should be 0°F. (—18°C.). At this low temperature perishable food may be kept for a considerable time. Food for freezing should be very fresh and frozen as quickly as possible. It should never be thawed and re-frozen. Instructions for the use of the deep-freeze cabinet are supplied by the manufacturer.

ELECTRIC FOOD MIXER—A food mixer is a useful item. There is a large variety on the market which gives the housewife a wide choice, ranging from a small hand model costing comparatively little, to an expensive model with many refinements.

ELECTRIC BLENDER OR LIQUIDISER—This consists of a motor unit, a number of blades and a beaker made of glass or plastic. It may be purchased as an independent unit or as an attachment to a food mixer. The motor operating the mixer works at a certain number of revolutions per second, but a blender or liquidiser needs a higher number of revolutions. By using the blender as an attachment to the mixer more strain is put on the motor causing extra wear and consequently extra maintenance. In practice it has been found that a separate machine for blending and mixing is more efficient and in the long run more economical. The liquidiser can be used for a variety of operations, to make a purée, to crumb bread, to grind, chop, blend, whip and mix, and does each very rapidly and efficiently. There are many varieties on the market from which the housewife can choose according to the amount of money she can afford to spend.

OTHER ELECTRICAL EQUIPMENT AVAILABLE — Kettle, Toaster, Percolator, Frypan, Rotisseur, Vegetable Peeler, etc.

PRESSURE COOKER—A saucepan in which high temperatures can be reached by using steam under pressure. The higher temperature permits cooking in a shorter time. Care should be exercised in using such cookers, and the manufacturer's instructions should be followed.

Pressure	Boiling point of Water
Atmospheric (15 lbs.)	100°C. (212°F.)
10 lbs. (extra to atmp.)	115°C. (239°F.)
15 lbs. (,,)	121°C. (250°F.)
20 lbs. (,,)	126°C. (259°F.)

Planning of Meals

THE housewife should work out the amount of money which she can afford to spend on food each week. By making an allowance for general supplies, e.g., sugar, tea, bread, butter, etc., she will then be able to know what money she has at her disposal for the various meals and divide it up accordingly.

Dinner, the main meal, may be eaten at midday or in the evening. It is for this meal that the rules for menu-planning should be studied and observed. A well-planned menu is an achievement and adds to the enjoyment of the meal itself.

RULES FOR MENU-PLANNING

1. Dinner menus usually consist of three or four courses, except for special occasions, when there may be more. The order of courses is: Hors d'oeuvre, Soup, Fish, Entrée, Joint or Poultry, Vegetables, Pudding or Sweet, Cheese or Savoury, Dessert, Coffee. This order should always be followed.

2. Choose dishes that are within the capabilities of the cook and do not put too great a demand on the equipment and space available.

3. Arrange light meals in hot weather, and in cold weather plan hot and more substantial meals.

4. Do not repeat the same colour throughout the menu, and make sure that vegetables harmonize in colour and flavour with the main meat or fish course. A meal without variety in colour is unpalatable and unappetizing.

5. Vary the method of cooking in the various courses, e.g., apple fritters (fried) should not come after fried fish or meat.

6. Make sure that the texture of each course is different from the preceding or following one, e.g. (1) a fish dish with sauce should not be followed by a casserole or stew of meat or poultry. Instead fried or roast meat would be suitable. (2) A creamy sweet or

11

pudding should not follow a casserole, but a fruit salad, firm pudding, or crisp pastry dish would be acceptable.

7. When entertaining, plan the menu carefully so that some of the meal can be prepared in advance and left ready. Avoid pork and curry because many people find these indigestible.

Suggested specimen menus which may be helpful are given at the end of the book.

AVERAGE QUANTITIES TO ALLOW PER PERSON

Soup : 5 helpings from 1 quart.

Fish : (1) as a fish course—1 fillet or 2-3 ozs. per person.
(2) as a main course—2-3 fillets or 6 ozs. per person.

Meat : with bone, 6-8 ozs.
without bone, 5 ozs. per person.
Steak : 6-8 ozs. per person.
Cutlets : 2 cutlets per person.
Chicken : 1 for 4-5 persons.

Potatoes : 6-8 ozs. per person.

Vegetables : 4 ozs. per person.

Sauce : 4-5 helpings from $\frac{1}{2}$ pt.

Puddings : Milk—$\frac{1}{4}$ pint per person.
Steamed—1 oz. flour per person.

Choice, Buying, and Storage
of Food

THE housewife who studies the market, compares prices and finds out what supplies are available, will be amply repaid by the economical and successful result she will get in running her home. Common sense and discrimination in the choice of food is essential where the amount of money to be spent on it is limited, and the smaller the amount of money the greater is the necessity for spending it to the best advantage.

The number to be catered for, as well as the amount of space available for storage, must also be taken into consideration by the housewife. See opposite page for average quantities to allow per person.

Points to be remembered when buying :

1. A list of the foods required should be made out beforehand. This will be made easier if a pad is kept in the kitchen, and the name of the foods written down, according as the supply is exhausted. Impulse buying should be avoided. Make a list of foods to be purchased and buy only necessities, especially when money is restricted.

2. It is most important to buy only from shops run on hygienic lines. The shop and the assistants should be clean. All food should be protected from flies.

3. It is preferable to buy from a shop where the trade is brisk, where it is unlikely that stores will accumulate, thus ensuring freshness of the food.

4. Perishable foods are best bought and used on the day of purchase. This also applies to frozen foods unless there is a frozen food compartment in the refrigerator.

5. Cheap food is often uneconomical and quite wasteful because of blemished parts in vegetables and fruit and excess of fat and bone in meat, so that the best is often cheapest in the end.

13

6. Where possible, cash payments are best, the tradesman is thus saved book-keeping and the housewife is saved a lot of trouble and time in keeping household accounts. However, the housekeeper should keep an account book to show how much is spent, and how one week may balance another week.

STORAGE OF FOOD

It is important to have adequate facilities for the storage of various foods. These are divided into :

(*a*) Perishable commodities, e.g., meat, fish, poultry, eggs, milk etc. A refrigerator is the most suitable storage place, but if this is not available a safe or cool ventilated pantry or larder is suitable (see "The Kitchen", page 7). To keep cooked food, e.g., soups, stews, custards, etc., cool quickly and keep covered in a cold place, preferably in a refrigerator. If kept in unsuitable conditions and then reheated and used, food poisoning could result from bacteria which flourish easily in a warm moist atmosphere.

(*b*) Semi-perishable commodities, e.g., fruit and vegetables, buy as required. Keep in a sectional rack in a cool ventilated place. Green vegetables can be put in the vegetable section of the refrigerator or kept in a tin box or polythene bag to reduce the evaporation of moisture which makes greens limp and tired.

(*c*) Non-perishable commodities, e.g., flour, sugar, tea, cereals, etc., store in covered jars or tins suitably labelled. New supplies should not be put into jars (or tins) until the existing supply is finished.

Fresh Meat : All houses should have a meat safe or refrigerator. The safe should be hung on the cool shady side of the house. It should be kept scrupulously clean and should be scrubbed out once a week. Joints may be hung up, and chops and steaks put on a flat dish in the safe. If meat is kept in a refrigerator cover loosely to allow air to circulate. Never leave tightly wrapped. Liver, kidneys, hearts, etc., should be bought on the day they are required for use.

Fish : Highly perishable, therefore should be used as soon as possible after purchase. In a refrigerator, it will keep for a few days.

Milk : Buy daily, keep covered in refrigerator or in a cold place.

Eggs : Keep in an egg rack or egg carton.

Fats : All kinds taint easily, they should be kept away from all strong-smelling foods. Buy as required. Keep in a refrigerator or in a cool place.

Cooking Oil : Keep at room temperature.

Cheese : Keep covered in a cool place.

Cereals : Buy in small quantities. Keep in covered, clearly-labelled jars.

Flour, Wheatmeal and Oatmeal : Keep in a cool, well-ventilated place. Put in a flour bin or container, leaving it in the bag if liked, and do not buy more than one month's supply.

Sugar : Keep in covered jars.

Pepper, Salt, and Mustard : Buy as required.

Spices : Buy in small quantities ; they must be kept in tightly-covered containers.

Yeast : Fresh yeast keeps for about four days tied loosely in a polythene bag. Dried yeast keeps for at least six months in a small tin with very little air space.

Baking Powder : Keep tightly covered.

Bread Soda, Cream of Tartar, Bex-Tartar : Keep in covered jars, clearly labelled.

Biscuits : Buy as required, keep in airtight containers.

Coffee : Always buy freshly-ground coffee in small quantities, or buy beans and grind as required. Keep in tightly-covered tin. Coffee loses flavour if stored after grinding. Instant coffee powders are handy for an emergency, but lack the flavour of freshly-ground coffee.

Tea : Keep in an airtight tin in a dry place.

Bread : Keep in a bread bin.

Jam and Jellies : Keep in a cool, dark, dry, well-ventilated place.

Convenience Foods:

(a) **Tinned Foods:** Keep in a cool, well-ventilated place. Avoid a tin with a bulge—this denotes fermentation, which would render the food highly dangerous. An indented tin is harmless unless the metal is damaged.

(b) **Frozen Foods:** Place in the freezing compartment of the refrigerator.

(c) **Dehydrated Foods:** Need no special storage and keep well. Soups, Vegetables, etc., are particularly useful in emergencies, therefore it is advisable to have some in stock.

Dried and Crystallised Fruits: Buy as required.

Nuts: Buy as required.

Bottled Foods: Keep in a cool, dry, dark place.

Pickles, Chutneys: Cover tightly and keep in a cool, dry, dark place.

Essences, Colourings: Buy as required, keep tightly corked.

Curry Paste, Curry Powder: Keep in a cool place in tightly-covered container. They lose flavour if kept for too long.

Vegetables: Place in a sectional rack or basket in cool, dark, ventilated place.

Green Vegetables: Buy as required. To keep them fresh and crisp put into a polythene bag or covered container at bottom of refrigerator or in a cool place.

Citrus Fruits: Buy as required. Keep in a cool place. They become dry and lose flavour if kept for too long.

Bananas, Cucumbers and Tomatoes: Buy as required. Keep in a cool place, but do not put into the refrigerator.

1 **Spoonful.**—When a spoon holds as much substance above the level of the spoon as the bowl (of the spoon) contains.

½ **Spoonful.**—A level spoonful— levelled off with a knife.

¼ **Spoonful.**—A level spoonful, divided on the length with a knife.

NOTE.—The spoons used in the recipes in this book are ordinary household spoons, not special measuring spoons.

Comparative Weights (approx.)		Lb.		Ozs.		Grams
		1	=	16	=	454
				3½	=	100
1 cup chopped meat	=	½	=	8	=	227
1 cup rice or sugar	=	⅜	=	6	=	170
1 cup flour	=	¼	=	4	=	113
1 level tablesp. jam or treacle ⎫ 1 cup breadcrumbs ⎪ 1 egg ⎬	=	⅛	=	2	=	57
2 level tablesps. flour ⎪ 4 level tablesps. breadcrumbs ⎭	=	$\frac{1}{16}$	=	1	=	28

Comparative Measures (approx.)		Pints		Fl. ounces		Millilitres
1 litre	=	1¾	=	35	=	1000
1 pint	=			20	=	571
1 tumbler	=	½	=	10	=	286
1 cup	=	⅓		7	=	190

NOTE.—Cups and tumblers vary in size, only one checked for measure should be used.

OVEN TEMPERATURES IN APPROXIMATE DEGREES OF HEAT

	Temperatures F—Fahrenheit C—Centigrade or Celsius	Lettered Control	Numbered Control
VERY HOT	500°F. approx. 260°C.	About H	About 9
HOT	450°F. approx. 230°C.	,, G	,, 7
FAIRLY HOT ..	425°F. approx. 215°C.	,, F	,, 6
MODERATE	400°F. approx. 205°C.	,, E	,, 5
FAIRLY MODERATE ..	375°F. approx. 190°C.	,, D	,, 4
VERY MODERATE ..	350°F. approx. 175°C.	,, C	,, 3
SLOW	300°F. approx. 150°C.	,, B	,, 2
VERY SLOW ..	250°F. approx. 120°C.	,, A	,, 1
COOL	200°F. approx. 95°C.		,, ½–¼

SOUP-MAKING

THE first consideration in making soup is the making of a good stock. Soup may be made without stock but if it is used as a foundation it gives an excellent flavour. The use of the Pressure Cooker is a great help in the making of stock because of the short time for cooking, thus achieving a great economy of fuel. A supply of stock sufficient for several days should be made at one time in order to save fuel, but in warm weather it is necessary to boil it up every day unless it can be kept in a refrigerator.

Bread, Melba Toast (page 215), **Dinner Buns** (page 191) or **Croûtons** (page 215) may be served with most soups.

Preparation of Vegetables for Soups, etc.

Wash all vegetables except onions in cold water, using a vegetable brush.

Parsnips	..	Cut off tops and roots. Peel thinly.
Carrots ..	..	Cut off tops and roots. Scrape lightly. If old peel thinly.
White Turnip	..	Cut off tops and roots. Peel thickly.
Onions ..	..	Cut off tops and roots. Remove brown skin.
Leeks ..	..	Cut off tops and roots. Remove outer skin.
Potatoes	..	Peel thinly
Celery ..	..	Cut off tops and root. Separate stalks.

BOUQUET GARNI

4 parsley stalks   2 thyme stalks

½ bay leaf

Wrap the parsley and thyme stalks in the bay leaf and tie with thread or fine white twine. Use to flavour soups, sauces, etc.

Stock

The making of stock is based on the following principles:

(1) Solvent power of water,
(2) Prolonged slow cooking.

Therefore stock is a liquid in which the flavouring qualities of meat, bones, and vegetables are held in solution. It is used as a foundation for soups, sauces and gravies.

18

A bouillon cube may be used as a substitute for stock. Dissolve in boiling water when required.

Stock may be classified as follows :

(a) **Brown Stock**—made from beef bones, shin of beef, browned vegetables, seasonings, flavourings and water.

(b) **White Stock**—made from bones, white vegetables, seasonings, flavourings and water.

(c) **Fish Stock**—made from bones of white fish, seasonings, flavourings, vegetables and water.

Pot Liquor is the water in which fresh meat has been boiled. It may be used instead of water when making stock, or in place of stock in the making of soups, sauces or gravies.

BROWN STOCK

4 quarts of cold water	4 ozs. onion
$\frac{1}{2}$ lb. leg beef	2 sticks celery
4 lbs. beef bones	2 tomatoes
4 ozs. carrot	$\frac{1}{2}$ oz. fat.

Bouquet garni (page 18)

1. Break up the bones, remove fat. If oven is hot, put bones on a roasting tin and place in the oven to brown for about $1\frac{1}{2}$ hours.

2. Cut the meat into small pieces.

3. Put the meat, bones and cold water into a large heavy saucepan. Bring slowly to the boil. Remove the scum. Add bouquet garni. Simmer slowly for 3 hours. Skim frequently.

4. Prepare vegetables as on page 18. Cut into small pieces. Fry carrot, onion and celery until brown in hot fat. Add with tomatoes to stock and simmer for a further 3 hours.

5. Strain immediately into an earthenware vessel, skim off all fat.

6. Keep uncovered, in a cool place. Bring to the boil daily in hot weather.

WHITE STOCK

4 quarts of cold water	4 ozs. onion
4 lbs. bones	3 sticks celery

Bouquet garni

Use the same method as for brown stock, but do not fry the vegetables, or brown the bones. A rabbit, carcase or trimmings of fowl or game, cooked or uncooked, may be used in white stock if liked.

Points on Stock-making

1. Ingredients used in stock-making should be fresh. The following should on no account be added :—

(a) Milky foods ;

(b) Starchy foods, e.g., pieces of bread, etc.

(c) Green vegetables, or water in which they have been cooked ;

(d) Fatty foods or scraps of meat fat.

(e) Turnip should not be used because it gives a grey colour and strong flavour to the stock.

2. Skimming is essential as soon as stock comes to the boil ; otherwise the scum boils into the stock, does not rise again, and gives a cloudy result.

3. If the stock is not strained immediately, place the saucepan on a pot-stand or on a cold surface, so that it will cool rapidly.

FISH STOCK

1 pt. cold water	½ oz. butter or margarine
1 lb. fish bones	2 ozs. onion
Bouquet garni	Lemon juice
2 peppercorns	

1. Wash the fish bones, soak 20-30 minutes.

2. Shred the onion, blanch it, put it in a strainer and then allow cold water to run over it.

3. Put butter or margarine and onion into a saucepan, cover with a round of greaseproof paper and then with lid. Cook gently for about 5 minutes but do not allow to colour.

4. Add fish bones, cover again with greaseproof paper and lid and cook for a further 5 minutes to extract flavour. Remove paper.

5. Add water, lemon juice, peppercorns and bouquet garni, boil and skim.

6. Simmer for 15 minutes. Strain and use at once as this stock will not keep.

Soups

Soups are usually classified under the following headings :—

(1) Broths.

(2) Clear Soups.

(3) Thickened Soups.

(4) Purées.

1. **Broths are thin** unclarified soups of considerable nutrient value, to which a small quantity of diced vegetables is added as a garnish. Cereal, e.g., barley, is also added to garnish and slightly thicken the broth.

Though broths are not clarified they are always transparent and should never be opaque.

2. **Clear Soups or Clarified Broths** are soups whose basic ingredient is a good stock. The stock is cleared by the addition of whites and shells of eggs and lean beef. When clarified it is termed consommé. Each consommé derives its name from the particular garnish used.

3. **Thickened Soups**: the foundation for these soups may be brown or white stock, pot liquor or water, and in it is cooked fresh meat or vegetables and flavourings. The rich soup thus obtained is strained and thickened by any of the Liaisons mentioned below. Usually some of the meat or vegetable cooked in the soup is cut into dice and served as a garnish in the soup.

4. **Purées** may be defined as soups which are thickened by sieving the ingredients of which they consist, or using a liquidiser, to form a purée. The ingredients are then held in suspension by a farinaceous substance.

LIAISONS

There are four methods of thickening soups.

A. Roux : Melted fat to which flour is added and cooked, the sieved soup then being added.

B. The addition of blended flour or cornflour after the soup has been sieved.

C. Cereals : sago, pearl barley, etc.

D. Yolks of eggs and cream used for richer and more expensive types of white soups—the amount of the farinaceous substance being reduced in this case.

NOTE.—All thickened soups should be corrected for consistency before serving. If too thick, add suitable liquid, i.e. milk, stock or water, and boil. If too thin, add blended flour and boil for a few minutes.

CHICKEN BROTH

1½ pts. of chicken stock	2 ozs. chopped onion
½ oz. pearl barley	2 ozs. chopped celery
Salt and pepper	1 teasp. finely-chopped parsley

1. Make stock by simmering carcase and bones of chicken for 1½ hours in 1 quart of water. Strain, cool and remove fat.

2. Add barley, cook for ½ hour. Add vegetables and cook for a further hour. Season and add parsley.

SHEEP'S HEAD BROTH

1 sheep's head	2 carrots
5 pts. water	1 white turnip
2 tablesps. pearl barley	3 leeks
Salt and pepper	2 sticks of celery

1 tablesp. finely-chopped parsley

1. Split the skull, lift the brains out. Wash the head, pay particular attention to the tongue and the parts around it. Remove eyes. Steep the head in cold salt water for one hour.

2. Wash the brains and leave to steep in cold water and vinegar (1 teaspoonful vinegar—1 pint water). These are not used in the broth but may be used for Brain Cakes or cooked in other ways.

3. Blanch the head (page 217). Put it with the barley, cold water and 1 teaspoonful salt into a saucepan. Bring slowly to the boil. Remove the scum. Simmer for 2 hours, skim frequently.

4. Add vegetables, cut in ⅛" dice, and simmer for another hour.

5. Remove the head. Season broth and remove any surface grease by drawing pieces of kitchen paper over the top. Sprinkle liberally with parsley.

MUTTON BROTH

1 quart of pot liquor (from Boiled Mutton, page 55), or water		
½ lb. neck of mutton		Carrot ⎱ Cut in
Salt and pepper	½ pt. ⎰	White turnip ⎰ ⅛" dice
1 oz. pearl barley		Onion ⎰

1 teasp. finely-chopped parsley

1. Wipe the meat, cut into four or five pieces and remove the spinal cord and fat.

2. Wash the barley and put it, with the meat, the liquid and a little salt into a saucepan and bring to the boil. Remove the grey scum that comes to the top.

3. Simmer for 1 hour, skimming frequently.

4. Add the vegetables to the broth and simmer for another hour. Correct seasoning.

5. Lift out the pieces of mutton and remove any surface grease by drawing kitchen paper over the top of the broth. Sprinkle liberally with parsley.

SCOTCH BROTH

½ lb. flank of beef or
   ½ lb. neck of mutton
1 qt. of cold water
1 oz. pearl barley
1 teasp. finely-chopped
   parsley

Salt and pepper
½ pt. {
Grated carrot
Carrot cut in ⅛" dice.
White turnip cut in ⅛" dice
Leek—sliced
Peas

1. Wipe the meat, cut into pieces and put into a saucepan with the cold water, salt and washed barley. Bring to the boil, skim well and simmer for 1 hour.

2. Add the vegetables to the broth and continue to cook for 1 hour.

3. Lift out the meat and skim. Draw a piece of clean kitchen paper over the top to remove grease.

4. Correct seasoning and sprinkle liberally with parsley.

MIXED VEGETABLE SOUP

3 ozs. carrots
3 ozs. onion
3 ozs. celery
3 ozs. leek
1½ ozs. white turnip
2 ozs. butter or margarine

2 ozs. flour
1 qt. stock or water
Bouquet garni
Salt and pepper
½ pt. milk
½ teaspoonful chopped parsley

1. Prepare the vegetables according to kind and cut into small pieces.

2. Melt the butter, put in the vegetables, cover with a round of greaseproof paper and a lid. Cook over a slow heat for about 10–15 minutes until the vegetables begin to soften. Do not allow them to colour.

3. Add the flour, mix well and cook slowly for about 5 minutes.

4. Add the stock, bring to the boil, skim and add seasoning and bouquet garni.

5. Simmer for about 1 hour until the vegetables are soft, lift out the bouquet garni, sieve the soup or use a liquidiser.

6. Re-heat the soup, add the milk and correct the seasoning and consistency. Bring again to the boil, serve and sprinkle the parsley on top.

BROWN VEGETABLE SOUP

White turnip	2 ozs. fat
Carrot	2 ozs. flour
Celery	1 quart of brown stock
Potato	Bouquet garni
Onion	Salt and pepper

1. Prepare the vegetables according to kind (page 18) and cut into ⅛-inch dice (½ pt. of mixed vegetables required).
2. Melt the fat in a saucepan, fry the vegetables, stir in the flour and cook until a good brown colour.
3. Cool slightly and add stock gradually stirring all the time.
4. Add bouquet garni and seasoning. Bring to boil. Skim.
5. Simmer gently until the vegetables are soft—about 1 hr.
6. Lift out the bouquet garni. Remove any surface grease from the top and correct seasoning. Serve.

TOMATO SOUP

¾ lb. tomatoes or 2 oz. tin tomato purée	Salt and pepper
4 ozs. chopped carrot	1 quart of stock
4 ozs. chopped onion	2 ozs. flour
Bouquet garni	2 ozs. butter or margarine
	½ pt. milk
½ teasp. sugar	

1. Melt butter, add vegetables and cook until golden brown.
2. Add the flour, mix well and cook for a few minutes.
3. Add tomato purée or sliced tomatoes, and cook for a few minutes longer.
4. Stir in the stock, bring to the boil and skim.
5. Add seasoning, sugar and bouquet garni and simmer for 1 hour, skimming frequently.
6. Strain, add milk, bring to the boil. Correct seasoning. Serve.

POTATO AND LEEK SOUP

8 ozs. potatoes	1 qt. chicken stock
8 ozs. leeks (white parts)	¼ pt. milk
2 ozs. margarine	Bouquet garni
1 oz. flour	2 tablespoonfuls cream
Salt and pepper	

1. Peel the potatoes, wash the leeks and cut both into small pieces.
2. Melt the margarine, put in the vegetables, cover with a round of greaseproof paper and a lid. Cook over a slow heat until they begin to soften.

3. Add the stock, seasoning and bouquet garni. Bring to the boil and simmer until the vegetables are soft. Remove the bouquet garni.

4. Sieve, add the flour blended with the milk. Boil for a few minutes, stirring well. A liquidiser may be used instead of a sieve. This gives a smooth purée which does not require thickening with flour, just add the milk and bring to the boil.

5. Correct the soup for seasoning and pour on to the heated cream in the hot soup tureen.

POTATO SOUP

1 quart of white stock or water	$\frac{1}{2}$ pt. milk
1 oz. butter or margarine	$1\frac{1}{2}$ ozs. sago
1 lb. potatoes	Salt and pepper
2 sticks of celery	1 teaspoonful finely-chopped
2 ozs. onion	parsley

1. Prepare vegetables according to kind (page 18), and chop finely.

2. Melt the butter, add the vegetables, cover and place over a slow heat for about 15 minutes but do not allow to brown.

3. Add the stock, bring to the boil, skim and simmer for about $\frac{3}{4}$ hour.

4. Press through a sieve or use a liquidiser, mix until smooth, return to rinsed saucepan.

5. Wash the sago and add to the soup with the milk. Boil until the grains of the sago are clear, about 15 minutes, stirring all the time.

6. Correct seasoning. Sprinkle parsley on top and serve.

LENTIL SOUP

1 quart of stock or water	2 ozs. flour
1 oz. butter or margarine	$\frac{1}{4}$ lb. lentils
Bouquet garni	2 ozs. chopped onion
$\frac{1}{2}$ pt. milk	Salt and pepper

1. Put the lentils into a strainer and pour cold water through.

2. Melt the butter in a saucepan, add the onion, cook for a few minutes but do not brown.

3. Add the lentils, stock, bouquet garni and seasoning, bring to boiling-point. Skim.

4. Simmer until the vegetables are soft, about 1 hour. Lift out the bouquet garni and rub soup through a sieve, or use a liquidiser.

5. Rinse the saucepan and return the sieved soup. Add the flour blended with the milk. Stir until it boils for 5 minutes. Season and serve.

FRENCH ONION SOUP

1 lb. onions	1 qt. well-flavoured stock (Bouillon)
1 oz. margarine	Salt and pepper
½ oz. flour	Grated cheese

Slices of Vienna Roll

1. Peel the onions and shred them. Blanch them.

2. Melt the margarine, put in the onion, cover and cook over a slow heat until soft and slightly coloured.

3. Add the flour, mix and cook for a few minutes.

4. Add the bouillon, bring to the boil, skim and season.

5. Simmer until the onions are tender—about 25 minutes. Correct seasoning.

6. Toast the bread. Put the soup into soup bowls, put toast on top and sprinkle with grated cheese.

NOTE.—If Bouillon is not available buy Bouillon Cubes and make up to a quart.

CHEESE SOUP

1½ pints white stock	1 oz. butter or margarine
¼ lb. hard cheese	1½ ozs. flour
4 ozs. onion	½ pt. milk

Salt and pepper

1. Prepare the onion, slice and chop finely.

2. Cook in the boiling stock for about 20 minutes.

3. Make a roux with the butter and flour, cook for 3 minutes, cool slightly and add the stock, milk and onion.

4. Boil for 5 minutes, stirring all the time. Remove from the heat.

5. Season and add the sieved cheese. Serve.

LEEK SOUP

6 leeks (medium size)	1 oz. butter or margarine
1 quart stock or pot liquor	2 ozs. flour
½ pt. milk	Salt and pepper

1. Prepare the leeks as on page 18, and slice.

2. Melt the butter, add leeks, cover and place over a slow heat for about 15 minutes but do not brown.

3. Add the stock and seasoning and cook until the leeks are soft.

4. Sieve or use a liquidiser and return to the rinsed saucepan.

5. Blend the flour with the milk and add to the soup, boil for 5 minutes, stirring all the time. Correct seasoning and serve.

GREEN PEA SOUP

1 quart white stock	$\frac{1}{2}$ pt. milk
6 ozs. peas	2 ozs. butter or margarine
1 onion	2 ozs. flour
2 sticks celery	Salt and pepper
Bouquet garni	Few drops green colouring

1. Prepare vegetables as on page 18, and cut into small pieces.

2. Put into a saucepan with the stock, peas, bouquet garni and salt.

3. Bring to the boil and simmer until the vegetables are soft, about 1 hour.

4. Remove the bouquet garni and rub the soup through a sieve, or use a liquidiser.

5. Rinse the saucepan and make a roux with the butter and flour, cook for 3 minutes, cool slightly and add the sieved soup and milk slowly.

6. Stir until it boils for 5 minutes. Correct seasoning and colouring. Serve.

CARROT SOUP

8 ozs. carrot	1 oz. butter or margarine
2 ozs. onion	2 ozs. flour
2 sticks of celery	$\frac{1}{2}$ pt. milk
1 quart of white stock	Salt and pepper
1 oz. bacon rinds	Pinch nutmeg

1. Prepare the vegetables as on page 18, and chop.

2. Heat the butter in a large saucepan, put in the vegetables and rinds, fry without browning for about 15 minutes.

3. Add the stock and bring to the boil, skim, cook until the carrots are tender. Remove the bacon rinds.

4. Sieve or use a liquidiser. Rinse the saucepan, put in the sieved soup.

5. Add the flour blended with the milk, stir until it boils for 5 minutes.

6. Correct seasoning and serve.

GRAVY SOUP

½ lb. round steak	½ oz. fat
2 sticks of celery	1 quart of brown stock
2 ozs. carrot	2 ozs. flour
2 ozs. onion	Bouquet garni
1 oz. white turnip	Salt and pepper

1. Remove skin, fat and bone from the meat. Wipe and shred very finely or mince it. Steep in the cold stock, to which a little salt has been added, for 1 hour, stirring occasionally.

2. Prepare vegetables according to kind (page 18), and cut into small pieces.

3. Melt the fat in a saucepan, add all vegetables and fry until lightly browned.

4. Add stock, meat and bouquet garni. Bring slowly to simmering point, and simmer 1½ hours. Remove bouquet garni. Sieve or use a liquidiser.

5. Rinse the saucepan and pour the sieved soup into it. Add the flour blended in a little cold stock or water. Bring to the boil, stirring well all the time; boil for 5 minutes.

6. Correct for seasoning and colour.

KIDNEY SOUP

¼ lb. beef kidney	1 oz. white turnip
1 quart of brown stock	2 sticks of celery
½ oz. fat	2 ozs. onion
2 ozs. flour	2 ozs. carrot
Salt and pepper	Bouquet garni

1. Skin and remove the core from the kidney, cut it into pieces. Soak in water for about 20 minutes. Pour off the water.

2. Prepare vegetables according to kind (page 18), and cut into small pieces.

3. Melt the fat in a saucepan, when hot, fry vegetables until brown. Add stock, kidney and bouquet garni. Bring to the boil, skim, simmer for about 1½ hours. Lift out a few pieces of kidney, cut into ¼″ dice and keep for garnish. Remove the bouquet garni.

4. Sieve the soup or use a liquidiser. Rinse the saucepan. Return soup to saucepan, add the flour blended with a little cold stock or water.

5. Add the diced kidney. Stir until it boils. Boil 5 minutes. Correct for colour and seasoning. Serve.

LIVER SOUP

1 oz. white turnip	1 quart brown stock
2 ozs. carrot	½ lb. liver
2 ozs. onion	Bouquet garni
2 sticks of celery	2 ozs. flour
1 oz. fat	Salt and pepper

1. Prepare vegetables according to kind (page 18), and cut into small pieces. Chop liver.

2. Heat the fat in a saucepan, add the prepared vegetables and fry until browned. Cool a little.

3. Add the cold stock, liver, bouquet garni and salt, bring to the boil and simmer for about 1½ hours. Remove bouquet garni, sieve or use a liquidiser.

4. Return to the rinsed saucepan, add the flour blended in a little cold stock or water. Stir until it boils for 5 minutes. Correct for colour and seasoning.

FISH

THE inclusion of fish adds variety to the diet, but compared with meat in equal quantities, it is a far less nutritive food. The fibres are finer, shorter and more easily separated than those of meat—this makes fish a more readily digested food than meat. The fibres of the different kinds of fish vary :—

(a) fine—as in plaice or sole ;
(b) coarse—cod or hake ;
(c) very coarse—in the claw of a crab.

Fish may be divided into three main classes :—

1. **White Fish**—*e.g.*, cod, plaice, whiting, etc.

This fish is sometimes described as the lean fish, as most of the fat is contained in the liver, and this is removed in cleaning. It makes a light, easily-digested meal, particularly suited to invalids.

2. **Oily Fish**—*e.g.*, herrings, salmon, mackerel, etc.

The food value of oily fish is higher than that of white fish as it contains a much larger proportion of fat ; this fat is evenly distributed throughout the flesh. Herrings are specially recommended as they are plentiful and therefore not expensive. Salmon is usually expensive but it is most popular and satisfying and is about three times as nourishing as white fish.

3. **Shell Fish**—there are two groups.

(a) Crustacea—*e.g.*, lobster, crab, crayfish, prawns, shrimps.
(b) Molluscs—*e.g.*, oysters, mussels, scallops, periwinkles.

Shell fish have very little nutrient value, and with the exception of raw oysters are not easily digested, however they provide a change in the diet.

CHOICE OF WHITE AND OILY FISH

1. Absolute freshness is essential. Oily and fresh-water fish should be used as soon as possible after they are caught. Turbot and brill have a better flavour if kept in proper storage for a day before use.

2. Fish should have a pleasant smell.

3. If there are scales they should be plentiful and should **not** come off easily.

4. The eyes should be bright and prominent.

5. The body should be stiff and the flesh firm.

6. The gills should be red.

7. The skin should be moist and unbroken; bruised fish decomposes rapidly.

8. The spots on plaice should be bright orange. They turn a tawny or brown colour when the fish is stale.

9. Choose medium-sized fish; very large fish are coarse in texture, and very small ones are inclined to be tasteless.

10. Fish of any sort should not be bought when out of season, as it is watery, is lacking in flavour and may be unwholesome.

FISH IN SEASON

Brill	All the year, but it is inferior in Spring.
Cod	Middle September to middle March.
Crab	April to October.
Crayfish	March to September.
Eels	June to March; best September to November.
Escallops	November to March.
Gurnet	All the Year.
Haddock	August to February.
Hake	May to September.
Halibut	All the year.
Herrings	July to February.
Lobster	All the year.
Mackerel	April to July.
Mussels	October to April.
Oysters	1st September to end of April.
Plaice	All the year, but it is inferior in February, March, and April.
Prawns	March to September.
Salmon	February to 1st September.
Shrimps	April to August.
Skate (Ray)	Practically all the year.
Sole, Black ⎱ ,, Lemon ⎰	All the year, but it is inferior in April and May
Trout	March to October.
Whitebait	Summer months—May to August.
Whiting	Available all the year but best from May to January.

PREPARATION OF FISH

1. To Clean

(*a*) Flat fish such as plaice and sole, cut a slit just below the gills on the dark side and remove the viscera.

(*b*) Fish that swim with their backs uppermost, such as haddock, mackerel, etc., slit from the head half-way to the tail on the underside and lift out the viscera. Keep the roe of herrings.

2. Rub off the black membrane in the cavity with a little dry salt.

3. Remove the scales by scraping with the back of a knife from the tail towards the head.

4. Cut off the fins from all fish except turbot.

5. To remove the eyes—cut the skin round eye socket, press the thumb behind eye and push out.

Flat fish may be bought filleted, but if bought on the bone the bones may be utilised for making fish stock. Black sole is usually skinned before filleting, but plaice, lemon sole, brill, turbot, etc., having a tougher skin, is first filleted, the skin being more easily removed from the single fillets. The white skin is not usually removed from either plaice or sole unless it is required for an invalid.

To Skin Black Sole

1. Ease away a little of the skin from the tail end.

2. Slip the right thumb under the skin and loosen along the side, repeat with the left thumb on the other side.

3. Dip the fingers in salt, take a firm grip of the skin at the tail end and remove by drawing off sharply towards the head.

4. Trim away the fins.

To Fillet Flat Fish

1. Place the fish on the board with the dark skin upwards and the tail facing you.

2. Using a sharp-pointed knife, cut through the flesh to the bone, cutting along the line of the backbone.

3. Holding the knife obliquely, remove the left-hand fillet in sharp quick strokes, keeping close to the bone.

4. Turn the head of the fish towards you and remove the second fillet.

5. Turn the fish over with the white skin uppermost and fillet the underside in the same way.

6. Trim loose edges from fillets.

To Remove the Skin from Fillets of Fish

1. Place the fillet with the skin side resting on the board.

2. Dip the fingers of the left hand in salt and catch the tail end, hold the knife obliquely and remove the flesh using a sawing movement.

BOILED WHITE FISH

1½ lbs. white fish (cod, hake, etc.)   Boiling water
Salt and vinegar
To serve:— ½ pint pouring sauce—Parsley, Egg, Caper or Anchovy.
Garnish:— Lemon and parsley.

1. Put sufficient water to cover the fish into a saucepan and bring to the boil.

2. Wash the fish, remove scales, put on a small plate and tie in a piece of muslin.

3. Add 1 teaspoonful of salt and vinegar to each quart of water. The acid in the vinegar helps to keep the flesh firm and white.

4. Draw the pan to the side of the fire, put in the fish, return to the heat and simmer gently until cooked, allowing 6 minutes for every pound of fish and 6 minutes over at the end. Rapid cooking toughens the fibres of the fish and breaks the flesh.

5. Drain well, remove the skin, serve on a hot buttered dish, garnish with cut lemon and parsley.

FRIED FISH

Fillets of fish (cod, hake, haddock, etc.)

To coat:— Egg and breadcrumbs.   Seasoned flour.
To fry:— A little clarified fat.
To garnish:— Cut lemon and parsley.
To serve:— Parsley, Caper or Anchovy Sauce (pouring) (page 150).

1. Wash the fish and dry in a cloth. If large cut into pieces. Pass through seasoned flour. Coat with egg and breadcrumbs.

2. Heat a little fat on a frying pan, put in the fish and fry until brown, turn and brown the other side. Shake the pan gently while cooking. Fish becomes firm in texture when cooked. Test by pressure.

3. Remove carefully with a fish slice and drain well on a piece of kitchen paper.

4. Serve on a plain dish paper on a hot dish. Garnish with cut lemon and parsley.

FISH PIE

½ lb. cooked fish (page 33) 1 lb. mashed seasoned potatoes
1 hard-boiled egg Salt and pepper
½ oz. butter or margarine 1 teaspoonful lemon juice
White Stewing Sauce (½ quantity on page 149)
Garnish: Parsley.

1. Remove skin and bone from the cooked fish. Make the sauce.

2. Cut the egg in half, lift out the yolk and rub through a sieve. Keep back a little to decorate the top of the pie. Chop the white of egg.

3. Add the fish, egg, salt, pepper and lemon juice to the sauce and mix together.

4. Put into a greased pie-dish and cover with the mashed potatoes.

5. Spread the potatoes evenly, mark with a fork, put on the butter in small pieces.

6. Bake in a moderate oven for about a ½ hour. Decorate with sieved yolk of egg.

7. Serve on a plain dish paper on a hot dish. Garnish with parsley.

FISH CROQUETTES

½ lb. cooked fish (page 33) 1 hard-boiled egg
½ teasp. lemon juice Salt and pepper
¼ pint white binding sauce (page 149)
To coat:— Egg and breadcrumbs.
To fry:— Bath of fat.
To garnish:— Cut lemon and parsley.

1. Remove skin and bone from the cooked fish and flake with two forks.

2. Mix the fish, chopped hard-boiled egg, lemon juice, pepper and salt with the binding sauce.

3. Turn on to a floured board, form into a long roll, cut into even-sized pieces and shape like a cork.

4. Coat with egg and breadcrumbs.

5. Fry in hot fat until golden brown, drain well on kitchen paper.

6. Serve on a plain dish paper on a hot dish and garnish with cut lemon and parsley.

FISH CAKES

½ lb. cooked fish (page 33)	½ teasp. finely-chopped parsley
½ lb. mashed potatoes	½ oz. butter or margarine (melted)
½ teasp. anchovy essence	Beaten egg to bind

Pepper and salt

To coat:— Egg and breadcrumbs.
To fry:— Bath of fat.
To garnish:— Cut lemon and parsley.

1. Remove skin and bone from the fish, break it into small flakes.
2. Mix with the potatoes, anchovy essence, parsley, butter, salt and pepper, bind with a little of the beaten egg.
3. Turn the mixture on to a floured board, form into a roll, cut into 8 even-sized pieces and shape into round cakes. Coat with egg and breadcrumbs.
4. Fry in the hot fat until golden brown in colour, drain on kitchen paper.
5. Arrange in two rows, overlapping the cakes, on a plain dish paper on a hot dish. Garnish with cut lemon and parsley.

COD AU GRATIN

1½ lbs. filleted cod	¼ pt. water
1 oz. chopped onion	½ pt. milk

Squeeze of lemon juice

Sauce:

1 oz. flour	¾ pt. liquid in which fish has been cooked
1 oz. margarine	2 ozs. grated cheese

Potato Border:

1 lb. cooked potatoes	1 egg
1 oz. margarine	Salt and pepper

1. Skin the fish and cut into four pieces. Wash in cold water.
2. Put the onion and fish into a saucepan, squeeze a little lemon juice over the fish, add the water and milk. Cover and cook gently for about 10 minutes.
3. Prepare the potatoes as for Potato Roses (page 113). Pipe around the edge of an entrée dish and keep hot.
4. Drain the fish out of the liquid and keep hot.
5. Melt the margarine in a saucepan, mix in the flour, cook until dry and sandy, cool a little, add the liquid gradually. Boil for 3 minutes, stirring all the time. Add nearly all the cheese, salt and pepper.
6. Pour a little of the sauce into the centre of the entrée dish, put in the fish and then the remainder of the sauce. Sprinkle with cheese. Brush the potatoes with egg wash and brown under the griller.

FRIED FILLETS OF PLAICE

1 ½ lbs. filleted plaice

To coat:—Egg and breadcrumbs.
To fry:—A little clarified fat or oil.
Garnish:—Cut lemon and parsley.
To serve:—Parsley sauce (page 150).

1. Remove the dark skin. Wash the fish and dry well.

2. Pour some beaten egg on to a plate, put in one piece of fish at a time, brush over with the egg and drain well.

3. Have plenty of fine breadcrumbs on a sheet of kitchen paper, put in the piece of fish, toss the crumbs over, then press in the crumbs with the hand.

4. Toss from one hand to the other to get rid of all loose crumbs.

5. Heat a little fat on a frying pan, put in the fish and fry until brown. Turn and brown the other side. Shake the pan gently while cooking.

6. Remove carefully and drain on kitchen paper.

7. Serve in two rows on a dish paper on a hot dish, having the fillets overlapping. Garnish with cut lemon and parsley.

NOTE.—If liked these fillets may be fried in deep fat.

FRIED FILLETS OF BRILL

Prepare and cook as for Fried Fillets of Plaice. If fillets are large cut on slant.

BAKED GURNET

1 gurnet	2 ozs. fat
4 ozs. stuffing (page 67)	Browned crumbs

Garnish:— Cut lemon and parsley.

1. Mix all the ingredients for the stuffing together and moisten with the melted butter.

2. Prepare the fish as on page 32. Wash well and dry. Put the stuffing into the opening of the fish and sew up.

3. Turn the fish into the shape of the letter S, run a skewer through from head to tail and tie with a piece of twine to hold in position.

4. Heat the fat in a baking tin and put in the prepared fish. Baste with the hot fat, baste again when half cooked. Bake in a moderate oven 20-30 mins., according to size.

5. Dust the top with browned crumbs and return to the oven for a few minutes.

6. Remove skewer, twine and thread. Lift with a fish slice on to a hot dish. Put a thin slice of lemon into each eye cavity and garnish with parsley.

FISH

WHITING IN BATTER

1 lb. filleted whiting.   Simple Coating batter (page 134).

To fry:— Bath of fat.
Garnish:— Parsley and cut lemon.
To serve:— Dutch Sauce (page 151).

1. Remove the skin from the fish, wash and dry. Cut into pieces about 2 inches in size. Put into batter and coat well.
2. Heat the fat.
3. Lift the fish out of the batter with a fork and drop into the hot fat. Fry until a golden brown colour. Time 8-10 mins. Drain well on kitchen paper.
4. Serve on a plain dish paper on a hot dish. Garnish with cut lemon and parsley.

BAKED HADDOCK (See BAKED GURNET)

RUSSIAN FISH PIE

Rough Puff Pastry:

6 ozs. flour	Pinch salt
4 ozs. butter or margarine	Cold water
1 teaspoonful lemon juice	

Filling:

1/2 lb. filleted fish	1/4 pt. white binding sauce (page 149)
1 hard-boiled egg	1 teasp. anchovy essence
1 teasp. chopped parsley	1 tablesp. lemon juice or vinegar
Salt and pepper	

To glaze:— Beaten egg
To garnish:— Cut lemon and parsley.

1. Make pastry (page 175) and roll out into a 12″ square, trim off the edges.
2. Remove skin from the fish. Wash and dry. Cut into 1-inch cubes, sprinkle lemon juice, salt and pepper over.
3. Mix with the cold sauce, anchovy essence and parsley. Put into the centre of the pastry, slice the hard-boiled egg and place on top.
4. Brush the edge of the pastry with cold water, fold the four corners to the centre, overlapping the edges slightly. Lift on to a greased tin.
5. Cut five leaves from the trimmings of pastry and arrange around the centre of the pie. Brush over with beaten egg.
6. Bake in hot oven until the pastry is lightly browned, reduce the heat and cook for three-quarters of an hour. Garnish with cut lemon and parsley and serve.

CURRY OF FISH

1 oz. butter or margarine	2 teasps. lemon juice
2 ozs. chopped onion	1 dessertsp. chutney
2 teasps. curry powder	$\frac{1}{2}$ apple (chopped)
1 oz. flour	1 teasp. tomato sauce
$\frac{3}{4}$ pt. stock	1 lb. filleted fish
Salt	1 tablesp. cream (if liked)

To serve:— 6 ozs. boiled rice (page 217).
To garnish:— Parsley and cayenne pepper.

1. Heat the butter in a saucepan, add the onion, curry powder and flour and cook well together.

2. Stir in the stock gradually, add the salt and lemon juice. Bring to the boil, skim, add chutney, apple and tomato sauce, simmer for about three-quarters of an hour.

3. Strain the sauce and return to the rinsed saucepan.

4. Remove skin from the fish, cut into pieces.

5. Put the fish into the sauce, cook gently for about 15 mins. and add the cream.

6. Arrange the rice as a border on a hot dish, put the curry mixture in the centre. Garnish with parsley and cayenne pepper.

GRILLED MACKEREL

2 mackerel

Marinade:

1 tablesp. salad oil	1 teasp. chopped onion
1 tablesp. lemon juice	1 teasp. chopped parsley

Salt and pepper

To garnish:— Cut lemon, watercress or parsley.
To serve:— Maître d'Hôtel Butter (page 157).

1. Remove heads, fins and tails from fish. Scale and wash well. Put fish flat on board, place left hand on top, remove fillet from head to tail, using a sharp knife. Remove bone from the under fillet.

2. Soak in the marinade for about 1 hour, turning frequently.

3. Heat and grease the griller. Put on the fish and grill the skin side first. Turn after about 4 minutes and grill the cut side for about 7 minutes.

4. Serve on a hot dish, put a pat of Maître d'Hôtel Butter on top. Garnish with cut lemon and watercress or parsley.

GRILLED HERRINGS

2 herrings   Salad oil or melted butter
To serve:—Lemon juice, chopped parsley and Mustard Sauce (page 150).

1. Remove the heads, fins and tails from fish. Scale, wash well and dry. Remove the intestine and any blood from the inside.

2. Slit the underside and place the herring with its back upwards on a chopping board. Press down along the backbone until the fish lies flat. Turn over and remove the backbone, commencing at the head end.

3. Score the skin two or three times to prevent its curling-up. Fold in two. Brush over with salad oil or melted butter.

4. Heat the griller, grease the bars and place the herrings on it. Brown quickly on both sides, then cook for about 6–8 minutes, turning from side to side occasionally.

5. Lift on to a hot dish, sprinkle lemon juice and a little finely-chopped parsley over.

NOTE : (*a*) If liked, instead of serving as above, place a pat of Maître d'Hôtel Butter on each herring.

(*b*) Herrings may also be grilled without removing the backbones. Score the skin in two or three places on each side of the back. Time about 10 minutes.

FRIED HERRINGS

Prepare as above, coat with seasoned flour and cook as for Fried Fish (page 33). Serve as for Grilled Herrings.

POTTED HERRINGS

2 herrings   1 bay leaf
3 tablespoonfuls brown vinegar   1 blade mace
3 tablespoonfuls water   2 peppercorns
Salt   1 small onion
2 cloves   Parsley

1. Prepare the herrings as for grilling (page 39). Cut through the centre, making two fillets. Wash each piece, sprinkle with salt and roll up.

2. Put into a fireproof casserole with the peppercorns, bay leaf, mace, cloves and slices of onions. Pour the vinegar and water over and cover.

3. Bake in a very moderate oven for about 1 hour. Leave aside to cool. Serve.

NOTE :

1. Potted herrings may be served hot.

2. If the herrings are to be kept for a few days add a little extra vinegar.

BAKED SOLE

1 black sole	½ oz. butter or margarine
2 ozs. stuffing (page 67)	A little fish stock or water

Garnish:— Parsley. Cut lemon.
To serve:— Dutch Sauce (page 151).

1. Prepare the fish as on page 32. Wash well and dry. Make a cut along the backbone on the skinned side. Raise each fillet from the bone to form a pocket.

2. Fill each pocket with the stuffing and lift on to a greased baking tin. Pour a little fish stock around and place the butter on fish in small pieces.

3. Cover with a piece of greased paper and bake in a moderate oven for 20–30 minutes, according to size.

4. Lift on to a hot dish, garnish with parsley and lemon.

POACHED SKATE

1 lb. skate wings	¼ pt. water
½ oz. chopped onion	1 oz. butter
Salt and pepper	1 teasp. capers

To garnish:— Chopped parsley.

1. Wash the skate, dry, and remove dark skin. To do this loosen the skin from the flesh at the thick side and then pull towards fins.

2. Grease a shallow saucepan with a little butter, put in the onion and place the fish on top. Add seasoning and water.

3. Place a round of greased paper on top, put on the lid, bring to the boil and simmer gently for about 10 minutes.

4. Lift the fish on to a hot dish. Make sure to drain well to remove all moisture.

5. Melt the butter and allow to become brown. Put chopped capers on top of the fish and mask with the butter. Garnish with a little chopped parsley.

SALMON CUTLETS

½ lb. cooked salmon	1 teasp. finely-chopped parsley
¼ pt. white binding sauce (page 149)	Grated rind and juice of ¼ lemon
	Salt and pepper

To coat:— Egg and breadcrumbs.
To fry:— Bath of fat.
Garnish:— A stick of macaroni, cut lemon, parsley.

1. Remove skin and bone from the fish and flake it. Mix with the sauce, parsley, lemon and seasoning. Spread on a wet plate and leave until cold.

2. Cut into eight pieces, lift off each piece on to a floured board, shape like a cutlet. Coat with egg and breadcrumbs.

3. Put an inch of macaroni in the narrow end of each to simulate the bone of the cutlet.

4. Fry to a golden brown colour in hot fat (page 74), drain well on kitchen paper.

5. Dish in two rows with the cutlets overlapping, on a hot dish, with a dish paper under them. Garnish with cut lemon and parsley.

SMOKED HADDOCK AU GRATIN

1 lb. smoked haddock	Bouquet garni (page 18)
$\frac{1}{4}$ pt. water	$\frac{1}{2}$ pt. milk

Sauce:

1 oz. flour	1 oz. butter or margarine
$\frac{3}{4}$ pt. liquid in which fish has been cooked	

2 ozs. sieved cheese	$\frac{1}{2}$ oz. breadcrumbs
$\frac{1}{2}$ oz. butter	Parsley

1. Steep the fish in boiling water for 2 minutes. Remove skin and fins, cut the fish into large pieces. Put the fish into a saucepan with the milk and water, add the bouquet garni.

2. Bring slowly to the boil and simmer until tender—about 10 minutes. Lift out and break it into pieces.

3. Put into a greased fireproof dish and keep hot.

4. Melt the butter, mix in the flour, cook for 3 minutes, add liquid. Boil for 3 minutes, stirring all the time, add half the cheese.

5. Pour the sauce into the fireproof dish, sprinkle with the remainder of the cheese and the breadcrumbs. Place a few pieces of butter on top and brown under the griller. Serve.

SMOKED OR FRESH COD WITH GARLIC

$1\frac{1}{2}$ lbs. fish	Juice 1 lemon
2 cloves garlic	2 tablespoonfuls oil or melted butter
4 ozs. chopped onion	Salt and pepper
2 tablespoonfuls chopped parsley	$\frac{1}{2}$ oz. breadcrumbs
	1 oz. butter

1. If using smoked fish, steep in cold water, drain and blanch it. Remove skin and bone from the fish, cut into pieces.

2. Remove the skin from the garlic, chop or crush it, mix it with the onion, parsley, lemon juice, oil or melted butter, salt and pepper. Put half of this mixture into a shallow fireproof dish. Place the fish on top and cover with the remainder of the mixture.

3. Sprinkle with breadcrumbs and put the butter in small pieces on top. Bake in a moderate oven for about $\frac{3}{4}$ hour.

BOILED KIPPERS

1 Trim tail and fins from the kippers and wash.

2. Put the kippers on a pan, cover with cold water, bring to the boil and boil for 5 minutes.

3. Drain well, lift on to a hot dish and serve with butter.

GRILLED KIPPERS

1. Prepare as for Boiled Kippers.

2. Heat the griller Put the kippers on the greased bars of the grill-pan with the skin side uppermost and sprinkle with pepper. Grill for about 5 minutes on each side.

3. Serve on a hot dish with a pat of butter on top.

BOILED LING

Cold water	½ lb. ling
¾ pt. milk	1 onion
Peppei	
1 oz. flour	¼ oz. butter
Garnish:— Parsley.	

1. Steep the ling in tepid water overnight. Scrape, wash well, cut into pieces. Put into a saucepan, cover with cold water.

2. Bring to the boil and simmer for half an hour. Pour off the water, add the milk, sliced onion and pepper. Simmer gently for half an hour.

3. Lift out the pieces of fish, put on to a hot dish and keep in a warm place.

4. Thicken the liquid with the flour blended with a little cold milk. Boil for 5 minutes. Add the butter and pour over the fish. Garnish with parsley.

MEAT

THE meat course of the daily dinner menu is the pivot on which the rest of the meal turns. Care in its choice and preparation is very necessary, as meat is the most expensive item in the housekeeper's daily budget. A thorough knowledge of how beef, mutton, pork, etc., are divided into joints is a great help when purchasing meat. A knowledge of the best method of cooking each particular cut or part of the animal, will help the housekeeper greatly in the economical preparation and cooking of meat.

Points to be remembered in Purchasing Meat

1. Buy from a reliable butcher.

2. Choose small meat if possible, as, in an overgrown animal the flesh is coarser, the bones larger, and there is a greater proportion of fat.

3. Flesh of meat should be a good characteristic colour, firm and elastic in texture.

4. All meat should have a fresh smell.

In addition to these points, each type of meat has its own special characteristic by which it can be judged.

Aims in Cooking Meat

(a) To render it tender and palatable.
(b) To make it pleasing to the eye.
(c) To retain its juices and nutritive properties.

The lean or muscle of meat consists of stringy fibres, which, when looked at under the microscope are composed of bundles of hollow tubes containing meat juice. These fibres are held together by connective tissues embedded with fat.

The meat juices contain a protein called meat albumen and the protein myosin is obtained from the fibres. When raw meat is cut, some of the meat juices exude and spread over the surface of the meat.

Cooking has the following effects on meat :—

(a) The surface protein coagulates.
(b) Fat cells are ruptured and the fat escapes.
(c) The connective tissue is converted into gelatine.

(*d*) Some of the moisture evaporates, causing loss of weight.

(*e*) An appetizing flavour develops in the meat.

(*f*) The colour of the lean changes.

In overcooked meat, the protein hardens and shrinks, and causes the meat to become indigestible.

INDIVIDUAL CHARACTERISTICS OF MEAT

BEEF

The best is got from an animal about 2 years old. Although not as digestible as mutton, it is more nourishing and strengthening. It must be well hung, the length of time depending on, firstly, the quality of the meat, and, secondly, the weather. (See note on Hanging of Meat, page 46.)

The **lean** is red in colour and slightly intergrained with fat, giving it a marbled appearance. The **fat** should be of a creamy colour.

VEAL

Is the flesh of the calf. It is obtainable throughout the year but is best from March to July. An animal aged 6 weeks to 3 months is best for killing. Veal does not keep well, being the flesh of an immature animal and, therefore, should be cooked within 2 or 3 days after killing.

Thorough cooking is necessary to render veal tender and digestible. The **lean** should be pale pink in colour, finely-grained and firm. If flesh has a bluish tinge, it should be rejected, as this is a sign of staleness.

The **fat** should be white, and that surrounding the kidneys should be hard and plentiful.

Soft moist fat denotes that the veal is not fresh.

MUTTON

From 3–5 years is the best age for killing sheep to obtain good well-flavoured meat. Mountain sheep, or those fed on the downs are considered the best in quality. Sheep reared on salt marshes or near the sea have a delicate flavour peculiar to themselves.

When buying, small mutton should be chosen, as it is usually plumper, more tender and less wasteful.

Mutton must be well hung.

The **lean** should be fine in texture. It is not as red as the lean of beef, but has a slightly darker red colour, and it is not intergrained with fat.

The **fat** should be hard, white and waxy.

LAMB

Is in season in early spring, but is rather dear at this time of the year. Later, it is more plentiful and cheaper. It is obtainable from spring to autumn. An animal 5–6 months old is considered the best. Hogget is the flesh of a lamb about a year old.

Lamb should be eaten soon after it is killed. The flesh is more delicate in flavour than that of mutton, but it is not as nourishing. It is more digestible than veal.

The **lean** is paler in colour than mutton.

The **fat** is of a pearly white colour.

A piece of caul should be supplied with each joint—this is a thin membraneous skin interlaced with fat, and it is used to cover the joint during roasting.

PORK

It is more difficult to digest than either beef or mutton on account of the large amount of fat between the fibres. It is because of this, and also, because of the fact that the pig is an unclean feeder that pork must be well cooked.

Young small pork is the best.

The **lean** should be of a pale pink colour, firm and fine-grained. The **fat** should be pearly white and free from black specks or kernels (small glands). It is softer than that of beef or mutton. The **rind** should be smooth and thin. The rind on a mature animal is rough and thick, and for this reason the butcher sometimes removes the rind from the pork before he sells it.

BACON

Is the flesh of the pig, salted and cured. It must be free from any unpleasant smell.

The **lean** should have a pink colour. That of mild cured bacon (which is the best) should be paler.

There should be as little gristle as possible.

The **fat** should be firm and of a pinkish white colour. Spots in the fat or kernels indicate disease.

The **rind** should be smooth and thin.

Hams.—The hind legs of a bacon pig are cut off in a round shape on the bone and cured individually. When choosing a ham, select one that is short and thick, with a moderate amount of fat.

Gammon.—The pig is brine cured, and then the hind legs are cut off square. The gammon is often divided into small cuts.

HANGING OF MEAT

However good the quality of meat, a certain length of time must elapse before cooking so that it may become tender. Meat improves by hanging. The length of time varies with—

(a) the nature and quality of the meat ;

(b) the season of the year ;

(c) the weather ;

(d) the conditions under which the meat is to be hung.

When an animal has been slaughtered, *rigor mortis* sets in ; *i.e.*, the muscles become tense, resulting in the stiffening of the meat fibres. When this has passed, the meat becomes tender and well-flavoured. This state lasts for a certain time and then bacterial action, resulting in decomposition, sets in. During hanging, the surface of the lean and fat of the meat becomes a darker colour, and dries up. If it starts to become moist again, it is a sign that the meat has been hanging for too long.

Meat will not " hang " during close " muggy " weather, or when there is thunder in the air.

Chart showing length of time good quality meat may be hung under normal and hygienic conditions :

Nature of Meat	In Winter	In Summer
Beef　　..　　..	About 10 days	About 6-7 days.
Mutton　　..　　..	,,　　,,　　,,	,,　　,,　　,,
Hogget—1 year old lamb	About 3-4 days	Should be used fresh.
⌠ Veal　　..　　..	Shouid be used fresh	Should be used fresh.
⌡ Spring Lamb　　..	Should be used fresh	Should be used fresh.

A reliable butcher will usually allow the meat to hang for the required length of time before selling it to his customers.

INTERNAL PARTS

Tripe, kidneys, heart, liver and sweetbreads must be fresh and perfectly free from taint and discolouration. They do not keep well. All fat, cores, membranes and blood-vessels should be cut away.

TRIPE

Is the inner lining of the stomach of the Ox. It is very nourishing and tender, and it is easily digested. It is usually sold prepared and partially cooked by the pork butcher.

LIVER

Lamb's and calf's liver are best but the most expensive. Sheep's liver is also often used and is cheaper. Beef liver is very nutritious but is coarse, and strong in flavour, and requires gentle and prolonged cooking to make it tender.

KIDNEYS

Mutton and beef kidneys are usually sold separately, calf's and lamb's are generally sold attached to the loin.

Mutton kidneys are best and most delicate in flavour, they are usually grilled or fried. They should be a good brown colour (without any suspicion of green tinge), plump, firm and dry. They should be free from spots or any smell, and the skin should be unbroken.

Beef kidneys are stronger in flavour and coarser in texture than sheep's kidneys. As they are rather indigestible, they should be cooked slowly. They are used for soups, stews, meat pies and meat puddings.

SWEETBREADS

Are light and easily-digested glands. They are got from either the calf, lamb or ox—the first-mentioned being most generally used. Ox sweetbreads are usually coarse and are rarely used. A " Pair " consists of the heart and throat sweetbreads. They are considered a great delicacy, but are expensive. They are mostly used for entrées and invalid dishes. The heart sweetbread is the more appreciated of the two, it is white, firm, flat and broad in shape, it is more suitable for serving whole. The throat sweetbread, which is the thymus gland of the animal, is longer and darker in colour. It is often rather membraneous and is more suitable in dishes where it can be cut up in small pieces.

SUET

Is the fat of beef or mutton, the solid fat surrounding the kidney being the best. Good quality fresh suet is firm, dry, sweet-smelling and should be devoid of kernels or blood streaks. Beef suet should be cream-coloured. It is more digestible and richer than mutton suet, and is used for suet pastry and may be used for steamed puddings. Mutton suet is harder than beef, and is white and waxy in appearance.

LARD

Is made from the fat of pork. It is rendered by putting the fat into a container standing in boiling water. The liquid fat is then poured off into clean jars, and must be kept air-tight or it will become rancid.

METHODS OF CUTTING ANIMAL CARCASES
INTO JOINTS

The cutting up of meat varies in different countries and even in the different localities of one country. The following diagrams give the prevailing method in Ireland. The notes given with the method of cutting up each animal should be of assistance to the housewife in deciding what piece she should buy for each particular dish.

BEEF

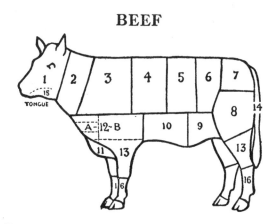

1. Head.
2. Neck Beef.
3. Rib Steaks.
4. Ribs (7 Ribs).
5. Sirloin.
6. Steak piece.
7. Tail-End.
8. Round Steak.
9. Flank of Beef.
10. Brisket.
11. Button-End.
12. Shoulder Beef divided into—
    A. Shoulder rings.
    B. Housekeeper's cut.
13. Leg Beef.
14. Ox Tail.
15. Ox Tongue.
16. Cowheel.

METHODS OF COOKING

Head
Neck   } These parts are rather coarse-grained and gelatinous.
Button-End }   Used for cheap stews and soups.
Rib Steaks: Suitable for stewing and braising.

Ribs : Good for roasting. The ribs may be boned and rolled. The rib next the sirloin is called the " wing-rib ". It is usually roasted on the bone or it may be cut into steaks and used for Club Steaks.

Sirloin : This is considered the choice piece. It may be roasted on the bone or boned and rolled before roasting. Some parts of the sirloin are more tender than others, *e.g.*,

> (*a*) The fillet or " under-cut " is the best piece. It can be removed from the sirloin, cut into steaks and used for Tournedos, Chateaubriand, etc.

> (*b*) The top of the sirloin is very tender. This piece may be cut into steaks and used for Entrecote Steaks, Minute Steaks, etc.

> (*c*) The tail-piece is not tender. It would be better to cut it off the sirloin and braise or stew it or put it into pickle and use for Boiled Corned Beef. When the tail-piece is cut off the sirloin it will leave a smaller tender roast which could also be cut into steaks and used for Porterhouse Steaks or T-Bone Steaks.

Steak Piece : Cut into steaks for grilling or frying. Sold as Sirloin Steak or Rump Steak.

Tail-End : May be braised, or pickled and boiled.

Round Steak : Consists of a large solid piece of meat with very little bone, and is usually cut into steaks for stewing, or may be braised, or pickled or salted.

Flank of Beef : May be stewed, or salted and boiled.

Brisket : Usually salted or spiced and boiled.

Shoulder Rings : May be stewed. Usually sold as mince.

Housekeeper's Cut : May be roasted or braised.

Leg Beef : May be stewed. Used mostly for stock as it is gelatinous.

Ox Tail : Stewed or used in Oxtail Soup.

Ox Tongue : Usually pickled and boiled, used either hot or cold. May also be braised.

Cowheel : is very gelatinous. Used for making jelly and stock. May also be boiled or stewed and served with a good piquant sauce.

VEAL

1. Head.
2. Neck.
3. Blade Bone or Back Gigot.
4. Veal Cutlets.
5. Centre Loin.
6. Side Loin.
7. Tail-End.
8. Fillet.

9. Hind-knuckle.
10. Flank.
11. Breast.
12. Centre Cut.
13. Fore-knuckle.
14. Calf's feet.
15. Tail.

METHODS OF COOKING

Head : sometimes boiled, and served either hot or cold. Also stewed.

Neck : used in stews and broths.

Blade Bone : may be stewed or braised.

Veal Cutlets : suitable for roasting, frying and grilling.

Centre Loin : contains the kidney. Suitable for roasting—may be boned and stuffed. Also, may be cut into chops.

Side Loin : may be stuffed or cut into chops.

Tail-End : good for roasting.

Fillet : this is the choicest and most tender part. It is the most expensive to buy. Used for roasting, entrées, braising. There is practically no waste with this joint.

Hind-knuckle : used for stock and soups.

Flank : used for stews, sometimes left on the fillet for roasting.

Breast : cheap to buy. May be boned, stuffed, rolled for roasting, or may be stewed or braised.

Centre Cut : may be roasted.

Fore-knuckle : more tender than hind-knuckle. May be stewed or boiled.

Calf's foot : used for making calf's foot jelly or stock.

Tail : used for stews and soups.

MUTTON

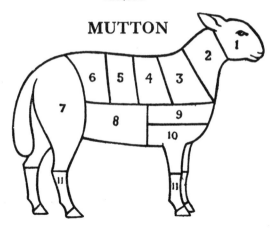

1. Head.
2. Neck.
3. Gigot Chops.
4. Fair-End—Cutlets.
5. Centre Loin.
6. Side Loin.

7. Leg of Mutton (about 6″ of lap usually left on leg).
8. Lap of Mutton and Breast.
9. Centre Cut.
10. Hand Gigot.
9 and 10 cut and left together form the shoulder.

METHODS OF COOKING

1. **Head :** used in broths, stews and may be boiled. Cheap to buy.
2. **Neck :** used in stews and soups.
3. **Gigot :** used in stews. Has a good proportion of lean.
4. **Fair-End :** used for roasting, and when divided into cutlets, for grilling and frying. It is dearer to buy cutlets already cut and trimmed, than to buy a piece of Fair-End and cut and trim it at home.
5. **Centre Loin :** may be roasted or cut into chops and grilled or fried. This piece is expensive on account of the larger proportion of bone.
6. **Side Loin :** May be roasted or cut into chops and grilled or fried.
7. **Leg of Mutton :** is one of the most economical joints, as it contains a smaller amount of bone and fat compared to other parts. The whole leg may be roasted or boiled. When the joint is too large it may be divided into the fillet or top piece and the shank. The fillet is then usually roasted, and the lower piece boiled or braised.
8. **Lap of Mutton :** cheap to buy. Used for stewing.
9. **Centre Cut :** usually boiled, or roasted, or braised.
10. **Hand Gigot :** may be braised.
    Shoulder (Nos. 9 and 10) : used for roasting. May be boned and stuffed.
11. **Trotters :** usually stewed.

LAMB

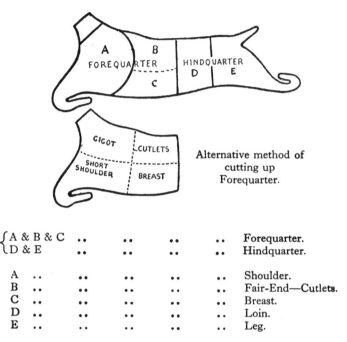

Alternative method of
cutting up
Forequarter.

$\left\{\begin{array}{l}A \& B \& C \\ D \& E\end{array}\right.$ .. .. Forequarter.
.. .. Hindquarter.

A .. .. Shoulder.
B .. .. Fair-End—Cutlets.
C .. .. Breast.
D .. .. Loin.
E .. .. Leg.

As lamb gets bigger and older it is divided like mutton.

METHODS OF COOKING

Forequarter may be roasted whole. Consists of Shoulder, Breast, and Fair-End.

Hindquarter contains the kidney. May be roasted whole. Consists of Leg and Loin.

Shoulder : suitable for roasting.

Breast : may be stewed or braised.

Fair-End : may be divided into cutlets and grilled or fried.

Loin : suitable for roasting or may be divided into chops for grilling and frying.

Leg : suitable for roasting.

BACON

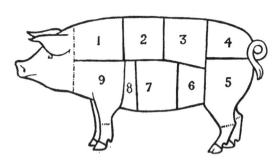

1. Collar.
2. Back and Ribs.
3. Long Loin.
4. Corner Gammon ⎫ Gammon or
5. Gammon Hock ⎭   Ham.

6. Flank.
7. Thin Streaky.
8. Thick Streaky.
9. Shoulder or Fore Hock.
10. Head.

METHODS OF COOKING

Collar : may be boiled, or sliced and fried.

Back ⎫
Long Loin ⎭ Expensive part. Usually cut for rashers.

Corner Gammon ⎫
Gammon Hock ⎭ May be boiled or baked, sometimes boned.

Flank : Economical part—used for boiling.

Thin Streaky : May be cut for rashers, or used for boiling.

Thick Streaky : Cut for rashers or used for boiling.

Shoulder : Used for boiling, sometimes boned.

Porksteak : Removed from the loin before curing, and sold fresh.

Head : Used for boiling.

Pork

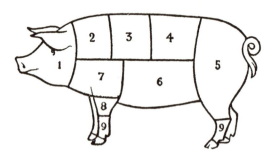

1. Head.
2. Back Gigot.
3. Fair-End (Cutlets).
4. Loin.
5. Leg.

6. Streaky.
7. Shoulder.
8. Shank.
9. Foot.

METHODS OF COOKING

Head : Salted. May be boiled and served hot or cold. It is often made into brawn.

Back Gigot : Generally roasted or cut and fried.

Fair-End : May be divided into cutlets or roasted whole.

Loin : Contains the kidney. Often roasted. May be divided into pork chops.

Leg : Used for roasting, may be stuffed. Sometimes salted and boiled.

Streaky : Generally salted and boiled and served either hot or cold.

Shoulder : Usually salted and boiled.

Shank
Foot } Generally salted and boiled.

N.B.—It is necessary to score the rind of parts to be roasted to facilitate carving.

Boiling

BOILING of meat is cooking by immersion in water just below boiling-point. The cooked meat should be tender and full of juice, this is obtained by regulating the amount of heat so that there is just a slow movement on the surface of the water. If the rate of boiling is fast the fibre of the meat contracts and becomes tough.

General Rules for Boiling Meat

1. Wipe fresh meat with a damp cloth, wash rabbit and internal meat such as sweetbreads and tripe. Wash salt meat, *e.g.*, bacon, ham, corned beef and tongue. If it is very salty or heavily smoked, soak it in cold water to remove some of the salt and to soften the fibres.

2. Weigh the meat and calculate the cooking time, 30 minutes per lb. for fresh meat and 35 minutes per lb. for salt meat. For a large piece of ham see page 58. A leg of mutton weighing approximately 7 lbs. would take 2¾-3 hours.

3. Put fresh meat into boiling water and salt meat into cold water. Bring to the boil and skim.

4. Boil very gently until cooked. Lift the meat out of the liquor and leave to relax in a warm place for 15 minutes before carving.

5. Serve with appropriate accompaniments.

BOILED MUTTON

3 lbs. mutton   Boiling salted water
Carrots and white turnips

To serve:—Parsley Sauce (pouring) page 150.

1. Wipe the meat with a damp meat cloth.

2. Put to cook in boiling salted water. Bring back to the boil. Skim. Boil for 3 minutes, then simmer steadily until cooked, about 1½ hours.

3. Prepare the carrots and turnips (page 18) and cut into neat pieces (the carrots divided down the centre and across in halves and the turnips cut in quarters). Cook with the meat. Time, about ¾ hour according to size.

4. Lift out the meat, drain and serve on a hot dish. Keep the pot liquor for Mutton Broth.

5. Drain the vegetables and serve with the meat or separately in a hot vegetable dish. Garnish with parsley.

Approximate times for cooking Mutton :

3 lbs. centre-cut allow 1½ hours.
6-7 lbs. leg allow 2½-3 hours.
3½-4 lb. fillet-end of leg allow 2 hours.
3¼ lbs. shank-end of leg allow 1¼ hours.

SHEEP'S HEAD

1 sheep's head	1 medium-sized onion stuck
Bunch of mixed fresh herbs	with 3 cloves
Boiling salted water	

To serve:— Parsley Sauce (page 150).
To garnish:— Rolls of bacon. 2 or 3 slices of lemon.

1. Have the head split in two by the butcher. Lift out the brains, and detach the tongue.
2. Wash the head and tongue well, and scrape away all mucous material from the nasal passages.
3. Steep the head and tongue in cold salted water for 30 minutes, and wash again in fresh cold water. Blanch it.
4. Put head and tongue down to cook in boiling salted water. Bring slowly to the boil. Skim well.
5. Add the onion and the washed herbs. Allow to simmer steadily until the meat slips easily away from the bone, about 1½ hours.
6. Lift out the head and tongue. Remove all the meat from the bones and divide into neat pieces. Skin the tongue, and slice it neatly.
7. Arrange the meat and tongue in centre of a hot dish, and garnish with cooked rolls of bacon and slices of lemon.

BOILED BACON

1½ lbs. bacon	Cold water

Browned crumbs (page 216)
To serve:— Cooked Cabbage.
½ pt. White Pouring Sauce (page 149).

1. Wash the bacon, and scrape off any discoloured or rusty parts. If very salty, steep in cold water for a few hours.
2. Put into a saucepan, and cover with cold water. Bring slowly to the boil. Skim. Boil for 5 minutes, then simmer steadily for about 1¼ hours.
3. When cooked, lift out the bacon, and remove the rind. It will peel off easily if the bacon is cooked.
4. Sprinkle with browned crumbs, or crisp under the griller.
5. Serve on a hot dish with freshly-cooked cabbage, or if liked serve the cabbage separately in a hot vegetable dish.

Approximate times for cooking bacon :

1½ lbs. streaky bacon (thin piece) allow 1¼ hours.
3 lbs. streaky bacon (thin piece) allow 1¾ hours.
1½ lbs. shoulder bacon (thick piece) allow 1½ hours.
3 lbs. gammon (thick piece) allow 2 hours.
5 lbs. gammon (thick piece) allow 2½ hours.

PIG'S CHEEK

1 pig's cheek
Cold water

Browned crumbs (page 216)

To serve:— Cooked cabbage (page 101).
White Pouring Sauce (page 149).

1. Wash the cheek well in cold water, paying special attention to the nasal passages, eye cavity, and around the tongue and teeth, using a pointed knife where necessary. Make a slit at the ear, and clean well inside, using a pointed knife.

2. If very salty, steep overnight in cold water. Blanch it.

3. Put to cook in a large saucepan with enough cold water to cover it. Bring it slowly to the boil, skim, then allow it to boil gently until cooked, about 2 hours.

4. Remove the skin from the cheek, and sprinkle with browned crumbs.

5. Crisp under the griller, or in the oven, for a few minutes.

6. Place a spray of washed and dried parsley in the eye cavity. Serve on a " pillow " of cooked cabbage on a hot dish.

The remainder of the cabbage may be served in a hot vegetable dish.

NOTE.—If the cheek has been dried and cured, it will require to be steeped for several hours. Put to cook in cold water and give it 1 hour's extra cooking.

BOILED OX TONGUE

1 ox tongue, pickled
Cold water
1 onion
1 carrot

1 white turnip
2 sticks of celery
Bouquet garni (page 18)

To serve:— Espagnole Sauce (page 152) *or*
Parsley Sauce (page 150).

1. Wash the tongue in cold water. Trim away the root.

2. Put into a saucepan with sufficient cold water to cover it. Bring it to the boil. Skim. Add the prepared vegetables, cut into chunks, and the flavourings.

3. Allow to boil gently until cooked. Time for cooking : a small tongue 2½ hours, a large tongue 3-3½ hours.

4. When cooked, pour off the water, place under running cold water for a few minutes. Lift out and remove skin and bone. Carve and serve.

CORNED BEEF

2 lbs. of brisket, *or* tail-end of corned beef
Cold water

To serve:— Parsley Sauce.

1. Weigh and wash the meat. Put into a saucepan and cover with cold water.
2. Bring slowly to the boil, skim, and simmer steadily for about 1¼ hours.
3. Take up, drain and serve.

BOILED PICKLED PORK

| 2 lbs. pickled or salt pork | Carrot | } if liked |
| Cold water | Parsnip | |

To serve:— Cooked greens.

1. Wash the pork and put it to cook in a saucepan with enough cold water to cover it. Bring to the boil. Boil for 3 minutes and skim. Simmer steadily for about 1½ hours.
2. Prepare the carrots and parsnips (page 18) and cut into neat pieces. Cook with the meat. Time, about ¾ hour, according to size.
3. When the meat and vegetables are cooked drain well and arrange them on a hot dish.

BOILED HAM

Ham   Bunch fresh mixed herbs
            Browned crumbs (page 216)

1. Soak the ham in cold water overnight.
2. Scrape the ham, remove all rusty and discoloured parts. Put into a saucepan, cover with cold water, add the washed herbs. Cover the saucepan, bring to the boil and boil for 3 minutes. Skim. Simmer steadily until cooked—for time, see below.
3. When cooked, lift out and remove the rind, sprinkle with browned crumbs or crisp in the oven.
4. **If to be served cold** shorten the time by about half-an-hour, allow the ham to cool in the water. When cold lift out, remove the rind and sprinkle with browned crumbs.

Approximate times for cooking ham :

5 lbs. ham allow 2½ hours
8   ,,   ,,   ,,   3½   ,,
12–13   ,,   ,,   ,,   4½   ,,

Stewing

STEWING is long, slow cooking in liquid in a closed vessel.

A stew is generally a mixture of meat and vegetables. It depends for its success on :—

(a) the rate at which it is cooked ;

(b) careful seasoning ;

(c) blending of flavours.

Regarding (a) it must be remembered that " a stew boiled is a stew spoiled." The maintenance of a low steady temperature (180°) is most essential to the success of a stew. If stew boils strongly for any length of time, the protein and gelatine of the meat harden, thus rendering the meat " tough " instead of tender.

Stewing is one of the most economical ways of cooking as :

(1) The inferior and coarser parts of the meat can be used.

(2) Any juices which escape from the meat are served in the gravy.

(3) Little attention and very little fuel is required, as only a simmering heat is necessary.

(4) Vegetables are cooked and served with the meat, thereby giving extra flavours to the stew.

(5) Less meat may be used if dumplings are cooked in and served with the stew.

Methods of Stewing

There are two ways of cooking stews :

(a) Over gentle heat.

(b) In the oven.

In both cases the lid must fit the vessel closely to prevent waste through evaporation.

Preparation of Meat for Stewing

Meat is wiped with a damp meat cloth. Surplus fat is removed and the meat is divided into neat pieces about 2 ins. × 2 ins.

Sometimes the meat is lightly fried before it is stewed, this prevents escape of some of the juices. This process is used especially when meat of superior quality is being used in stew. Preparatory frying also helps to brown the gravy.

The liquid to which the meat is added may be either thin, or of the consistency of a stewing sauce. It is advisable to use a thin liquid for meat that is tough, as it penetrates and softens the fibres better.

Serving

When cooked in a saucepan, meat is served in centre of a hot dish with the gravy poured over. The vegetables, which were cooked with it, are served to garnish the dish.

If stew is cooked in a casserole, it is served in the dish in which it was cooked, hence the term " en casserole ".

Fricassée

This is a white casserole or stew, usually made from poultry. The raw meat is first stiffened without colouring in fat. The cooking is then completed in White Stewing Sauce made from chicken or white stock instead of milk. Lastly cream is added to finish the sauce before serving.

Blanquette

This is a white casserole or stew made from white meats. The meat is first cooked in water or white stock. White Stewing Sauce is then made using this liquid instead of milk. The meat is put back into the sauce and heated before serving.

IRISH STEW

2 lbs. breast of mutton, *or* 1½ lbs. gigot chops
2 lbs. potatoes   Pepper and salt
5 medium-sized onions   ¾ pint cold water
1 teaspoonful chopped parsley

1. Cut the meat into neat pieces, removing the skin and superfluous fat. All fat is not removed because the potatoes will absorb a certain amount.
2. Peel the onions and chop one. Wash and peel the potatoes thinly. If small, leave whole, if large, cut in two. Slice one thinly.
3. Put the meat in the bottom of a heavy saucepan, then put in the sliced potato and chopped onion, season with pepper and salt. Add the water, bring to the boil. Skim. Simmer for 1 hour.
4. Arrange the potatoes and onions on top, cover and simmer for a further hour.
5. Serve the meat in the centre of a hot dish, arrange potatoes and onions around. Pour a little sauce over and serve the remainder in a hot sauce-boat. Garnish with parsley.

HOT POT

1½ lbs. gigot chops   Pepper and salt
2 lbs. potatoes (sliced)   Cold water
2 onions (chopped)   1 dessertspoonful finely-
2 carrots (sliced)   chopped parsley
2 sticks celery (chopped)

1. Arrange in layers in a greased casserole, pie-dish, or fireproof dish, and season well. Finish with a layer of potatoes. Pour on enough cold water to half fill the dish.
2. Cover with a lid, or with a piece of cooking foil. Cook in a very moderate oven for 2–2½ hours. Remove the lid for the last ½ hour to brown the potatoes.
3. Place the casserole on a plain dish paper on a hot dish and garnish with parsley.

BROWN STEW

1 lb. round or rib steak	1 oz. flour
4 ozs. onion	³/₄ pt. brown stock
4 ozs. carrot	Pepper and salt
2 ozs. white turnips	1 teaspoonful Worcester Sauce
1 oz. fat	

2 soft tomatoes or 1 dessertspoonful Tomato Sauce

To garnish:—Julienne strips (page 217).

1. Cut the meat into pieces about 2 inches square.
2. Prepare the vegetables (page 18), slice the onion and cut the carrots and turnips into neat pieces.
3. Heat the fat in a saucepan, add the meat and onion, and brown quickly, then lift out on to a plate.
4. Add the flour and seasoning and stir over a moderate heat until lightly browned. Cool slightly and add the stock, stirring all the time.
5. Add Worcester Sauce and tomatoes, bring to the boil and skim.
6. Return the meat and onion to the saucepan, add the carrots and turnip. Cover and stew gently for approximately 2 hours, stirring occasionally.
7. When cooked, put the meat on a hot dish. Strain the sauce, correct consistency and seasoning, bring to the boil. Pour a little sauce over the meat, serve the remainder in a hot sauce-boat. Garnish the stew with Julienne strips.

EXETER STEW

Make as for Brown Stew, with the addition of Savoury Balls (*see below*).

SAVOURY BALLS

4 ozs. flour	¹/₂ teasp. baking powder
Pepper and salt	¹/₂ oz. breadcrumbs
¹/₂ oz. finely-chopped onion	1¹/₄ ozs. finely-chopped beef suet
Cold water	1 teasp. finely-chopped parsley

1. Sift the flour, baking-powder and salt into a bowl. Add the remainder of the dry ingredients and mix well with a wooden spoon.
2. Add enough cold water to make to a stiff paste.
3. Put on to a floured board, knead very lightly and form into a roll.
4. Cut into twelve equal-sized pieces and roll each into a ball. Add to the stew 1 hour before serving.

STEWED TRIPE AND ONIONS

1 lb. tripe	¾ pint milk
2 onions (medium-sized)	Pepper and salt
2 cloves	1 tablesp. cream (if liked)
1 oz. butter or margarine	1 oz. flour

To garnish:— Six sippets of toast.
Sprigs of parsley.

1. Wash the tripe well in cold water three or four times. Cut into 2-inch pieces. Blanch it (page 217).
2. Put into a saucepan with the milk, cloves, butter and the onions cut in slices. Cover with a close-fitting lid. Bring to the boil slowly, and allow to simmer gently until tender, about 1–1¼ hours, stirring occasionally.
3. Ten minutes before the tripe is fully cooked, stir in the flour blended in a little milk, and continue stirring until cooked. Season and add cream.
4. Remove the cloves and serve the tripe in a hot dish with some of the sauce poured over. Garnish with toast cut into diamond shapes, and with sprigs of parsley.

CASSEROLE OF BEEF

1½ lbs. thick part of leg beef	6 ozs. sliced onion
1 tablespoonful seasoned flour	2 glasses red wine
4 ozs. salted breast of pork	A clove of garlic
6 ozs. tomatoes	Pepper and salt
1 tablespoonful cooking oil	1 dessertspoonful mushroom ketchup

To serve:—12 ozs. long-grained rice (boil as on page 217).

1. Wipe the meat, remove fat, cut into cubes and toss in the seasoned flour. Cut the pork into small pieces.
2. Remove the eyes from the tomatoes, skin them, cut in two and remove the seeds. Cut the flesh into pieces.
3. Heat the oil in a heavy pan, add the pork and cook well. Add the onion, tomato and meat, stir over the heat until the meat is lightly browned.
4. Mix in the red wine, then add sufficient water to nearly cover the meat (about ¼ pt.). Stir until it boils for a few minutes, put into a casserole. Crush the garlic and put on top of the meat.
5. Cover with cooking foil and a tightly-fitting lid and cook in a very moderate oven for 3–4 hours.
6. Stir in the mushroom ketchup, taste the sauce and correct seasoning.

QUICK MINCE DINNER

1 lb. rib or round steak (minced)	1 clove garlic (chopped)
3 ozs. margarine or other fat	Pepper and salt
1 tin tomatoes (13 ozs.)	4 ozs. mushrooms
4 ozs. chopped onions	2–4 ozs. grated cheese
Chopped parsley	

To serve:—Colcannon or cooked spaghetti.

1. Fry the meat in 2 ozs. of hot fat for about 7 minutes. Add the tomatoes, onion, garlic, pepper and salt. Stir over the heat for about 5 minutes. Cook over a low heat or in a covered casserole in a very moderate oven for about 30 minutes.

2. Remove the stalks and skins from the mushrooms, if large, break into pieces. Heat the remainder of the margarine in a small saucepan, add the mushrooms, put a piece of greased paper on them, cover the saucepan and leave over a low heat for a few minutes.

3. Add the mushrooms and cheese to the meat and cook slowly for about 5 minutes. Sprinkle with parsley and serve.

HARICOT OF MUTTON

1½ lbs. fair-end of mutton (about 5 cutlets) or fillet of mutton	Bouquet garni
4 ozs. onion—chopped	1 teasp. mushroom ketchup
1 oz. flour	1 teasp. tomato sauce
¾ pt. brown stock	Pepper and salt

To garnish:—Julienne strips :—4 ozs. carrot.
2 ozs. white turnip.

1. If using fair-end, saw off the chine bone, shorten by about 2 inches, and divide into neat cutlets. If using the fillet cut into neat pieces. Trim off surplus fat.

2. Melt a little of the surplus fat and fry the meat and onion in it.

3. Pour off fat, leaving about 1 tablespoonful. Add the flour, and stir well until it becomes a brown colour. Cool for a few minutes and gradually add the stock, stirring well.

4. Bring to the boil. Skim, add seasoning, flavourings and bouquet garni.

5. Cover with tightly-fitting lid. Stew until the meat is tender, about 1½ hours. Skim frequently.

6. Prepare the carrots and turnips as on page 18 and cut into match-like strips. Add the trimmings to the stew and cook the strips in boiling salted water until tender.

7. When the haricot is cooked, serve on a hot dish, with the meat in the centre, strain the gravy over and garnish with Julienne Strips.

CURRY OF MUTTON

1 lb. lean mutton	1 oz. flour
1 oz. fat	³/₄ pt. stock
2 ozs. onion (chopped)	1 dessertspoonful chutney
2 teasps. curry powder	¹/₂ apple (chopped)
1 teasp. tomato sauce	

Border of Rice:—6 ozs. long-grained rice (boil as on page 217).

To Garnish:—Parsley.　Cayenne pepper.

1. Cut the meat into pieces ½ inch square.

2. Heat the fat, fry the meat until brown. Fry the onion.

3. Add the flour and curry powder and cook well.

4. Add the stock gradually, stirring all the time. Bring to the boil. Skim.

5. Add the apple, chutney and tomato sauce. Cover tightly with a lid, and stew for 1½ hours.

6. When cooked serve on a hot dish in a border of rice. Garnish rice with parsley and cayenne pepper.

CURRIED BEEF

Make as for Curry of Mutton, using 1 lb. round steak instead of lean mutton.

CARBONADE OF BEEF

1 lb. rib or round steak	Pepper and salt
1½ ozs. seasoned flour (page 216)	³/₄ pint beer
1½ ozs. fat	Bouquet garni (page 18)
1 tablesp. lemon juice	Chopped parsley

To serve:—Fried onion rings.

1. Cut the beef in inch cubes and toss in the seasoned flour.

2. Heat the fat in a heavy saucepan, put in the meat and fry until lightly browned. Add lemon juice, salt and pepper and stir well. Add the beer and bring to the boil, stirring well.

3. Put into a casserole, add the bouquet garni and cook in a very moderate oven for about 2 hours.

4. Remove the bouquet garni, sprinkle with parsley and serve.

Roasting

ROASTING formerly meant cooking before direct or radiant heat in a current of air. A " roasting-jack " was usually used, this had a clockwork mechanism, which kept the meat rotating, thus exposing all surfaces to the heat in turn. The modern rotisseur is on this principle.

Baking or Oven Roasting

Use only the best cuts of good quality meat for this method.

High temperatures tend to toughen meat and cause a lot of shrinkage. Meat roasted at approx. 400°F. is more uniformly cooked, shrinks less and is more tender because of the slow penetration of heat. The flavour is better and the meat retains more juice.

When roasting meat in an electric cooker the directions for roasting as supplied with the particular type of cooker should be followed.

BONING OF MEAT

A joint which is boned and stuffed has distinct advantages :—

 (i) It is more economical, no waste in carving.
 (ii) The removed bones can be used more advantageously in stock for soup or for gravy to serve with the joint.
 (iii) The addition of stuffing makes the meat go further.
 (iv) It supplies a pleasant change from the plain joint.

The joints which are usually boned and stuffed are :—

Breast, shoulder, leg and fillet of mutton.
Fillet of pork.
Breast of veal.

Ribs of beef are usually boned and rolled, but are not stuffed.

To ensure that a stuffed joint is cooked, the joint must be weighed after stuffing.

To Bone a Joint

A short, sharp-pointed knife should be used. Care must be taken that the joint is disfigured as little as possible, and especially that the outer skin is not pierced. The bones should be removed from the joint as free from meat as possible.

A knowledge of the position and shape of the bone is necessary. Keeping the knife pressed close to the bone all the time, cut away the flesh with sharp, even strokes. Take care that the knife does not slip. When two bones meet at a joint, cut through the sinews and remove the loosened bones. Any part that is unsuitable, *e.g.*, gristle and superfluous fat, is removed. In some cases, *e.g.*, breast of mutton or veal, the meat is flattened out, the stuffing laid on and the joint rolled. In others, *e.g.*, shoulder or fillet of mutton, the cavity left by the removed bones is filled with stuffing. The meat is then secured into shape with fine white string.

TO ROAST MEAT

1. Wipe the meat with a damp cloth. Weigh and calculate the time according to the type of meat (see chart, page 72). Extra time should be allowed for a very thick joint.

2. The roasting tin must be larger than the joint, so that any juices and fat from the meat will collect in it. Use a roasting grid if liked.

3. Have the oven at 400°F. Heat a little fat (about 3 ozs.) in the roasting tin, when it is hot put in the meat and baste all the surfaces with the hot fat.

4. Baste the meat frequently during cooking. Turn the meat when half cooked.

5. Press the meat with a spoon to test if it is cooked and judge by the colour of the juice. If the juice is red the meat is undercooked, if pink the meat is medium-rare, if brown the meat is well done.

All meat with the exception of beef should be well done. Beef may be rare or medium-rare according to taste.

6. When meat is cooked, lift it on to a hot dish. Keep hot while gravy is being made.

Pot-Roasting

Pot-roasting is a useful and economical method of cooking meat or birds, which would be too small to oven-roast, and which would be too big to grill. It also obviates the necessity for heating an oven for the sole purpose of cooking a small piece of meat. The meat should be of good quality, as for roasting.

Method for Pot-Roasting

1. Wipe the meat with a damp cloth, weigh and calculate time for cooking. (See chart, page 72).

2. Heat about 2 ozs. fat in a heavy saucepan. Put in the meat and brown the surface all over.

3. Cover with a close-fitting lid and cook over a moderate heat, allowing the same amount of time as for oven-roasting. Baste and turn the meat occasionally.

4. Serve as for roast meat, and make the gravy in the usual way.

THIN BROWN GRAVY FOR ROAST MEATS

1. When the cooked meat has been removed from the roasting tin, place the tin over the heat for a few minutes to caramelize the sediment. Pour off the fat.

2. Add salt and pepper to the tin and mix well. Pour in ½ pt. stock, bring to the boil, skim, correct for colour and seasoning. Strain into a hot sauce-boat.

THICKENED BROWN GRAVY FOR ROAST STUFFED MEATS

1. When the cooked meat has been removed from the roasting tin, place the tin over the heat for a few minutes to caramelize the sediment. Pour off the fat leaving about 1 dessertspoonful.

2. Add salt, pepper and 1 dessertspoonful flour. Mix well until brown and smooth in texture.

3. Add ½ pt. stock, stirring well, bring to the boil. Skim. Boil for about 3 minutes, correct for colour and seasoning. Strain into a hot sauce-boat.

YORKSHIRE PUDDING

2 ozs. flour	1 egg
Pinch of salt	¼ pt. milk

2 ozs. fat or oil

1. Sift the flour and salt into a bowl. Make a well in the centre and drop in the unbeaten egg with a little milk.

2. Mix smoothly round and round, with a wooden spoon, allowing the flour to fall in gradually, adding about half the milk as required.

3. Work with the back of the spoon to remove any lumps. Beat with the bowl of the spoon for a few minutes to introduce some air.

4. Add the remainder of the milk and leave to stand for about ½–1 hour in a cool place.

5. Put the fat to heat in a Yorkshire tin or divide it between eight deep patty tins. Put into a hot oven until the fat is hot.

6. Stir the batter and pour into the prepared tin or tins and bake in a hot oven 450° F. for about 25–30 minutes.

7. When cooked, cut into eight pieces. Arrange on a dish paper on a hot dish with slices overlapping. Individual Yorkshire puddings may be served in the same way. Garnish with parsley.

STUFFING

4 ozs. breadcrumbs	2 ozs. margarine
1 teasp. chopped parsley	Salt and pepper

1 oz. chopped onion

Melt the margarine in a saucepan, add the onion, cover with a round of greaseproof paper. Put on the lid and allow to cook without colouring for about 5 minutes. Mix with the other ingredients. Stuffing or forcemeat should just stick together when pressed in the hand, but should fall apart when released.

SAGE AND ONION STUFFING

4 ozs. breadcrumbs	2 ozs. margarine
2 ozs. chopped onion	Salt and pepper
1 teaspoonful chopped sage	

Melt the butter in a saucepan, add the onion, cover with a round of greaseproof paper. Put on the lid and allow to cook without colouring for about 5 minutes. Add sage, crumbs, salt and pepper. Mix all well together.

POTATO STUFFING

8 ozs. mashed potatoes	Pinch of mixed herbs
1 oz. chopped onion	Salt and pepper
1 teasp. chopped parsley	1 oz. margarine

Melt the margarine in a saucepan, add the onion, cover with a round of greaseproof paper. Put on the lid and allow to cook without colouring for about 5 minutes. Mix with the other ingredients.

ROAST STUFFED HEART—(Pot-Roast)

1 sheep's heart	2 ozs. fat
2 ozs. sage and onion stuffing (above)	
Thickened Brown Gravy (page 67)	

To garnish:—Parsley. Julienne strips (page 217).

1. Wash the heart thoroughly in several lots of tepid water. Cut away the blood-vessels opening into the heart. Cut down into the division which separates one side of heart from the other. Rinse it and dry well.

2. Fill the cavity with the stuffing and tie a strong piece of greased paper over the top, or the opening may be stitched if liked.

3. Melt the dripping in a heavy saucepan, and when hot put in the heart, baste well.

4. Pot roast according to directions on page 66. Baste occasionally and turn often to ensure that it is evenly roasted. Allow ¾-1 hour according to size.

5. When cooked, lift on to a plate, remove twine and paper, and keep hot while making the gravy. When gravy is made, strain it into a hot sauce-boat.

6. Serve the heart on a hot dish, and garnish with Julienne strips and parsley.

NOTE :—

(a) Sheep's Heart may also be roasted in the oven (page 66).

(b) Ox Heart and Calf's Heart may be roasted in the same way. Allow double the quantity of stuffing and cook Ox Heart for 2-2½ hours, and Calf's Heart 1½-2 hrs. depending on size.

(c) Hearts may also be stuffed and stewed.

BEEFSTEAK AND KIDNEY PIE

5 ozs. Rough Puff Pastry (page 175)

Filling:

1 lb. round steak	1 tomato (cut in slices)
¼ lb. beef kidney	Stock
2 ozs. carrot (cut in slices)	1 tablespoonful seasoned flour
2 ozs. onion (chopped)	1 teaspoonful chopped parsley

To glaze:—Beaten egg.
To garnish:—Parsley.

1. Skin and remove core from kidney, cutting it into pieces. Soak in water for about 20 minutes.

2. Remove surplus fat from the meat and cut into pieces.

3. Toss the meat and kidney in seasoned flour. Arrange in a pie-dish (one-pint size), and distribute the vegetables evenly throughout. Threequarters fill the pie-dish with stock.

4. Roll out the pastry a little larger than pie-dish. Cut off strip ½ inch wide.

5. Brush edge of pie-dish with cold water and place the strip of pastry on it, cut edge outwards. Brush over with cold water.

6. Cover pie with the pastry, and press the edges well together. Trim the edge with a sharp knife, flake and decorate.

7. Brush over the pie with beaten egg.

8. Roll the remaining pastry into a strip 1 inch wide. Cut into four diamonds and mark each with a knife to resemble a leaf.

9. Make a hole in the centre of the pie and arrange the leaves neatly around the hole. Brush them with beaten egg.

10. Place the pie on a tin and bake in a hot oven (450° F.) for 10 minutes. Cover with a sheet of greased paper. Reduce the heat to a very moderate temperature (350° F.) and cook for 1½-2 hrs.

11. When almost cooked, pour in a little extra boiling stock if necessary.

12. Serve on a plain dish paper on a dish. Garnish with parsley.

BAKED LIVER AND BACON

½ lb. lamb's or calf's liver	½ pt. brown stock
¼ lb. streaky rashers	½ teaspoonful Worcester Sauce *or*
2 ozs. stuffing (page 67)	½ teaspoonful Mushroom Ketchup

Salt and pepper

1. Cut the liver into slices about ½ inch in thickness. Place on a greased tin. Spread a large teaspoonful of stuffing on each piece of liver.

2. Remove the rind from the rashers and cut each in two. Place a piece of rasher on top of the stuffing.

3. Pour a little stock into the tin, cover with a sheet of greased paper, and bake in a moderately hot oven for 30 minutes.

4. Serve on a hot dish. Add remainder of stock to the tin and boil up. Add the sauce or ketchup, season and strain around the liver on dish.

HOT GALANTINE

1 lb. round steak	½ lb. sausages
6 ozs. breadcrumbs	¼ lb. rashers
2 ozs. onion	1 teaspoonful chopped parsley
Pepper and salt	1 teaspoonful Worcester Sauce
1 egg	1 teaspoonful Tomato Sauce

To coat:—Egg and crumbs.

To fry :—Bath of fat.

To serve:—½ pint Tomato Sauce (page 152), *or* Espagnole Sauce (page 152).

1. Mince the meat and skin the sausages. Remove rind and bone from rashers, and cut into neat pieces.

2. Mix the meat, breadcrumbs, finely-chopped onion, herbs and seasonings together. Bind with beaten egg.

3. Flour the chopping board, put the meat on it and flatten it out into an oblong about 1 inch thick. Spread sausage meat over and then a layer of rashers. Roll up and press edges together.

4. Coat with beaten eggs and crumbs, and fry in hot fat until golden brown.

5. Bake in a casserole for about 1¾ hours. Serve on a plain dish paper on a hot dish and garnish with parsley.

MOCK DUCK (or STUFFED PORKSTEAK)

1 porksteak   A little hot fat
Sage and Onion Stuffing (page 68).
To garnish:—Parsley.
To serve:—Thickened Brown Gravy (page 67).
Apple Sauce (page 156).

1. Split the porksteak, leaving on a hinge. Flatten out. Put stuffing on lower half. Fold other half down. Skewer each side in position.

2. Roast as on page 66, allowing 1-1¼ hours, according to size.

3. When cooked, remove skewers, lift on to a hot dish and garnish with parsley.

STUFFED BREAST OF MUTTON

2–3 lbs. breast of mutton   2 ozs. fat
4 ozs. Potato Stuffing (page 68)
To serve:—Thickened Brown Gravy (page 67).

1. Bone the meat (page 65), place the stuffing in the centre, roll up. Secure with white twine. Weigh.

2. Roast as on page 66, allowing 25 minutes to each pound.

3. When cooked, remove twine, lift on to a hot dish and garnish with parsley.

MEAT	SUITABLE JOINTS	TIME TO BE ALLOWED	ACCOMPANIMENTS
Beef	Sirloin Wing-rib Ribs Housekeeper's Cut	20–25 minutes to each lb.	Roast Potatoes—page 111. Yorkshire Pudding—page 67. Horseradish Sauce—page 157. Thin Brown Gravy—page 66.
Veal	Breast Loin Veal Cutlets or Ribs Leg Centre Cut	30 minutes to each lb.	Rolls of Bacon—page 88. Thin Brown Gravy—page 66—but if stuffed—Thickened Brown Gravy—page 67, or Tomato Sauce. Roast Potatoes.
Mutton	Centre-loin Fair-end Leg Shoulder Centre Cut Breast	25 minutes to each lb.	Roast Potatoes. Red Currant Jelly except with Shoulder, then Onion Sauce—page 150. Thin Brown Gravy, but if stuffed—Thickened Brown Gravy—page 67.

Lamb {
Young {
Lamb {
	Loin, Leg
	Shoulder, Fair-end
	Hind-quarter
	Fore-quarter
		30 minutes to each lb.	New Potatoes—page 98.
			Green Peas—page 104, or Green Salad—page 116.
			Mint Sauce—page 156.
			Thin Brown Gravy—page 66.

Pork	Leg Loin, Fair-end Back Gigot Porksteak	30 minutes to each lb.	Apple Sauce—page 156. Roast Potatoes—page 111. Thin Brown Gravy—page 66, but if stuffed—Thickened Brown Gravy—page 67.

TREATMENT BEFORE COOKING

Prepare bone of Sirloin or Ribs for carving, see page 218. Remove excess fat. Tie into shape. Cook according to directions " To Roast Meat ", page 66.

Prepare bone of Loin or Fair-end for carving (see page 220). Breast and top of leg may be boned and stuffed. Tie into shape. Cook according to directions " To Roast Meat ", page 66.

Centre-loin ⎱ Joint and remove spinal cord. Remove skin and trim off excess
Fair-end ⎰   fat. Follow directions " To Roast Meat ", page 66.

Top of Leg ⎱ Remove bones and put in Stuffing, page 65.
Shoulder ⎰ Tie into shape with fine twine. Follow directions " To Roast
    Meat ", page 66.

Centre Cut ⎱ Trim off surplus fat. Follow directions " To Roast Meat ",
Leg ⎰   page 66.

Breast.—Remove bones, stuff with Potato Stuffing—page 68. Tie into shape with fine twine. Follow directions " To Roast Meat ", page 66.

Cover the joint with caul before Roasting. Follow directions " To Roast Meat ", page 66.

Loin ⎱ Joint and remove spinal cord. Remove skin by pulling off from
Fair-end ⎰   backbone. Follow directions " To Roast Meat ", page 66.

Loin ⎱
Leg ⎬ Score the skin with a sharp knife at intervals of $\frac{1}{4}''$ apart. If this
Back Gigot ⎰ were not done it would be impossible to carve through the skin when the joint is cooked.

Loin.—Make a slit between the fat and the lean and fill this pocket with Sage and Onion Stuffing—page 68. Tie in shape with fine string.

Porksteak.—See Mock Duck.

Frying

FRYING is cooking in not fat or oil to brown and crisp the outside and cook the inside. There are two methods of frying :

    1. Shallow or Dry Frying.
    2. Deep or Wet Frying.

Shallow Frying

This is the cooking of food in a very small amount of fat on a hot pan. It is not an economical method, as only the best cuts of meat can be used, a considerable absorption of fat takes place, and the fat cannot be used again. Though not economical, this is a quick and simple method of preparing small pieces of food, *e.g.* kidneys, steaks, liver, etc. When frying rashers no fat is required on the heated pan.

Deep Frying

The fat used may be vegetable fat, vegetable oil or rendered beef fat. Sufficient quantity to cover the food is required. A basket is generally used. Care should be taken not to overheat the fat or oil because it will decompose and burn, which renders it useless. After use cool the fat slightly and strain through a fine mesh strainer.

To Clarify Beef Fat

Put the fat into a large saucepan and cover with cold water. Bring to the boil, and boil for 10 minutes. Strain. When the fat hardens, it forms a cake on top of the water. Lift off this cake of fat and scrape any sediment from underneath. Wipe with a dry cloth.

RULES FOR DEEP FRYING

1. The fat must be hot and still. When the fat is not hot enough, foods fried in it become sodden, greasy and indigestible. If the fat is too hot the outside of the food will burn and the inside remain uncooked.

2. Articles for deep frying are usually coated with :
    (*a*) beaten egg and breadcrumbs, *or*
    (*b*) batter.
This coating crisps when it is put into the hot fat, thus preventing the fat from being flavoured, whether sweet or savoury dishes are being cooked.

3. To avoid lowering the temperature, do not put too many articles into the fat at the same time.

4. Deep fried articles must be thoroughly drained on kitchen paper, immediately after frying.

5. The fat must be re-heated before another quantity of food is put in to fry.

To coat articles for Frying

(a) *Egg and breadcrumbs :*—The breadcrumbs must be fine, and it is best to put them on to a sheet of kitchen paper for coating. Have the beaten egg on a plate, put in the articles to be coated one by one, and brush them over with beaten egg. Lift out and drain. Put on to the crumbs, and taking the paper by the sides, toss until completely covered. Press the crumbs well in with the hands, and shake off any loose ones.

(b) *Batter :*—Coat the food in a thick batter (page 134). No frying basket is used when batter-coated foods are being fried.

FRIED PORK CHOPS

4 pork chops	2 large cooking apples
Seasoned flour (page 216)	A little butter or margarine

Parsley

1. Wipe the meat, remove surplus fat. Coat with the seasoned flour.

2. Melt some of the fat trimmings in a frying-pan. When hot put in the chops and fry for about 20 minutes, turning them frequently.

3. When cooked, lift on to a hot dish and keep in a warm place.

4. Wash the apples, remove the core and slice into rings ¼ inch in thickness. Toss in flour. Fry in butter or margarine until tender, but not broken. Serve on the dish with the chops, and garnish with parsley.

FRIED LIVER AND BACON

$1/2$ lb. lamb's, calf's or sheep's liver
$1/4$ lb. rashers
1 dessertspoonful of seasoned flour

To garnish :—Parsley.

1. Remove rind and bones from rashers.

2. Put into a frying-pan and cook quickly, turning frequently. Fry them until the fat is clear. Lift on to a hot dish and keep hot.

3. Cut the liver into slices ½ inch thick and coat with seasoned flour.

4. Put the liver on the pan, fry on both sides, in the hot bacon fat.

5. Lift on to a hot dish, and serve with the fried rashers. Garnish with parsley.

FRIED STEAK AND ONIONS

1 lb. sirloin or fillet steak—1 inch thick	A little fat
Pepper and salt	2 onions

Parsley

Gravy:

¼ pt. brown stock   Pepper and salt

1. Cut off the roots and tops from the onions, peel off the brown skin, and cut into rings.

2. Heat a heavy frying-pan, put on a little fat and heat it. Put in the onions and fry until golden brown, turning frequently. Cover the pan and continue cooking until the onions are soft. Drain and keep hot. Wipe the pan and heat it again.

3. Wipe the steak. Batten. Sprinkle with pepper and salt. Grease the pan, put on the steak and fry for 7–12 minutes, according to taste, turning it frequently, using two knives or cooking tongs.

4. Serve on a hot dish, arrange the onions around and garnish with parsley.

5. Pour off the fat from the pan, add pepper and salt. Stir over the heat, add the stock and bring to the boil. Strain and serve in a hot sauce-boat.

MUTTON CUTLETS

1½ lbs. fair-end of mutton
1 dessertspoonful seasoned flour
1 lb. potato purée

To coat :—Beaten egg and fine breadcrumbs.

To fry :—Bath of fat.

To serve:—Tomato Sauce (page 152), *or* Espagnole Sauce (page 152).

1. Wipe the meat. Saw away the chine bone, being very careful not to cut into the meat.

2. Saw across the rib bones, leaving them about 5 inches long. Trim away surplus fat.

3. Divide the cutlets, making them equal in thickness. Batten. Remove all fat and skin from the tip, leaving about ½ inch bare. Scrape away all skin from the underside of bone.

4. Toss the cutlets in seasoned flour, brush with beaten egg and coat with breadcrumbs.

5. Fry in hot fat until tender and browned about 10–12 minutes. Drain on kitchen paper.

6. Have the potato purée very hot and arrange it in a bank down the centre of a hot dish.

7. Place the cutlets against it, having the bones overlapping slightly at the top.

8. Pour a little Tomato or Espagnole Sauce around. Serve remainder in a hot sauce-boat.

Grilling

GRILLING is cooking either over or under a radiant heat.

It is a very quick method of cooking. On account of the intense heat and rapid cooking, best quality meat only is suitable ; inferior meat would become indigestible and tough.

Small pieces of meat, which will cook quickly, *e.g.*, chops, steaks, kidneys, joints of poultry and game, etc., are suitable for grilling.

Chops and steaks should not be less than 1 inch and not more than 1½ inches thick for grilling.

Kidneys must be split open and skewered in that position.

Rules for Grilling

1. All articles should be brushed over with melted fat or oil, except rashers and sausages.

2. Heat the griller and grease the bars of the grill-pan.

3. Always grill the cut side of kidneys first.

4. Place the meat on the bars and turn frequently until cooked, using two knives or cooking tongs ; never stick a fork into the meat. Reduce the heat as required.

5. Properly grilled meat should have a light puffy appearance.

N.B.—The time for grilling meat depends on the thickness, rather than on the weight of the meat. If sufficiently cooked, the surface of the meat should be crisp and should have a rich brown colour and should be slightly elastic when pressure is applied. It is still raw if spongy, and it is over-cooked if it is hard without resistance.

GRILLED STEAK

1 lb. sirloin or fillet steak—1 inch thick
½ oz. clarified fat
Pepper and salt

To serve:—Potato Chips (page 111).
Maître d'Hôtel Butter (page 157).

1. Wipe the meat. Remove outside skin and any superfluous fat.

2. Batten. Sprinkle with pepper and salt. Brush over with clarified fat.

3. Place on well-heated and greased bars, grill as above. If necessary reduce the heat and turn frequently until cooked, 7–12 minutes, according to taste.

4. Serve meat on a hot dish, place the pats of Maître d'Hôtel Butter on top.

GRILLED CHOPS

2 mutton chops (1 inch thick)   Pepper and salt
½ oz. clarified fat

To serve:—½ oz. Maître d'Hôtel Butter (page 157).
Grilled Tomatoes (below), *or*
Potato Chips (page 111).

1. Wipe the meat, remove skin and superfluous fat and trim neatly. Batten and season.
2. Skewer into a round shape and brush over with fat.
3. Grease the heated bars of the grill-pan. Put on the chops, grill as on page 77. If necessary reduce the heat and turn frequently until cooked, 12–15 minutes.
4. Serve on a hot dish. Put pats of Maître d'Hôtel Butter on top.

MIXED GRILL

1 cutlet   1 sausage
1 mutton kidney   1 tomato
1 rasher   ½ oz. fat
          Pepper and salt

To serve:—Maître d'Hôtel Butter (page 157).

1. Skin and core the kidney, split, leaving on a hinge. Skewer into a flat shape. Brush with melted fat. Sprinkle with pepper and salt.
2. Prepare cutlet and brush over with melted fat. Sprinkle with pepper and salt.
3. Remove rind from the rasher and prick the sausage.
4. Cut tomato across in half.
5. Arrange the grill so that everything will be cooked at the same time.

Cutlet ..	..	..	..	7 to 10 minutes.
Kidney ..	..	..	..	7 to 10 ,,
Sausage..	..	..	..	6 to 8 ,,
Rasher ..	..	..	..	4 to 5 ,,
Tomato ..	..	..	..	4 to 5 ,,

6. Serve at once, arranging neatly on a hot dish. Put a pat of Maître d'Hôtel Butter on top of cutlet.

Steaming

STEAMING is cooking by means of the latent heat of steam from boiling water. It is a slower method of cooking than boiling, *e.g.*, meat takes 1½ times as long to cook when steamed.

Steaming renders food tender and digestible, but large pieces of beef or mutton are rather tasteless when cooked by this method. It is more suited to small cuts and pieces of meat and poultry, and because of the resulting digestibility of the food, it is a method by which most solid dishes for invalids are prepared.

Advantages

1. It is economical as regards fuel, space and attention. A complete meal can be cooked over one hot plate or burner when a two- or three-tiered steamer is used.

2. No food value is lost as in boiling.

As steaming does not develop appetizing flavours, it is necessary to serve a good well-flavoured sauce with steamed meat.

There are three methods of Steaming

1. By using a saucepan that has one or more steamers fitted on top.

2. Between two plates over a saucepan of boiling water.

3. By using a saucepan containing sufficient boiling water to come half-way up the sides of the mould. The saucepan must be kept tightly covered and the water must boil steadily all the time.

In all these methods care must be taken that all the water does not evaporate, more boiling water must be added as required.

BEEFSTEAK AND KIDNEY PUDDING

4 ozs. suet pastry (page 175)

Filling:

¾ lb. round steak	1 oz. onion
¼ lb. ox kidney	1 tomato (cut in slices)
1 dessertsp. seasoned flour	2 tablesps. stock or cold water
1 teasp. chopped parsley	

To garnish:—Parsley.

1. Prepare filling as for Beefsteak and Kidney Pie (page 69).

2. Make suet pastry (page 175), and cut off one-third for the lid. Roll out each piece into a round about ¼ inch in thickness.

3. Line a greased 5-inch pudding-bowl evenly with the larger round of pastry.

4. Put in the filling. Pour the stock over.

5. Brush the edges with cold water, place the smaller round of pastry on top and press the edges together. Cover with greased paper.

6. Steam for 2½ to 3 hours. Turn out on to a hot dish and garnish with parsley.

Re-Heats of Cold Meats

General Rules :

1. Use nothing that is not absolutely fresh.

2. Remove all bone, skin, fat and gristle from the meat. The bones may be utilized to make stock for the sauce or gravy as required.

3. Mince or slice meat as required.

4. Cooked meat is rather insipid, therefore it requires to be well seasoned and flavoured by the addition of herbs, sauce, vegetables, etc.

5. White meats are re-heated in white sauce, and other meats in brown sauce.

SHEPHERD'S PIE

¾ oz. fat	1 dessertsp. Mushroom Ketchup
1 oz. chopped onion	1 teasp. chopped parsley
¾ oz. flour	Salt and pepper
½ pt. stock	¾ lb. minced cooked meat
1 dessertsp. Tomato Sauce	1 lb. cooked mashed potatoes
A little milk	

1. Melt the fat, add the onion, cover with a round of greased paper and cook over a slow heat for 5 minutes.

2. Add the flour and cook until brown.

3. Add the stock, bring to the boil. Skim. Add Tomato Sauce, Mushroom Ketchup, chopped parsley, salt and pepper, and simmer for 5 minutes.

4. Add the meat to the sauce and boil. Put into a greased pie-dish.

5. Cover with the mashed potatoes and smooth with a knife. Brush over with a little milk. Score with a fork.

6. Re-heat in a moderate oven for about half-an-hour.

7. Garnish with parsley and serve on a plain dish paper on a dish.

HASH

1 oz. fat	1 tablesp. Tomato Sauce
2 ozs. chopped onion	1 tablesp. Mushroom Ketchup
1 oz. flour	Salt and pepper
¾ pt. stock	1 lb. cooked meat
A slice of toast	

1. Melt the fat, add the onion, cover with a round of greased paper and cook over a slow heat for 5 minutes.

2. Add the flour and cook until brown.

3. Add the stock, bring to the boil. Skim. Add Tomato Sauce, Mushroom Ketchup, salt and pepper.

4. Remove all fat, gristle and bone from the meat and cut into slices.

5. Add to the sauce, cover saucepan with a lid and allow the meat to re-heat. Boil for 5 minutes.

6. Turn on to a hot dish and garnish with diamonds of toast.

RISSOLES

½ lb. minced cooked meat	1 teaspoonful chopped parsley
4 ozs. mashed potatoes	Pepper and salt
¼ pt. brown binding sauce (page 151)	Pinch of nutmeg
1 dessertsp. seasoned flour	1 teaspoonful ketchup

To coat:—Beaten egg and breadcrumbs.
To fry:—Bath of fat.
To garnish:—Parsley.

1. Add the meat, mashed potatoes, salt and pepper, parsley, nutmeg and ketchup to the sauce. Boil for 1 minute.

2. Mix well, turn on to a lightly-floured board, and form into a roll.

3. Cut into even-sized pieces and form each piece into a ball. Pass through seasoned flour.

4. Coat with beaten egg and crumbs, and fry in hot fat until golden brown in colour. Drain on crumpled kitchen paper.

5. Serve on a plain dish paper on a hot dish and garnish with parsley.

MINCE AND POTATO BORDER

½ oz. fat	1 dessertsp. Tomato Sauce
1 oz. chopped onion	1 dessertsp. Mushroom Ketchup
½ oz. flour	1 teasp. chopped parsley
½ pt. stock	Salt and pepper

1 lb. minced cooked meat

Border:—1½ lbs. mashed potatoes (page 111).
To garnish:—Parsley.

1. Melt the fat, add the onion, cover with a round of greased paper and cook over a slow heat for 5 minutes.

2. Add the flour and cook until brown.

3. Add the stock, bring to the boil. Skim. Add Tomato Sauce, Mushroom Ketchup, chopped parsley, salt and pepper, and simmer for 5 minutes.

4. Add the meat and mix. The mixture should be soft, without being too moist. Boil for 5 minutes.

5. Have the mashed potatoes very hot. Make a border of them on a hot dish and score with a fork.

6. Serve the mince in the centre. Garnish the border with sprigs of parsley.

MEAT CAKES

½ lb. minced cooked meat	Pinch of mixed herbs
½ lb. mashed potatoes	Pepper and salt
1 teasp. chopped parboiled onion	1 egg
1 teasp. chopped parsley	

To coat:—Beaten egg and crumbs.
To fry:—Shallow or deep fat.
To garnish:—Parsley.

1. Mix the meat, potatoes, onion, parsley and herbs well together. Season, and bind with beaten egg.

2. Turn on to a floured board and form into a roll. Cut into 8 even-sized pieces and form each piece into a round cake.

3. Coat with beaten egg and breadcrumbs.

4. Fry to a golden brown in hot fat. Drain on crumpled kitchen paper.

5. Serve on a plain dish paper on a hot dish and garnish with parsley.

DURHAM CUTLETS

¼ pt. brown binding sauce (page 151)	8 ozs. minced cooked meat
1 dessertsp. Tomato Sauce	2 ozs. breadcrumbs
1 dessertsp. Mushroom Ketchup	1 teasp. chopped parsley
Salt and pepper	A few pieces of macaroni

To coat:—Beaten egg and breadcrumbs.
To fry:—Bath of fat.
To garnish:—Parsley.

1. Add the Tomato Sauce, Mushroom Ketchup, salt, pepper, meat, breadcrumbs and parsley to the sauce and mix well together. Boil for 1 minute.

2. Turn mixture on to a wet plate and smooth over with a wet knife, making the mixture about 1 inch thick. Leave it aside to become cold and firm.

3. Cut the mixture into 8 triangular pieces. Shape each piece into a neat cutlet on a floured board.

4. Coat with beaten egg and crumbs ; put a 1 inch piece of macaroni into the narrow end of each to simulate bone of cutlet.

5. Fry in hot fat till golden brown in colour. Drain on crumpled kitchen paper.

6. Serve on a plain dish paper on a hot dish. Garnish with parsley.

Cold Meats

BRAWN

1 pig's cheek (salted)	Pepper
2 pig's feet	Cold water
½ teaspoonful powdered allspice	Bouquet garni

To garnish:—Parsley.

1. Wash cheek thoroughly and steep overnight in cold water. Rinse it and wash the feet.

2. Put both into a saucepan, cover with cold water. Add the bouquet garni, bring to the boil. Skim, and simmer until the meat comes easily from the bones, about 3 hours.

3. When cooked, skin the head, remove the meat from head and feet and cut into dice. Skin the tongue and ear, and cut them into thin strips. Add pepper and allspice and mix well.

4. Return the bones to the liquor and boil without a lid until the liquor is reduced to one pint, strain.

5. Add the meat to it and heat. Put into a cake tin or mould. Allow to become cold and set.

6. Dip tin into boiling water and turn out on to a dish. Garnish with parsley.

BOILED SPICED BEEF

4–5 lbs. spiced beef	1 white turnip
1 onion	Cold water
1 carrot	Allspice
2 sticks of celery	

To garnish:—A sprig of holly.

1. Wash and weigh the beef. Tie into a neat shape.

2. Put into a saucepan with enough cold water to cover. Bring slowly to the boil. Skim.

3. Add the prepared vegetables (page 18), cut into chunks. Boil gently until meat is cooked. Skim when necessary. Time about 2½ hrs.

4. Lift out the meat when cooked. Allow to cool. Remove the twine, dust over with powdered meat spice, and garnish with a sprig of holly.

NOTE.—This meat may also be pressed in an oblong tin, turned out, and sliced when cold.

COLLARED PIG'S HEAD

1 pig's head (salted)	Pepper and salt
1 onion	$\frac{1}{4}$ teaspoonful grated nutmeg
Bouquet garni	$\frac{1}{2}$ teaspoonful grated lemon rind
1 carrot	Cold water to cover
1 white turnip	

1. Wash the head in cold water, paying special attention to the nasal passages, eye cavity and around the tongue and teeth, using a pointed knife when necessary. Blanch.

2. Put down in cold water and add the prepared vegetables and bouquet garni. Bring slowly to the boil, skim and simmer steadily for two hours.

3. Take up the head, cool a little. Skin and slice the tongue thinly.

4. Remove all the bones from the head, and place the two halves on a board. Sprinkle with pepper, salt, lemon rind and nutmeg.

5. Place the slices of tongue on one half, and put the other half of the head on top, thick side on thin side. Roll up and tie firmly into a cloth.

6. Cook for a further 2 hours. Lift on to a board and cover with a second board. Leave until cold, then remove the cloth. Slice thinly as required.

POULTRY

THIS term includes chickens, turkey, goose, duck and pigeon. The flesh of poultry is more easily digested than that of butchers' meat, because the flesh is not intergrained with fat (the fat lies under the skin and round the intestines), and the fibres are shorter.

CHOICE OF POULTRY

When choosing poultry, the following points will indicate that the bird is young :—

The **legs** should be smooth and pliable and the scales on them only slightly overlapping. In the male bird, the spur should be short.

The **feet** should be supple and rather moist.

The **beak** and end of **breastbone** should be pliable.

The **flesh** should be smooth, plump and without long hairs. If the bird is unplucked the **plumage** should be plentiful and soft.

When **fresh** the **eyes** should be clear and not sunken, the **flesh** firm and white or yellow, without any trace of a green or a bluish tinge. There should be no unpleasant odour. When the skin is shrunken and broken and not a good colour, it is an indication that the bird has been kept in cold storage.

CHICKENS

A bird for roasting, grilling or frying should be tender and young, but for boiling, stewing or braising, where the process of cooking is slower, an older and, therefore, cheaper bird will answer the purpose. It is a **chicken** until it is nine months old and then **a pullet** until twelve months old, or a little older.

TURKEYS

The flesh and skin of a good quality turkey is white. The breast should be broad and plump and a good shape. A medium-sized bird should be chosen as its flavour is more delicate and it is usually more tender. The flesh of the hen is considered sweeter than that of the cock.

GEESE AND DUCKS

Young birds have yellow, pliable feet, the webbing of which should be soft and easily torn. The bill should always be yellow and pliable, and the underside of the bill should break easily if bent. The skin should be smooth and the breast should not be too fat.

PIGEONS

The legs should be slender and of a pinkish colour. The breast should be plump and fat. The flesh of a light-coloured bird is more delicate than that of a dark-coloured one. A tame pigeon is smaller than the wild species and should be cooked soon after it has been killed.

PREPARATION OF POULTRY FOR COOKING

In towns, birds are usually prepared for cooking by the poulterer. In country districts, where one has to buy from the market, or where one has one's own poultry yard, the housewife will be obliged to do the whole preparation herself.

To Pluck and Singe Poultry

1. Pluck while the bird is still warm.
2. Hold the legs in the left hand and pluck from the tail upwards towards the head, removing the feathers from the wings first, then from the legs, and lastly from the breast and neck.
3. Hang by the feet, in a cool, dry, well-ventilated larder, until the period of *rigor mortis* has passed. As in the case of meat, the time for hanging varies with the condition under which poultry is hung and according to the type of bird.
4. Singe, to remove any hairs. Be careful not to blacken or scorch the skin.
5. Remove any pin-feathers.

To Draw

1. Make an incision on inside of leg 1 inch below the knee joint. Loosen the sinews with a skewer, then draw them out, one at a time.
2. Cut off legs 1 inch below knee joint.
3. Cut off head close to head.
4. Cut skin down back of neck towards body and loosen neck from the skin. Wipe away all congealed blood with paper.
5. Remove crop and wind-pipe.
6. Cut off neck close to body and put it into cold water.
7. Insert fingers and loosen inside at neck end.
8. Make a slit between the vent and tail, wipe vent with paper. Cut round the vent with a sharp scissors.
9. Insert first two fingers of right hand and loosen the inside.
10. Catch the gizzard and draw it out—all the entrails should come with it, except the lungs.
11. Remove the lungs which lie against the ribs on either side of the backbone.
12. Pour some cold water through the bird keeping the outside of the bird dry.
13. Separate liver from gall-bladder, being careful not to break the latter.

14. Cut away the gizzard, and wipe with a piece of paper. Make a slit between the two lobes, open back with thumbs and remove bag of stones.

15. Wash heart and put into cold water with the neck. Use to make stock for gravy.

To Truss

1. Place the fowl on the board, breast upwards, and neck end towards you. Loosen the skin over the upper portion of the breast.

2. For a roast bird put in the stuffing. Bring the flap of neck skin well down on the back and secure with a stitch.

3. Turn the wings in and under on to the back.

4. Pass the tail through the hole left by cutting away the vent.

5. Hold the legs together and press them towards the wings and close to the breast of the fowl to make it look more plump.

6. Put a trussing needle, threaded with some fine twine, through the joint of the right wing and joint of right leg, through the body, and through the joint of the left leg, and through the joint of the left wing. If a trussing needle is not available, a skewer may be used to secure the wings and legs in the same way.

7. Cross the two ends of the string at the back and bring them down over the ends of the legs, and tie them close to the body, at the side.

NOTE.—Use the neck, gizzard and heart to make stock. The liver may be fried or used for savouries.

BOILED CHICKEN

1 chicken   Boiling water
Piece of cut lemon

½ pint parsley sauce (p. 150).

Accompaniment: Boiled ham (page 58), *or*
Rolls of bacon (page 88).

1. Singe, draw and truss the chicken (page 86). Rub it over with cut lemon to whiten it.

2. Put breast downwards in enough boiling water to completely cover it.

3. Bring to the boil. Skim. Boil for 5 minutes, then simmer ¾-1¼ hours, according to age and size of bird, skimming frequently.

4. When cooked, lift out and drain well, remove the twine, put on a plate in a warm place to dry.

5. Put on a hot dish and serve.

NOTE.—Keep the water in which the chicken was cooked for making Chicken Broth (page 21) or other soup.

ROAST CHICKEN

1 chicken	3 ozs. fat
Stuffing: (page **67**)	
4 ozs. breadcrumbs	1 oz. chopped onion
1 teasp. chopped parsley	2 ozs. butter or margarine

Salt and pepper

Slice of fat bacon

To serve:—½ pt. bread sauce (page 156), ½ pt. thin brown gravy
(page 66).
Rolls of bacon, parsley.

1. Singe, draw, stuff and truss the chicken as on page 86.

2. Place the slice of fat bacon over the breast of the chicken.

3. Heat the fat in a roasting tin, put in the chicken, back downwards, baste well with the hot fat.   Allow 1–1½ hours to roast in a moderate oven according to size of the bird.   Baste every 15 minutes.

4. Remove the rind and bones from the rashers, divide in two or three and flatten on a board.   Roll up and put on a skewer. Put in beside the chicken twenty minutes before it is cooked.

5. About 15 minutes before the chicken is cooked remove the slice of bacon.

6. When cooked, remove the twine and skewer from the chicken. Break off the 1 inch of bone left on legs and lift chicken on to a hot dish.

7. Garnish with parsley and rolls of bacon.

ROLLS OF BACON

6 streaky rashers

Remove the rinds and bones from the rashers, divide in two or three pieces according to size and flatten on a board with a knife. Roll up and put on a skewer.   Grill 8–10 minutes, or put on a tin in the oven for about 15–20 minutes.

RABBITS

RABBITS must be cooked fresh, otherwise they are unwholesome. They should be firm, plump and free from discolouration, and the neck should be short. Choose young rabbits for roasting; older rabbits may be stewed or used for soups.

TO CHOOSE

1. The claws should be smooth, pointed and sharp.
2. The pad under the paws should be well developed (this disappears as the animal ages).
3. The cleft in the jaw should be narrow.
4. The ears should be soft, thin, and easily torn.
5. The teeth should be small and white.
6. The flesh should be moist and have a slightly bluish tinge.

WHEN IN SEASON

RABBITS are in season from September to March.
GRAZIERS from March to September.

HANGING OF RABBITS

As they must be used fresh, hanging for one day is sufficient. They must be paunched immediately after they are killed. The skin is left on while hanging, as this prevents the flesh from becoming dry. The hind legs are tied together and the rabbit hung in a cool, dry, airy larder.

TO PREPARE RABBITS FOR COOKING

To Paunch

1. Make a slit underneath, right down to the tail and remove stomach and intestines.
2. Be careful to take out the small piece of intestine lying close to the tail, and any discoloured parts.
3. Wipe well with a damp cloth.

To Skin

1. Cut off fore and hind legs at the first joint, and the tail close to the body.

2. Starting where the slit was made in the body. loosen the skin and work towards the hind legs.

3. Turn the hind legs inside-out and pull off the skin.

4. Working towards the shoulders, draw the skin off the body, skinning the fore legs in the same way as the hind legs.

5. Cut off the head.

To Clean

1. Remove the kidneys and the fat surrounding them.

2. Break the diaphragm (the thin membrane separating the chest from the abdomen), and remove the heart and lungs.

3. Wash the rabbit very well in tepid salted water, changing the water three or four times, and leave it to steep if possible for half-an-hour with a little white vinegar in the water to whiten the flesh.

ROAST STUFFED RABBIT

1 rabbit	Slice of fat bacon
2 ozs. stuffing (page 67)	3 ozs. hot fat
A little flour	

Accompaniments:—Thickened brown gravy (page 67).
Rolls of bacon (page 88).

To garnish:—Parsley

1. Clean and wash the rabbit (page 89). Dry it, and fill the body cavity with stuffing and sew up. Rub all over with flour.

2. Slit the flesh at the four joints, and at the thighs of the hind legs. Turn the fore legs backwards and draw the hind legs forward, having them just overlapping the fore legs. Fix them in position by passing a skewer through the point of the left fore and hind legs, through the body, and out through the points of the fore and hind legs at the other side. Secure with twine.

3. Place a piece of fat bacon over the back of the rabbit and roast it for 1–1¼ hours according to size. Remove the bacon for the last ten minutes to allow the rabbit to brown.

4. Remove the twine and skewer from the rabbit and serve it on a hot dish with the rolls of bacon. Garnish with parsley.

BOILED RABBIT

1 rabbit   Boiling salted water
Onion Sauce (page 150) *or* Parsley Sauce (page 150)

To serve:—Piece of boiled bacon, *or* Rolls of bacon (page 88).

1. Clean the rabbit (page 89), and wash it thoroughly, leaving it to steep for half-an-hour if possible. Dry it.
2. Slit the flesh at the four joints, and at the thighs of the hind legs. Turn the fore legs backwards, and draw the hind legs forward, having them just overlapping the fore legs.
3. Run a skewer through the points of the hind and fore legs, through the body, and through the points of the legs at the other side, and secure it with twine, or, use a trussing needle and fine twine.
4. Put into boiling salted water, back downwards, and simmer gently for 1–1¼ hours, according to size.
5. Take up, remove the skewer, drain and place rabbit on a hot dish. Carve or cut up as desired. If liked coat with the sauce or serve it separately.

CASSEROLE OF RABBIT

1 rabbit   1 dessertsp. Tomato Sauce
1½ ozs. seasoned flour (page 216)   1 dessertsp. Worcester Sauce
¼ lb. streaky rashers   4 ozs. chopped onion
1½ ozs. fat   4 ozs. carrot
¾ pt. brown stock   2 ozs. white turnip
Pepper and salt   Chopped parsley

1. Clean and wash the rabbit (page 89). Cut off the four legs at the joints, cut each hind leg in two, and cut the body into three or four pieces. Wash well and dry. Pass through seasoned flour.
2. Remove the rind from the rashers, fry in a heavy saucepan and lift out. Add the fat and heat it.
3. Put in the onion and rabbit, fry to a golden brown. Add remainder of the flour and cook for a few minutes.
4. Cool a little, add the stock, sauces, pepper and salt. Bring to the boil, boil for 4 minutes, stirring well. Put into a casserole.
5. Prepare the carrots and white turnip and cut into ½ inch dice. Add to the casserole.
6. Cover and cook in a very moderate oven 1½–2 hours. Add the cooked rashers 15 minutes before the rabbit is cooked.
7. Garnish with parsley and serve.

RABBIT PIE

5 ozs. Rough Puff Pastry (page 175)

1 rabbit	2 ozs. onion
1 tablesp. seasoned flour	1 teasp. chopped parsley
2 ozs. carrot	A little stock

To glaze:—Beaten egg.
To garnish:—Parsley.

1. Prepare and disjoint the rabbit as for Casserole of Rabbit. Toss in seasoned flour.
2. Continue as for Beefsteak and Kidney Pie (page 69).

NOTE.—¼ lb. streaky rashers may be added to improve the flavour.

CURRY OF RABBIT

1 rabbit	1 oz. flour
¼ lb. streaky rashers	¾ pt. stock
1 oz. fat	1 dessertsp. chutney
2 ozs. chopped onion	½ apple (chopped)
2 teasps. curry powder	1 teasp. tomato sauce

½ lb. boiled rice (page 217)

To garnish:—Parsley.   Cayenne pepper.

1. Prepare and disjoint the rabbit as for Casserole of Rabbit (page 91).
2. Remove the rind from the rashers and cut them into small pieces. Fry them and lift on to a plate.
3. Add the fat and heat it. Fry the pieces of rabbit until brown. Add the onion and fry.
4. Mix the flour and curry powder, add it, and cook for a few minutes.
5. Add the stock gradually, stirring all the time. Bring to the boil, skim. Add the chopped apple, chutney, tomato sauce and seasoning.
6. Cover tightly with a lid and stew for about 1¼ hours. Put back the rashers and continue cooking for about half-an-hour.
7. Serve on a hot dish with the rice. Garnish with parsley and cayenne.

VEGETABLE COOKERY

UNFORTUNATELY, the section marked "Vegetables" in the cookery book is very often neglected, if not completely ignored. The result is, as might be expected, that the vegetables are always cooked in the same uninteresting manner, and frequently with a diminution in their nutritive value. Thus, the vegetable reaches the table as an insipid food, which ought to be eaten, but which everyone would much rather do without.

The case may be the complete opposite of this if the vegetables are chosen when fresh, are properly cooked and attractively served.

The freshness of the vegetable is of the utmost importance, since the sooner it reaches the table from the farm or garden the better its flavour and the greater its nutritive value.

Vegetables are a valuable source of minerals, vitamins, roughage and water. Root vegetables also contain carbohydrates and the pulse vegetables, i.e., peas, beans and lentils contain second-class protein.

Vegetables may be divided into three main classes :—
1. Root vegetables and tubers.
2. Green vegetables.
3. Vegetables with blanched stems or leaves.

These three divisions may be further divided into seven sub-divisions, according to the section of the plant used :
1. Roots : *e.g.*, carrot, beetroot, etc.
2. Bulbous Roots : *e.g.*, onions, leeks, etc.
3. Tubers : *e.g.*, potatoes, etc.
4. Flowers, *e.g.*, cauliflower, broccoli, etc.
5. Leaves, *e.g.*, spinach, cabbage, etc.
6. Blanched Stems : *e.g.*, seakale, celery, etc.
7. Fruit : *e.g.*, tomato, marrow, cucumber, etc.
8. Pulses : *e.g.*, peas, beans, etc.
9. Fungi : *e.g.*, mushrooms.

Vegetables are best when in season—at this time they are cheapest and have the best flavour. The following charts give points which will be found very useful when choosing and preparing vegetables.

All vegetables must be fresh ; when stale they are unwholesome and decay quickly, particularly greens.

Salt Solution for preparation of Vegetables

1 tablespoonful salt to 1 gallon water. Use plenty of water when washing vegetables.

Changes which take place when Vegetables are Cooked

1. Loss of vitamins.
2. Loss of soluble mineral salts and flavouring substances.
3. Softening of the cellulose or fibrous part of the vegetable.
4. Bursting of the starch cells and thorough cooking of the starch, which renders it more digestible.

ROOT VEGETABLES

VEGETABLES	CHOICE	IN SEASON
Carrot	Should be firm, unblemished and uninjured.	Outdoor : June to April.
Beetroot	„　　„　　„	" Round " type, June onwards. " Long " type, August to March.
Salsify	„　　„　　„	October to February.
Turnip	„　　„　　„	June to April.
Parsnip	„　　„　　„	November to March.
Radishes	Should be firm and not overgrown.	Outdoor : April to November. Forced : February to April.
Horseradish	Should be firm and thick.	October to March.
Kohl-rabi	Should be firm.	June onwards.

CARROTS

To prepare :

Cut off the tops and roots, wash well using a vegetable brush. Scrape lightly, if old peel thinly and wash again. Do not leave steeping in water. Prepare as required if possible. Small carrots are left whole, larger ones are divided down the centre and across in two, or cut into thin slices.

To cook :

Cook in boiling salted water until soft. Drain.

To serve :

METHOD 1.—Melt a little butter or margarine in a saucepan, put in the carrots and toss them until completely coated. Serve in a hot vegetable dish, sprinkle chopped parsley over.

METHOD 2.—Serve in a hot vegetable dish, mask with White Coating Sauce (page 149).

BEETROOT

To prepare:
Cut off green leaves 2 inches from the top. Wash well in cold water, being careful not to break the small roots nor to cut the skin because beetroot would lose colour. Do not peel.

To cook:
Cook steadily in boiling water 2–3 hours until tender. Test by pressure with the finger. No knife, fork or skewer to be used.

To serve hot:
METHOD 1.—Drain carefully, remove skin. Cut into slices ¼ inch in thickness or cut into large cubes. Melt 1 oz. butter or margarine in a saucepan, add ½ teasp. finely-chopped onion, cook for a few minutes without browning, add beetroot and heat well. Season and serve in a hot vegetable dish.

METHOD 2.—When sliced, put into a hot vegetable dish and mask with White Coating Sauce (page 149.)

To serve cold:
Allow beetroot to cool in water in which it has been boiled, drain and remove skin. Slice as thinly as possible, put into a glass or salad bowl. Sprinkle a little salt over and cover with vinegar.

SALSIFY

To prepare:
Pick salsify of medium size, cut off top and cut about 1 inch off the end. Wash in plenty of cold water with a little lemon juice or vinegar. Scrape lightly, wash again. Tie into small bundles with white twine. Cook immediately.

To cook:
Melt 1 oz. margarine or butter in a saucepan, add salt, a good squeeze of lemon juice or vinegar and sufficient boiling water to cover the salsify. Put in the salsify and simmer until tender— about 30–40 minutes. Drain well, remove the twine.

To serve:
Serve in a hot vegetable dish and coat with White Coating Sauce (page 149). Garnish with parsley. If liked toss in melted butter and sprinkle chopped parsley over.

TURNIPS—Swede

To prepare:
Wash with a vegetable brush, peel thickly, wash again. Cut into slices about ¾ inch thick and then into chunks.

To cook:
Cook in boiling salted water for about ½ hour, until tender, Drain well. Season and mash. Add 1 oz. melted butter or

margarine, beat well over a low heat until piping hot. The turnips may also be served without mashing, the chunks should be tossed in hot butter before serving.

To serve:
Serve in a hot vegetable dish, garnish with parsley.

White or Golden Ball (Orange Jelly) Turnips

To prepare:
Wash with a vegetable brush, peel thickly, wash again.

To cook:
Put into boiling salted water, cook until tender, about 20 minutes. Drain well.

To serve:
Serve in a hot vegetable dish, coat with White Coating Sauce (page 149) or melted butter. Garnish with parsley.

PARSNIPS

To prepare:
Wash well, peel thinly, wash again. Cut into medium-sized pieces.

To cook:
Put to cook in boiling salted water. Cook until tender, about $\frac{1}{2}-\frac{3}{4}$ hour. Drain well and mash. Melt a little butter or margarine in a saucepan, add parsnips, salt and pepper, beat over a low heat until piping hot. The parsnips may also be served without mashing. Before cooking, dice or cut them in match-like strips. Toss in butter and serve.

To serve:
Serve in a hot vegetable dish. Garnish with chopped parsley.

RADISHES

To prepare:
Wash well. Cut off tops and ends of roots, scrape lightly, wash again. Use uncooked in salads.

HORSERADISH

To prepare:
Scrub with a vegetable brush. Peel thinly. Grate or shred it in a liquidiser.

KOHL-RABI

To prepare:
Wash with a vegetable brush, peel thickly, wash again. Cut into half-inch slices and then into chunks.

To cook:
  Cook in boiling salted water until tender, about ½ hour. Drain well.

To serve:
  Serve in a hot vegetable dish. Coat with White Coating Sauce (page 149). or melted butter. Garnish with parsley.

BULBOUS ROOTS

VEGETABLE	CHOICE	IN SEASON
Onions	Should be firm and sound.	July to April or May.
Scallions	„ „ „	February to September.
Shallots	„ „ „	November to January.
Leeks	„ „ „	October to May.

ONIONS

To prepare:
  Cut off root and stem, peel off the brown skin.

To cook:
  Choose onions of an equal size. Blanch, if liked, to remove the strong flavour. Cook in boiling salted water. Boil until tender, small onions take about 25 minutes, large Spanish onions take about 45 minutes. Drain well.

To serve:
  Serve in a hot vegetable dish, coat with White Coating Sauce (page 149). Sprinkle breadcrumbs on top and brown under the griller.

SCALLIONS

To prepare:
  Cut off the roots and tops, wash. Use uncooked in salads.

LEEKS

To prepare:
  Cut off roots and green tops. Remove outer skin and wash. If large, split in two. Cut into 3-inch lengths.

To cook:
  Put into boiling salted water, boil until tender, 30–40 minutes. Drain well.

To serve:
  Serve in a hot vegetable dish, coat with White Coating Sauce (page 149). Garnish with chopped parsley.

TUBERS

Vegetable	Choice	In Season
Potatoes—Old	Should be firm with unwrinkled skins.	All the year.
New	„ „ „ „	May to July.
Jerusalem Artichokes	„ „ „ „	September to March.

OLD POTATOES

To prepare:

Wash well, using a vegetable brush; if peeling them, do so very thinly, dropping them into cold water as peeled. Wash again.

To cook:

Put down to cook in boiling salted water, having sufficient water to cover the potatoes. Cook until tender, 30–40 minutes, according to size. Drain off the water, cover with a cloth, leave for a few minutes on a warm stove.

To serve:

Serve potatoes in their jackets in a hot vegetable dish. If they are peeled sprinkle with chopped parsley.

NEW POTATOES

To prepare:

Wash the potatoes, using a vegetable brush, scrape off the skin and wash again.

To cook:

Put to cook in boiling salted water. Add a sprig of mint. Boil until tender, about 15–20 minutes. Drain off all the water, cover with a clean cloth and leave for a few minutes on a warm stove.

To serve:

Put into a hot vegetable dish, pour a little melted butter over and sprinkle with finely-chopped parsley.

STEAMED POTATOES

When potatoes are washed and scraped or peeled thinly, put into a steamer over boiling water, sprinkle with salt (add a sprig of mint for new potatoes) and cook until tender—about 45–50 minutes for old potatoes, about 20 minutes for new ones.

To serve:

Serve as for Boiled Potatoes.

JERUSALEM ARTICHOKES

To prepare:
Wash well, using a vegetable brush. Peel, keeping under cold water as much as possible. Drop into a basin of cold water to which a little lemon juice or white vinegar has been added. When prepared cook immediately.

To cook:
Put to cook in boiling water to which salt and a little lemon juice or vinegar has been added. Cook until tender, about 25 minutes. Drain well.

To serve:
Serve in a hot vegetable dish, coat with Béchamel Sauce (coating consistency, page 151) or melted butter. Garnish with parsley.

FLOWERS

Vegetable	Choice	In Season
Cauliflower	Head should be firm, white and compact—size has no relation to flavour.	Outdoor: June to October.
Broccoli	Head should be firm, not as close as cauliflower. Sprouting broccoli may be white or purple.	Sprouting: March to May. Hearting: Mid-December to June.
Globe Artichokes	Green better than those with a purple tint.	June to September.

CAULIFLOWER AND BROCCOLI

To prepare:
Remove the outer leaves, break into flowerettes, wash well.

To cook:
Cook in boiling salted water, about 12 minutes, until the stalks are soft. Cover while cooking. Drain well.

To serve:
Arrange in a hot vegetable dish, coat with White Coating Sauce (page 149) or melted butter. Garnish with chopped parsley.

SPROUTING BROCCOLI

To prepare:
Break into pieces about 4 inches in length. Wash well.

To cook:
Cook in boiling salted water until the stalk is tender—about 15 minutes. Drain well.

To serve:
Serve in a hot vegetable dish, pour a little melted butter over it.

GLOBE ARTICHOKES

To prepare:

Remove bottom leaves. Cut an inch off top of leaves. Wash well in cold water. Wash a second time in cold water. Turn upside-down on a sieve until all the water has run out of them.

To cook:

Put to cook, points downwards in boiling salted water to which a little lemon juice has been added. Boil quickly 5–6 minutes, reduce the heat and cook slowly until tender—about ½ an hour. Drain well.

To serve hot:

Remove centre of choke and serve artichokes on a folded table-napkin in a hot vegetable dish. Serve melted butter separately.

To serve cold:

Serve on a folded table-napkin and serve Vinaigrette Dressing separately.

LEAVES

VEGETABLE	CHOICE	IN SEASON
Brussels Sprouts	Should be young, small and compact.	September to March.
Cabbage	Should be firm and of good colour, heavy in proportion to size. Stalk should snap easily.	All the year.
Spinach	Should be small and leaves young for good flavour.	May to October.
Curly Kale	Should be firm and of good colour.	November to March.
Lettuce	Should be fresh, crisp and green.	Outdoor : Late April to October. Indoor : November to March.
Leaves of Kohl-Rabi	Fresh and Green.	June onwards.
Endive	„ „	September to November.
Water-Cress	Should be obtained from a reliable source. It should be fresh, crisp and green.	All the year.

BRUSSELS SPROUTS

To prepare:
Trim off stalk and any withered leaves, wash several times in cold salted water.

To cook:
Cook in boiling salted water until tender—about 10–15 minutes. Drain well. Toss in melted butter and season.

To serve:
Turn into a hot vegetable dish.

CABBAGE

To prepare:
Remove stump and outer withered leaves. Cut the head in quarters and remove centre stalk. Wash cabbage well in plenty of cold water.

To cook:
Cook in fast boiling salted water until tender—about 15–20 minutes. Old cabbage is tough and may take a little longer to cook. Drain well in a colander, press out all the water and chop.

To serve:
Melt a little butter or margarine in the saucepan, put in the cabbage, salt and pepper and re-heat. Serve in a hot vegetable dish.

CURLY KALE AND OTHER LEAVES

To prepare:
Cut off stalks, separate leaves. Wash well in plenty of cold water.

To cook:—As for Cabbage.

To serve:—As for Cabbage.

SPINACH

To prepare:
Remove stalks. Wash in plenty of cold water, lift out, wash again until all traces of sand have been removed.

To cook:
Cook in fast boiling salted water for 3 minutes with the lid on the saucepan. Drain well, pressing out all the water. Toss in melted butter with two forks. Season.

To serve:
Serve in a hot vegetable dish.

LETTUCE

To prepare:
Wash several times in cold water. Swing loosely in a clean tea towel or salad basket to remove water.

ENDIVE

To prepare:

Wash in plenty of cold water, lift out and wash again until all traces of sand have been removed. Remove stalk. Dry in a cloth.

WATER-CRESS

To prepare:

Wash well and drain.

FRUIT

Vegetable	Choice	In Season
Cucumber	Green in colour. Should have thin, firm unwrinkled skin.	Hot House : All the year.
Tomato	Should be firm, round and bright red in colour.	All the year round.
Vegetable Marrow	Should have firm unwrinkled skin.	July to October.
Pumpkin	Should be fresh and firm.	August to October.
Aubergine *or* Egg Plant	Firm, skin fresh and glossy.	Imported.
Green Peppers	„ „ „	„
Gherkin	Should be firm and fresh.	Mid-August to end of September.

CUCUMBER

To prepare:

Wash and peel if liked. Used sliced in salads and sandwiches.

TOMATO

To prepare:

Wash and dry. Remove the eye.

To skin:

Drop into boiling water for one second, then into cold. Lift out and peel.

Methods of Cooking:

Grilling, Frying, Baking.

To bake:

Put a collar of greaseproof paper around each peeled tomato. Bake in a fairly moderate oven for 10–15 minutes. Remove paper. Lift on to a hot dish, sprinkle chopped parsley over.

NOTE.—Tomatoes are used uncooked for salads and sandwiches.

VEGETABLE MARROW

To prepare:

Cut into slices, peel, remove seeds and soft part from the centre. Cut into chunks.

To cook:

Place in a steamer, sprinkle with a little salt and cook over boiling water until soft—about 10–15 minutes. Drain well.

To serve:

Put into a hot vegetable dish and coat with White Coating Sauce (page 149) or melted butter. Garnish with chopped parsley.

PUMPKIN

Cooked and served as for Vegetable Marrow, but requires a slightly longer time to cook.

PULSES

VEGETABLE	CHOICE	IN SEASON
Broad Beans	Well filled, heavy and glossy on the outside. Fresh green colour.	June to August.
French Beans	Should be small and have a pale green bloom on them. Pale green colour.	July to September.
Scarlet Runners	Larger variety of French Beans— coarser and darker in colour than French beans.	July to October.
Peas	Should be well filled and a good green colour.	Mid-June to September.
Lentils	Red or Egyptian best.	Imported.
Split Peas	Green or Yellow.	Imported.

BROAD BEANS

To prepare:
Shell just before cooking.

To cook:
Cook in boiling salted water for about 15–20 minutes. Beans should not be overcooked as this toughens the outer skin and makes it difficult to remove. Skin the beans.

To serve:
Melt a little butter in a saucepan, add salt, pepper and beans, re-heat and serve in a hot vegetable dish. They may be coated with White Coating Sauce if liked.

FRENCH BEANS AND SCARLET RUNNERS

To prepare:
Top and tail the beans, at the same time stringing them. Wash and shred them, using a bean slicer or small sharp knife.

To cook:
Put into boiling salted water, bring back to the boil, skim. Boil for about 10–12 minutes until tender. Drain.

To serve:
Toss in a little melted butter, season and serve in a hot vegetable dish.

PEAS

To prepare:
Shell just before cooking.

To cook:
Put into boiling salted water with a sprig of mint, bring back again to the boil, skim, cook for 10–15 minutes until tender. Drain.

To serve:
Put into a hot vegetable dish with a little butter and seasoning.

NOTE.—Air-dried and frozen vegetables are cooked according to the instructions on the package.

BLANCHED STEMS OR BLANCHED LEAVES

VEGETABLE	CHOICE	IN SEASON
Asparagus	The stalks should be firm, crisp, about ½ inch thick and not too long.	Outdoor : April to June. Forced : November to February.
Celery	Should be crisp and white.	August to March.
Seakale	„ „ „	Outdoor : March to May. Forced : January to March.
Chicory	„ „ „	January to March.

ASPARAGUS

To prepare :
Cut stalks all one length—about 6 inches. Scrape the white part very lightly, downwards, using the back of a knife. Wash carefully in plenty of cold water. Tie in bundles with white twine, having tips going all the one way.

To cook :
Cook in boiling salted water to which a little lemon juice has been added. Have sufficient water in the saucepan to cover the asparagus and a saucepan large enough to allow the asparagus to lie flatly in it. Boil gently until tender—about 30 minutes. Drain well.

To serve :
Serve on a folded table-napkin or on dry toast. Serve Hollandaise Sauce or melted butter in a hot sauce-boat. It may be served cold with Vinaigrette dressing served separately.

CELERY

To prepare :
Remove the green tops and point the root. Wash the outside. Take off the stalks and wash well, using a vegetable brush. The outer coarse stalks should be kept for soup. The centre of the heart can be served raw and the remainder cooked as a vegetable.

To serve raw:

Wash well and leave in cold water until required. Drain and serve in a celery glass, tumbler or flat dish.

To cook:

1. Cut the celery into lengths of approximately 2 inches. Put into boiling salted water to which a few drops of lemon juice have been added. Cook until tender, about ½ hour.

2. Drain, keeping some of the liquid to make the sauce, keep the celery hot in a vegetable dish.

3. Make a White Coating Sauce (page 149) using half milk and half cooking liquor from the celery. Pour over celery. Garnish with parsley.

SEAKALE

To prepare:

Wash, remove root end, scrape lightly and tie in bundles.

To cook:

Cook in boiling salted water, to which a few drops lemon juice or white vinegar is added, until tender—about 15 minutes. Lift out, drain well and remove string.

To serve:

Arrange in a hot vegetable dish, pour a little melted butter over and sprinkle with chopped parsley.

CHICORY

To prepare:

Point root end and remove any discoloured leaves. Cut in two down the centre. Wash well.

May be served raw as a salad.

To cook:

Put into boiling salted water to which a few drops of lemon juice or white vinegar has been added. Cook until tender—about 15–20 minutes. Drain well.

To serve:

Fold each piece of chicory in two, arrange in a hot vegetable dish. Coat with White Coating Sauce (page 149) or melted butter. Garnish with chopped parsley.

FUNGI

VEGETABLE	CHOICE	IN SEASON
Mushrooms	Should be fresh not shrivelled. Young button mushrooms should have pink gills. Older mushrooms may have light brown gills.	Field: August-September. Forced: All the year round.

MUSHROOMS

To prepare:
Remove the stalks, and the skin if liked. Wash the mushrooms well.

To cook:
Put them into a casserole or heavy saucepan with some butter, a squeeze of lemon juice, salt and pepper. Cook over a slow heat or in a moderate oven for about 15 minutes.

HERBS

HERB	CHOICE	IN SEASON
Parsley	Fresh and bright green colour.	All the year round.
Mint	Fresh with dull green colour.	Outdoor: April to November.
Sage	Silver green colour.	All the year.
Thyme	Small leaf of dark green colour.	,, ,,
Chives	Should be fresh and green.	,, ,,
Mustard and Cress	Fresh and bright green colour.	,, ,,

PARSLEY

Pick off sprigs, wash well, dry by wringing in a clean tea towel. Use for garnishing and for flavouring sauces and stuffing. Use stalks in bouquet garni for soups, etc.

MINT

Pick off leaves, wash. Use when cooking new potatoes and peas, also for making Mint Sauce and Mint Jelly.

SAGE

Pick off leaves, wash and chop. Use for flavouring in stuffings.

THYME

Wash and use for bouquet garni.

MUSTARD and CRESS

Wash, use in salads and sandwiches.

CURRIED BEANS

½ lb. butter beans   ½ pt. Curry Sauce (page 152)
2 ozs. cooked rice (page 217)
To garnish:—Chopped parsley.
Cayenne pepper.

1. Steep the beans in water to which ¼ teaspoonful bread soda has been added, overnight.
2. Strain them and put to cook in cold water, bring to the boil, skim, and simmer for about 2 hours until the beans are tender. Drain well.
3. Put into the curry sauce and stew for about ½ hour.
4. Make a ring of the prepared rice on a hot dish and serve the beans and sauce in the centre.
5. Garnish the rice with parsley and cayenne.

STEWED CARROTS

1 lb. garden carrots   ½ pt. brown stewing sauce
(page 151)

1. Prepare carrots as on page 94.
2. Put into the prepared stewing sauce in fireproof dish and stew for 1–1½ hours.
3. Remove lid from casserole, sprinkle chopped parsley on top and serve at once.

NOTE.—If using old carrots split in four on the length, cook in a little boiling salted water for half an hour. Strain and use this liquid when making stewing sauce.

CARROT MOULDS

8 ozs. carrots   1 egg
1 teasp. flour   Pepper
Salt   Finely-chopped parsley

1. Prepare carrots and cook until tender.
2. Drain and rub through a wire sieve. This purée should measure 1 breakfastcupful. Season to taste.

3. Add flour and beaten egg and mix thoroughly.

4. Grease four dariole moulds. Sprinkle a little finely-chopped parsley inside of each. Fill purée into the moulds to within $\frac{1}{4}$ inch of the top. Put into a bain-marie.

5. Cover with greased paper. Poach until firm to the touch, 20–25 minutes.

6. Turn out on to a hot dish.

NOTE.—Carrot moulds may also be used as a garnish for stews.

COLCANNON

1 lb. of cooked potatoes (mashed)	½ lb. cooked kale or cabbage
1 oz. butter or margarine	Salt and pepper
1 oz. chopped onion	A little milk

1. Melt the butter, add the onion, cover with a round of grease-proof paper, put lid on saucepan and cook over a slow heat for 10 minutes but do not allow to colour.

2. Add the mashed potatoes, chopped cabbage, pepper, salt and milk. Mix all well together and re-heat thoroughly, stirring all the time.

3. Pile in a hot vegetable dish. Score with a fork.

CHAMP

1 lb. cooked potatoes	2 teasps. chopped parsley
1 oz. butter or margarine	Salt and pepper
1 oz. chopped onion	A little milk

Make and serve as for Colcannon.

CAULIFLOWER AU GRATIN

1 cauliflower	½ pt. white coating sauce
2 ozs. grated cheese	(page 149)

To garnish:—Parsley.

1. Prepare and cook the cauliflower (page 99).

2. Arrange cauliflower in a fireproof dish.

3. Add a little more than half the grated cheese to the white coating sauce. Mix well and pour over the cauliflower.

4. Sprinkle the remainder of the grated cheese over the top of the cauliflower. Brown under a griller. Garnish with parsley.

STEWED CELERY

1. Prepare the celery as on page 105.
2. Put into a saucepan with enough milk and water to cover. Bring to the boil and simmer for about 1 hour.
3. Strain off the liquid and make a white coating sauce with it (page 149).
4. Arrange in a hot vegetable dish and coat with the sauce.

STEWED CHICORY

1 lb. chicory	¾ pt. Béchamel Sauce (stewing
1 tablesp. cream	consistency) (page 151)

To garnish:—Parsley.

1. Prepare chicory (page 106). Put into a fireproof dish.
2. Pour the Béchamel Sauce over the chicory. Stew until tender in a moderate oven—about 25–30 minutes.
3. Stir in the cream. Place dish on a dish paper on a hot dish. Garnish with parsley.

GREEN PEA PURÉE

½ lb. dried green peas	1 onion with 2 cloves stuck into it
Salt and pepper	A small bunch of herbs tied in
1 oz. butter	muslin
1 tablesp. cream or milk	1 teaspoonful sugar
4 ozs. mashed potatoes	

1. Steep peas overnight. Put into a saucepan, cover with boiling water. Add onion and cloves, pepper and bunch of herbs. Boil until peas are tender.
2. Lift out the onion and herbs, drain the peas and rub through a sieve.
3. Melt the butter in a saucepan, add sugar, salt, cream, mashed potatoes and sieved peas. Re-heat thoroughly, beating well all the time until quite smooth. Use as required.

BAKED POTATOES

Potatoes

To serve:—Butter.
To garnish:—Parsley.

1. Choose large potatoes about the same size. Wash and scrub them. Wash again and prick with a skewer.
2. Cook in a moderate oven for about 1¼ hours. Test with a skewer.
3. Make a slit on top of each potato, press open and place a pat of butter into each and serve. Garnish with parsley.

MASHED POTATOES OR POTATO PURÉE

| 1 lb. cooked potatoes | 3 tablespoonfuls milk |
| 1 oz. butter or margarine | Pepper and salt |

To serve:—Chopped parsley.

1. Peel potatoes thinly and mash them, using a potato masher or sieve. Old potatoes are best.
2. Put milk, butter, pepper and salt into a saucepan. Heat until the butter is melted.
3. Add potatoes and mix over the heat until piping hot, using a wooden spoon to stir.
4. Pile into a hot vegetable dish and sprinkle some finely-chopped parsley on top.

POTATO CHIPS

| Potatoes | Salt and pepper |

To fry:—Bath of fat.

1. Wash and peel the potatoes. Cut into ½ inch slices, then across into ½ inch strips. Wash in cold water and dry well.
2. Heat the fat. Put a small quantity of potatoes at a time into the frying basket. Cook in the hot fat until soft but not brown.
3. Lift out the basket. Heat the fat again, put in the chips a second time and fry until golden brown. Drain on kitchen paper.
4. Sprinkle with salt, keep hot until the remainder of the chips have been cooked in the same way.
5. Serve in a hot vegetable dish on a plain dish paper.

ROAST POTATOES

| Potatoes | Dripping |

1. Wash and scrub potatoes. Peel very thinly, wash and dry thoroughly.
2. Have dripping hot in a roasting tin, put in potatoes and baste with the hot fat. Cook in a hot oven for about 1 hour. Turn and baste frequently so that they may be evenly browned all over.
3. Drain on kitchen paper. Serve in a hot vegetable dish on a plain dish paper.
NOTE.—These potatoes are sometimes cooked beside the meat on the roasting tin and served round the joint.

FRIED POTATOES

1 lb. cooked potatoes	Salt and pepper

To fry:—Clarified fat.

1. Peel the potatoes and cut in ¼-inch slices.
2. Heat a very little clarified fat on a pan, put on some of the potatoes and fry until lightly browned, tossing them on the pan.
3. Season and serve in a hot vegetable dish. Garnish with parsley.

POTATO LOAF

1 lb. mashed potatoes	1 oz. melted butter
Pepper and salt	1 teasp. finely-chopped onion
2 teasps. finely-chopped parsley	Beaten egg

To glaze:—Beaten egg.

1. Mix potatoes, seasoning and flavourings together. Add the melted butter and sufficient beaten egg to bind.
2. Turn on to a lightly-floured board, form into a cone. Brush over with beaten egg. Score with a fork.
3. Place on a greased tin and bake in a hot oven until nicely browned.
4. Garnish with parsley and serve.

POTATO CONES

Make and bake as for Potato Loaf but shape the mixture into sixteen equal-sized cones.

DELMONICO POTATOES

1½ lbs. potatoes	½ pt. milk
Salt and pepper	

1. Wash and peel the potatoes. Cut them in ½ inch cubes.
2. Put potatoes, milk, salt and pepper into a heavy saucepan. Bring to the boil and cook gently until tender.
3. Draw saucepan to the side of the stove and rotate it slightly until the milk is thickened by the starch from the potatoes.
4. Put into a hot vegetable dish and garnish with parsley. Serve very hot.

MAÎTRE D'HÔTEL POTATOES

1½ lbs. cooked potatoes	½ pt. milk
Salt and pepper	2 ozs. sieved cheese

1. Peel the potatoes and slice them thinly.
2. Put them into a heavy saucepan with the milk, salt and pepper. Bring to the boil and rotate the saucepan until the milk thickens.
3. Add half of the cheese, put into a hot fireproof dish, sprinkle remainder of the cheese on top. Brown under the griller. Garnish with parsley and serve hot.

POTATO ROSES

1 lb. mashed potatoes	Salt and pepper
1 oz. butter or margarine	1 beaten egg

To serve:—Cooked green peas.
To garnish:—Parsley.

1. Melt the butter, add to the potatoes with salt, pepper and enough beaten egg to bind.
2. Put over the heat for a few minutes to cook the egg.
3. Divide two-thirds of the potato mixture into six equal parts. Shape each part into a round flat cake. Place on a greased baking tin.
4. Pipe remainder of potato mixture around cakes, using a large rose pipe. Brush with beaten egg and brown in a hot oven.
5. Fill centres with hot buttered peas, seasoned to taste. Garnish with parsley and serve.

POTATO CROQUETTES

½ lb. mashed potatoes	1 teasp. chopped parsley
½ oz. butter	Pepper and salt
½ teasp. finely-chopped onion	Half a beaten egg

To coat:—Egg and breadcrumbs.

1. Mix potatoes, seasoning and flavourings together. Add the melted butter and sufficient egg to bind. Mix until smooth.
2. Turn on to a floured board. Knead lightly and form into a roll. Divide into equal pieces. Form into cork-shaped pieces.
3. Coat with egg and breadcrumbs. Fry in hot fat until golden brown in colour. Drain on kitchen paper.
4. Garnish with parsley and serve.

NOTE.—Potato Balls may be prepared in the same way but shaped in round balls before coating.

CASSEROLE OF VEGETABLES

Mixture of all vegetables in season

1. Prepare and cut up vegetables into small pieces.
2. Stew in stock or gravy until tender.
3. Put the vegetables and some of the gravy into a casserole ; cover with a thick layer of mashed potatoes.
4. Bake in a moderate oven until thoroughly hot and until the potato is lightly browned all over.

GLAZED VEGETABLES

Cut the vegetables into small pieces and put them into a saucepan with 1 oz. margarine and 4 tablespoonfuls of water to each pound of vegetables, stir over a low heat for a few minutes, add salt and pepper. Cover the saucepan with a tightly-fitting lid and cook the vegetables slowly until tender. Shake the pan occasionally to prevent the vegetables sticking to it.

If liked the vegetables may be cooked in a fireproof dish in a very moderate oven.

SALADS

In this section of cookery the housewife may use her ingenuity, skill, and imagination to produce as much variety as possible, because the salad may consist of one or a number of various ingredients.

Salads may be composed of raw vegetables, cooked vegetables, cooked meat and fish or fruit.

Salads are usually classified under four headings :—

1. Green salads, made from lettuce, cucumber, cress, etc.

2. Salads made from cooked, or a mixture of raw and cooked vegetable, as Potato Salad, Winter Salad, etc.

3. Fish and meat salads.

4. Fruit salads.

A salad may be served as an accompaniment to a hot or cold meat dish, or as an individual dish.

Preparation of Vegetables and Fruits for Salads

VEGETABLE	PREPARATION
Lettuce	Wash in plenty of cold water, each leaf should be washed separately. Tear leaves or cut with a stainless knife. Drain well, by first shaking it lightly out of the water, then put into a salad basket or clean cloth and shake without crushing the leaves. When keeping lettuce in the refrigerator, keep it covered.
Water-cress or Cress	Wash in cold water—drain as for lettuce.
Mustard	Wash in cold water—drain as for lettuce.
Sorrel	Wash in cold water—drain as for lettuce.
Chives	Rinse in cold water. Cut into $\frac{1}{2}$ inch pieces.
Spring Onions ..	Top, tail, skin and cut.
Carrot	Wash, scrape and grate.
Celery	As on page 105.
Tomatoes	Wash, remove the eyes, slice or cut into quarters. To peel : Cover with boiling water, leave for a few seconds. Put into cold water, lift out and remove the skins.
Radishes	Wash and cut in slices or divide in eight half-way through and steep in cold water until opened up.

VEGETABLE	PREPARATION
Cucumber ..	.. Wash, peel if liked. Slice as required.
Nasturtiums ..	.. Separate petals and rinse if necessary. Leaves prepared as for lettuce.
Orange ..	.. Peel, removing all the pith.
Endive ..	.. Remove stalks. Wash well, drain as for lettuce.
Beetroot ..	.. As on page 95.

CARROT SALAD

2 or 3 young carrots   1 head of lettuce
French dressing (page 153)

1. Prepare vegetables. Grate carrot and shred lettuce. Toss in French dressing.
2. Put lettuce and grated carrot in layers in a glass dish.

POTATO SALAD

1 lb. cooked potatoes	1 teasp. chopped parsley
1 teasp. chopped shallots	A few lettuce leaves
1 hard-boiled egg	French dressing (page 153), *or*
Salt and pepper	Salad dressing (page 154)

1. Prepare lettuce as on page 101, arrange in a salad bowl.
2. Peel and dice the potatoes, add the shallots and mix with the dressing. Season.
3. Pile in the centre of the lettuce. Sprinkle chopped parsley over and garnish with sliced hard-boiled egg.

SUMMER SALAD

1 head lettuce	2 hard-boiled eggs (sliced)
3 tomatoes	1 bunch radishes
Some sliced cucumber	1 bunch spring onions

To serve:—Salad dressing.

Prepare lettuce and other vegetables. Arrange all the ingredients neatly in a polished glass dish.

GREEN SALAD

1 head lettuce	¼ cucumber
1 bunch of chives	1 teaspoonful chopped parsley
French dressing (page 153)	

Prepare vegetables. Toss in French dressing. Serve immediately in a glass dish.

WINTER SALAD

1 beetroot	1 carrot
2 sticks celery (raw)	2 tablespoonfuls peas (cooked)
1 potato	1 white turnip
3 tomatoes	Salad dressing

Salt and pepper

1. Prepare root vegetables. Steam or boil until tender, but not soft or broken. Cut into dice.

2. Cut celery into $\frac{1}{2}$ inch pieces and tomatoes into quarters or eighths. Keep back a little of each vegetable to use as a garnish. Mix remainder together. Season.

3. Pour salad dressing over, and mix well but carefully. Put into a glass dish and garnish with the remainder of the vegetables.

BEETROOT SALAD

3 medium-sized cooked beetroot	3 tablespoonfuls mayonnaise
3 sticks celery	Lettuce leaves
1 dessert apple	Chopped parsley

1. Arrange the prepared lettuce in a salad bowl.

2. Peel and dice the beetroot. Peel, core and dice the apple. Chop the prepared celery. Put all into a bowl, add the mayonnaise and mix together.

3. Pile into the centre of the salad bowl, garnish with parsley and a few small lettuce leaves.

PUDDINGS AND SWEETS

THERE are many types of puddings which may be divided roughly as follows :

1. Hot Puddings : (a) Milk Puddings and Custards ;
   (b) Suet Puddings ;
   (c) Madeira Mixtures ;
   (d) Batters ;
   (e) Fresh Fruit Puddings ;
   (f) Omelets and Soufflés ;
   (g) Pastry Dishes and Tarts.
2. Cold Sweets.

Milk Puddings

These are mixtures of milk and a farinaceous substance sometimes enriched by the addition of eggs. A well-made milk pudding should be neither too stiff nor too thin, but should be creamy in texture, the farinaceous product having absorbed most of the milk during the cooking process.

Food Value of Milk

The value of milk in the diet may be judged from the fact that during the first months of the life of all infants, the natural food is milk. These first months are the period of greatest growth, hence milk must contain all that is necessary to make this growth possible.

Milk, though a liquid, contains about 12% of solid matter ; but it varies more than any other food in composition, according to the breed and age of the cow, the way in which the cow is fed, and the period which has elapsed since calving. Milk contains proteins, which are the body-builders; sugar and fat, which provide heat and energy ; mineral matter in the form of calcium, which is an essential in proper bone formation ; and Vitamins A and D, and Riboflavin, which are necessary for healthy growth. Water forms the remaining 87% to 88% of milk, which makes it a very bulky food.

Average Composition of Milk

Water—87·2%.

Proteins—3·5% in the form of casein and albumen.

Fat—3·7% in the form of a very fine emulsion.

Sugar—4·9% in the form of lactose.

Mineral matter—0·7%.

Skim milk contains about 1% of the fat of milk, but as it contains all the protein and sugar of ordinary milk, it may be regarded as one of the cheapest sources of animal protein. It is also a good source of calcium.

Changes which occur in milk on boiling

1. Alteration in flavour.
2. Casein rendered less digestible.
3. Destruction of the minute emulsion of the fat.
4. A skin forms on the surface—this skin contains some of the albumen, casein, fat and mineral matter ; unless this skin is used a large percentage of the food value is lost.
5. Possible reduction in the vitamin content.

Pasteurisation

Pasteurisation is a heat treatment followed by rapid cooling, which, when properly carried out, ensures that most disease-producing micro-organisms present, are killed It can be applied to a variety of foods, *e.g.*, milk, ice-cream, beer, etc.

Before pasteurisation milk must not contain more than 500,000 micro-organisms per ml. and after pasteurisation must not contain more than 100,000 micro-organisms per ml. Milk so treated will keep 2–3 days under normal conditions due to the reduction in the number of souring micro-organisms.

1 ml. =1/1000 part of a litre.

1 litre = approximately 1¾ pints.

Custards

A custard is a highly nutritious food, being a combination of milk and eggs. As albumen coagulates at a comparatively low temperature (149°F.) care must be taken to ensure that the custard is not over-heated, otherwise it will curdle.

When baking, the dish containing the custard should be placed in a tin, which has been half-filled with water. A very moderate oven should be used.

General Rules for Making Milk Puddings

1. Proportions :

(a) *Puddings.*

Coarse grain, *e.g.*, rice, tapioca, sago, etc., use 2 ozs. to 1 pt. milk.

Fine grain, *e.g.*, semolina, ground rice, etc., use 1½ ozs. to 1 pt. milk.

(b) *Moulds.*

Cornflour or arrowroot, use 1½ ozs. to 1 pt. milk.

Semolina or ground rice, use 2 ozs. to 1 pt. milk.

2. If using skim milk the deficiency in fat should be made up by adding ½ oz. butter or margarine to each pint of milk.

3. Always wash coarse grain before use.

4. To prevent milk from sticking and burning, rinse the saucepan with cold water before use. A heavy saucepan also helps to prevent burning.

5. Rice should be cooked until it swells and becomes soft ; tapioca and sago until they become soft and semi-transparent. Fine grain requires only a short time for cooking (10 mins.). They should be stirred continually, as they are very liable to burn.

6. The farinaceous product must be thoroughly cooked before adding the eggs.

7. When adding flavouring, vary this as much as possible and always use sparingly.

8. Wipe the edge of the pie-dish before putting into the oven.

9. Bake in a moderate oven. If only a hot oven is available, place the pie-dish in a tin of water, and put on a low shelf in the oven.

10. Serve on a dish with a d'oyley underneath the pie-dish.

PLAIN RICE PUDDING

1 pint milk	½ oz. butter or margarine
2 ozs. rice (shortgrained)	2 level tablespoonfuls sugar

Flavouring

1. Wash the rice by putting it into a strainer, then allow cold water to run through it.

2. Put it into a greased pie-dish with the sugar, milk and flavouring. Add the butter cut in small pieces.

3. Place on a tin and bake in a very moderate oven for about 1½–2 hours.

4. When set, dredge with castor sugar and serve.

RICE PUDDING (Basic Coarse-Grain Pudding)

1 pint milk	½ oz. butter or margarine
2 ozs. rice (shortgrained)	2 level tablespoonfuls sugar
1 egg	Flavouring

1. Wash the rice by putting it into a strainer, then allow cold water to run through it.

2. Bring the milk to the boil, sprinkle in the rice, bring back to the boil, stirring all the time. Cover with a lid, place over a low heat (with a gas stove use an asbestos mat) and cook gently until the grains swell and become soft, thus absorbing a lot of the milk. Stir occasionally. Time—about 30 minutes.

3. Add sugar, butter and flavouring, mix well and allow to cool slightly.

4. Beat the egg, pour the rice on to it, beating to prevent the egg from curdling.

5. Grease a pie-dish and pour the rice into it.

6. Bake in a moderate oven until set and nicely browned—about half an hour.

7. Sprinkle a little castor sugar on top and serve.

NOTE.—If liked a little nutmeg may be grated on top of pudding before putting into the oven, instead of adding flavouring.

SEMOLINA PUDDING (Basic Fine-Grain Pudding)

1 pint milk	½ oz. butter or margarine
1½ ozs. semolina	2 level tablespoonfuls sugar
1 egg	Flavouring

1. Bring the milk to the boil, sprinkle in the semolina, stirring all the time.

2. Simmer for about 10 minutes until the semolina swells and so thickens the milk. Stir all the time.

3. Remove from the fire, add sugar, butter and flavouring. Mix well and allow to cool slightly.

4. Separate the yolk from the white of egg. Beat the yolk, pour the semolina on to it, beating to prevent curdling.

5. Beat the white of egg until stiff and fold through the semolina. Pour into a well-greased pie-dish.

6. Bake in a moderate oven until set and nicely browned—about ½ hour.

7. Sprinkle with castor sugar and serve at once.

FAROLA PUDDING

Proportions and method as for Semolina Pudding (above).

GROUND RICE PUDDING

Proportions and method **as for** Semolina Pudding (page 121).

TAPIOCA PUDDING

Proportions and method as for Rice Pudding (page 121). Allow
15–20 mins. for preliminary cooking of the tapioca. It should become
clear when cooked.

Types of Tapioca : Seed, Bullet, Flake.

SAGO PUDDING

Proportions and method as for Rice Pudding (page 121). Allow
15–20 minutes for preliminary cooking of sago.

MACARONI PUDDING

Proportions and method as for Rice Pudding (page 121). Allow
15–20 mins. for preliminary cooking of macaroni.

CORNFLOUR MOULD

1 pint milk	2 level tablespoonfuls sugar
1½ ozs. cornflour	Lemon rind

1. Blend the cornflour with about 2 tablespoonfuls milk.

2. Put the remainder of the milk into a rinsed saucepan with
the lemon rind. Infuse for about 15 minutes.

3. Bring slowly to the boil and remove the lemon rind. Pour
the milk on to the blended cornflour, stirring all the time.

4. Return to the saucepan, bring to the boil and continue
stirring until the cornflour boils for 7 minutes.

5. Remove from the fire, add the sugar and stir until dissolved.

6. Rinse a mould with cold water, then pour in the cornflour.
Put into a cold place, or place in a bowl of cold water until set.

7. Loosen round the edges. Turn out on a glass dish, **and**
decorate with fruit or chopped jelly.

CHOCOLATE MOULD

1 pint milk	½ oz. cocoa *or* 1 oz. chocolate powder
1½ ozs. cornflour	2 level tablespoonfuls sugar
Vanilla essence	

Mix the cornflour and cocoa together and continue as for Cornflour Mould, adding a few drops of Vanilla essence.

GROUND RICE MOULD

1 pint milk	2 level tablespoonfuls sugar
2 ozs. ground rice	Lemon rind

Method as for Cornflour Mould (page 122).

CARRAGEEN MOULD

1 pint milk	2 strips lemon rind
$\frac{1}{4}$ oz. carrageen moss	2 level tablespoonfuls sugar
Pinch of salt	

1. Steep the carrageen in cold water for 10–15 minutes. Rinse well in cold water.

2. Put it into a saucepan with the milk, salt and lemon rind. Bring slowly to the boil and cook until the carrageen coats the back of a wooden spoon.

3. Add sugar and stir until dissolved.

4. Rinse a mould with cold water. Strain the carrageen into it. Do not push the carrageen through with a spoon, but shake well in the strainer. Leave in a cold place until set.

5. Loosen round the edges by giving a few gentle shakes. Turn out on a well-polished glass dish. Serve with stewed fruit or cream.

BREAD AND BUTTER PUDDING

3 ozs. thinly-sliced bread and butter

$\frac{3}{4}$ pint milk	1 egg
2 level tablespoonfuls sugar	1 oz. sultanas
Nutmeg	

1. Cut the bread into fingers.

2. Put the bread into a greased pie-dish, sprinkling the sultanas between the slices, until three-quarters full.

3. Heat the milk and add the sugar, stir until the sugar is dissolved.

4. Beat the egg and pour the heated milk on to it, taking care that it does not curdle. Pour this over the bread in the pie-dish. Grate a little nutmeg on top. Place pie-dish on a flat tin. Bake in a very moderate oven for about $\frac{3}{4}$ hour until quite set and nicely browned. Dredge a little castor sugar on top and serve at once.

QUEEN OF PUDDINGS

1½ ozs. breadcrumbs
½ pint milk
½ oz. butter or margarine
Grated rind of ½ lemon, or a few drops lemon essence

1 level tablespoonful sugar
1 yolk of egg

1 tablespoonful raspberry jam
1 white of egg ⎫
2 ozs. castor sugar ⎭ Meringue

1. Put butter, milk and lemon rind into a saucepan and heat until the butter is melted. Add sugar and stir until dissolved. Cool slightly.

2. Beat the yolk of egg and pour the heated milk on to it, taking care not to let it curdle.

3. Put the breadcrumbs into a bowl, and pour the egg and milk over them. Pour into a well-greased pie-dish.

4. Place on a flat tin. Bake in a very moderate oven for about 40 minutes or until set.

5. Heat the jam slightly and spread on top of the pudding.

6. Beat the white of egg stiffly and fold in the castor sugar. Pile roughly on top of the jam.

7. Return to a very cool oven until the meringue is set and well dried out, about ½ hour. Allow to become lightly browned.

NOTE.—Instead of making breadcrumbs, cut the bread into pieces, soak in the egg and milk mixture until soft. Beat well or put in the liquidiser at slow speed for a few seconds.

CHOCOLATE MERINGUE PUDDING

½ pint milk
½ oz. butter or margarine
1½ ozs. sugar
1½ ozs. breadcrumbs
Meringue:
   1 white of egg.
   2 ozs. castor sugar.

½ oz. cocoa
¼ teasp. Vanilla essence
1 egg yolk
1 tablesp. apricot jam

Method as for Queen of Puddings (above) mixing the cocoa with the breadcrumbs.

CARAMEL RICE

4 ozs. sugar ⎫
¼ pint water ⎭ Caramel

1 pint milk
2 ozs. rice (shortgrained)
½ oz. butter or margarine

1 egg white
1 oz. sugar
Flavouring

1. Prepare, the caramel as for Caramel Custard (page 126) and pour into a heated pie-dish, revolve the pie-dish until the sides are coated with the caramel.

2. Wash the rice by putting it into a strainer, then allow cold water to run through it.

3. Bring the milk to the boil, sprinkle in the rice, bring back to the boil, stirring all the time. Cover with a lid, place over a low heat (with a gas stove use an asbestos mat) and cook gently until the grains swell and become soft, thus absorbing a lot of the milk. Stir occasionally.

4. Add sugar, butter and flavouring, mix well and allow to cool slightly.

5. Beat the white of egg stiffly and fold through the rice mixture.

6. Pour into the prepared pie-dish. Bake in a very moderate oven until set and nicely browned—about ½ hour.

7. Sprinkle castor sugar on top and serve.

NOTE.—The whole egg may be used if liked, and in this case the mixture is made as for Rice Pudding (page 121).

CARAMEL SEMOLINA

4 ozs. sugar ⎱ Caramel	
¼ pint water ⎰	
1 pint milk	2 level tablespoonfuls sugar
1½ ozs. semolina	Few drops of Vanilla essence
½ oz. butter or margarine	1 egg

1. Prepare the caramel as for Caramel Custard (page 126) and pour into a heated pie-dish. Revolve the pie-dish until the sides are coated with the caramel.

2. Prepare the semolina as on page 121.

3. Pour into the prepared pie-dish and bake in a very moderate oven until set and brown.

4. Sprinkle with castor sugar and serve.

BAKED CUSTARD

1 pint milk	2 level tablespoonfuls sugar
3 eggs	Flavouring

1. Heat the milk, add sugar and flavouring and stir until dissolved.

2. Beat the eggs and pour the milk on to them.

3. Strain into a greased pie-dish. Place in a tin half-filled with cold water.

4. Cook in a very moderate oven until set and very lightly browned.

5. Dredge castor sugar on top, and serve.

NOTE.—If liked, a little nutmeg may be grated on top of custard before putting into the oven.

CARAMEL CUSTARD

$\left.\begin{array}{l}\frac{1}{4} \text{ lb. sugar} \\ \frac{1}{4} \text{ pint water}\end{array}\right\}$ Caramel

1 pint milk
3–4 eggs

2 level tablespoonfuls sugar
Flavouring

1. Put the sugar and water into a saucepan and stir over a gentle heat until dissolved.
2. Bring to the boil, and boil until it is a good brown colour, but do not allow to burn.
3. Pour into a dry 5-in. cake tin or heated pie-dish, and holding this in a dry cloth, revolve the tin or pie-dish until the sides are evenly coated with the caramel. Leave to become cool.
4. Heat the milk, add sugar and flavouring, stir until sugar is dissolved.
5. Beat the eggs and pour on the milk.
6. Strain into the prepared tin or pie-dish. Cover with a piece of greased paper.
7. Place in a deep tin with hot water coming half-way up the tin or pie-dish. Cook in a very moderate oven until set, about 45 mins.
8. If using a tin turn on to a glass dish.
9. Add 1 tablespoonful water to the tin and stir over a gentle heat until the remainder of the caramel is dissolved. Serve with the custard.
10. Serve custard either hot or cold.
NOTE.—For individual helpings use dariole moulds.

CABINET PUDDING

½ pint milk
2 eggs
4 ozs. cake or bread (cut in ½ inch dice)

2 level tablespoonfuls sugar
2 ozs. cherries
Few drops of Vanilla essence

To serve:—Jam Sauce (page 154).

1. Cut the cherries in quarters and mix with the cake.
2. Heat the milk, add sugar and flavouring. Stir until sugar is dissolved, cool, add to the beaten egg, and pour over the cake.
3. Put into a greased mould or bowl. Cover with greased paper. Place in a deep tin with hot water coming half-way up the mould or bowl.
4. Cook in a very moderate oven until firm to the touch— about 1 hour.
5. Remove paper and turn out on to a hot dish. Dredge castor sugar on top.

Steamed Puddings

Steamed Puddings are generally included in winter menus, because of the heat and energy-providing properties of their ingredients.

They are very substantial and should only be included in the menu when the preceding fare has been of a light nature.

Fat for steamed puddings may be beef suet, butter, margarine or oil. The cooking time depends on the fat used, *e.g.*, suet takes about twice as long as butter, margarine or oil. Suet must be chopped finely to ensure that enough heat penetrates to the centre of it, to change the state of the fat from a solid to a liquid. Margarine or butter may be incorporated by rubbing into the flour or by softening in a warm place and then mixing with the dry ingredients. When using oil it is important to buy a good quality to obtain a pleasant flavour. Each fat gives a different texture and flavour to the pudding.

ROLY POLY PUDDING

6 ozs. suet pastry (page 175) 3 or 4 tablesps. jam

To serve:—Jam Sauce (page 154).

1. Dip a pudding cloth in boiling water and squeeze out as much water as possible. Brush with clarified fat. Sprinkle lightly with flour to form a paste. This prevents water from getting into pudding.

2. Make suet pastry and roll into an oblong shape about $\frac{1}{4}$ inch thick, keeping it as even as possible.

3. Damp around the edges of pastry with cold water. Spread the jam to within 1 inch of the edge of pastry. Roll up to form a roll, seal the edges well together.

4. Wrap up the pudding in the cloth, leaving enough room for it to swell. Tie the ends with twine, leaving a piece of twine between the ends to lift the pudding. Sew up the opening.

5. Put the pudding into a large saucepan of boiling water. If the pudding has not room to lie flat it will have a bad appearance when cooked. Boil or steam from 2–$2\frac{1}{2}$ hours.

6. Lift out of the water and drain. Remove the cloth and roll on to a hot dish. Pour a little jam sauce around the dish and serve the remainder in a hot sauce-boat.

FRUIT ROLY POLY

6 ozs. Suet Pastry (page 175)

Filling:

2 ozs. currants or sultanas	1 oz. butter or margarine
1 oz. chopped peel	1 oz. sugar

$\frac{1}{4}$ teasp. mixed spice

To serve:—Custard Sauce (page 153).

Prepare filling by melting the butter and adding the washed currants or sultanas, peel, sugar and spice. Make as for Roly Poly Pudding (page 127), using the above filling instead of jam.

APPLE DUMPLING

6 ozs. Suet Pastry (page 175)

Filling:

3 apples	2–3 tablespoonfuls sugar
2 cloves	

To serve:—Apple Syrup Sauce (page 155), *or* Custard Sauce (page 153).

1. Grease a small pudding-bowl (5 inches) and a piece of paper for the top.

2. Make the pastry and cut off one-third for the top of dumpling. Knead each piece lightly, roll the larger into a round shape $\frac{1}{4}$ inch thick, and line the pudding-bowl with it.

3. Peel, core and slice the apples, put into the lined bowl with the sugar and cloves. Add a little water.

4. Brush round the edge of pastry with cold water.

5. Roll remaining piece of pastry into a round, large enough to cover bowl. Place on top and press edges well together.

6. Put a pleat across the centre of the greased paper to allow room for the pudding to rise. Cover the dumpling with it.

7. Steam for about 2 hours.

8. Turn on to a hot dish. Dredge with castor sugar. Serve sauce in a sauce-boat.

To Caramel Pastry.—Grease the pudding-bowl thickly and coat with brown sugar.

BASIC STEAMED PUDDING

2 ozs. flour	Pinch of salt
2 ozs. beef suet *or* margarine	1 egg
2 ozs. breadcrumbs	A little milk
2 ozs. sugar	Flavouring

$\frac{1}{2}$ teasp. baking powder

To serve:—$\frac{1}{2}$ pint Custard Sauce (page 153).

1. Chop the suet finely (page 215) and add it to the sieved flour. If using margarine rub it into the flour or soften it and add it later with the egg.

2. Add all the dry ingredients and mix well together.

3. Beat the egg, add the flavouring. Add to the dry ingredients with enough milk to make to a dropping consistency.

4. Put into a greased 5-inch pudding-bowl—it must not be more than three-quarters full. Cover with a piece of greased paper.

5. Steam for about 1½–2 hours according to fat used in pudding.

6. Serve on a d'oyley on a hot dish. Dredge castor sugar on top.

MARMALADE PUDDING

Ingredients as for Basic Steamed Pudding (page 128), adding 1 tablespoonful marmalade. Add this to the dry ingredients before adding the egg. Continue as for Basic Steamed Pudding. Serve Marmalade Sauce (page 155).

LEMON PUDDING

Ingredients and method as for Basic Steamed Pudding (page 128), adding the grated rind and juice of ½ lemon. Serve Lemon Sauce (page 155) or Custard Sauce (page 153).

ORANGE PUDDING

Ingredients and method as for Basic Steamed Pudding (page 128), adding the grated rind and juice of 1 orange. Serve Orange Sauce (page 155) or Custard Sauce (page 153).

FIG PUDDING

Ingredients as for Basic Steamed Pudding (page 128), adding ¼ lb. figs. Pour boiling water over the figs and soak for 15 minutes, dry them and cut in small pieces, removing the stalks. Add to the dry ingredients. Continue as for Basic Steamed Pudding. Serve Custard Sauce (page 153), Lemon Sauce (page 155), or Vanilla Sauce (page 149).

SULTANA PUDDING

Ingredients as for Basic Steamed Pudding (page 128), adding 2 ozs. cleaned sultanas to the dry ingredients. Continue as for Basic Steamed Pudding. Serve Vanilla Sauce (page 149), or Custard Sauce (page 153).

BACHELOR PUDDING

Ingredients as for Basic Steamed Pudding (page 128), adding 2 ozs. cleaned currants and 1 oz. chopped peel to the dry ingredients. Continue as for Basic Steamed Pudding. Serve Lemon Sauce (page 155) or Vanilla Sauce (page 149).

CHELSEA PUDDING

Ingredients as for Basic Steamed Pudding (page 128), adding 2 ozs. cleaned raisins and 2 ozs. cleaned currants to the dry ingredients. Add 1 dessertspoonful of treacle to the beaten egg and continue as for Basic Steamed Pudding. Serve Lemon Sauce (page 155) or Custard Sauce (page 153).

GINGER PUDDING

Ingredients as for Basic Steamed Pudding (page 128), adding 1 teaspoonful ground ginger and ½ teaspoonful ground cinnamon to the dry ingredients. Add 1 tablespoonful treacle and 1 dessertspoonful golden syrup to the beaten egg and continue as for Basic Steamed Pudding. Serve Custard Sauce (page 153).

PLUM PUDDING

2 ozs. flour	1 oz. whole almonds
4 ozs. breadcrumbs	Rind and juice of ½ lemon
4 ozs. beef suet or butter	1 sour apple
4 ozs. brown sugar	½ teaspoonful mixed spice
2 ozs. sultanas	¼ teaspoonful salt
4 ozs. raisins	2–3 eggs
4 ozs. currants	2 tablespoonfuls whiskey *or*
2 ozs. candied peel (chopped)	Half small bottle stout

To serve:—Brandy Butter *or* Brandy Sauce.

1. Prepare the dried fruit (page 178). Blanch and chop the almonds (page 178). Peel and grate the apple. Put into a bowl with the candied peel and lemon rind. Mix all well together.
2. Chop the suet finely (page 215) and add it to the sieved flour. If using butter rub it into the flour or soften it and add it later with the eggs. Add the sugar, breadcrumbs, spice, salt and mix well together. Mix in the prepared fruit.
3. Beat the eggs and add them with the whiskey or stout and lemon juice, bind all together. Leave overnight.
4. Put into a greased bowl. Cover with a prepared cloth (page 217) or cooking foil. Steam or boil for about 4 hours.
5. When cold, store in a dry place for several weeks. Steam or boil for 2 hours before serving.
6. Turn on to a hot dish. Just before serving pour a little whiskey over the pudding and light. If not lighting, put a sprig of holly on top.

SAGO PLUM PUDDING

1 tablespoonful sago	½ lb. breadcrumbs
½ pint milk	½ lb. sultanas
¼ lb. sugar	1 oz. candied peel
4 ozs. butter or margarine	1 egg
½ teaspoonful mixed spice	½ teaspoonful breadsoda
2 teaspoonfuls lemon juice	

To serve:—Custard Sauce (page 153).

1. Wash the sago, put into a saucepan with the milk, bring to the boil, and cook gently until the sago is cooked and clear.
2. Add the butter and stir until melted.

3. Mix all the dry ingredients together in a bowl. Pour the sago mixture on to them and mix well.

4. Beat the egg, and add with the lemon juice to the other ingredients. Mix very well together.

5. Pour into a well-greased bowl, cover with greased paper. Steam for 1½–2 hours.

6. Remove paper and turn out on a d'oyley on a hot dish. Dredge the top with castor sugar.

Madeira Mixtures

This type of pudding owes its lightness to beating, first, in the creaming of the butter and sugar, and then when the eggs are added. If insufficiently beaten, this mixture will be solid instead of light and spongy. It may be either baked or steamed.

CANARY PUDDING

4 ozs. butter or margarine	About 1 tablespoonful water
4 ozs. castor sugar	Vanilla essence
6 ozs. flour	½ teaspoonful baking powder
2 eggs	

To serve:—Jam Sauce (page 154).

1. Have the butter or margarine at room temperature. Put it with the sugar into a bowl and beat until white and creamy using a wooden spoon or electric mixer.

2. Beat the eggs and flavourings and add gradually to the creamed butter and sugar. Beat well. If preferred the eggs may be broken and beaten into the mixture one at a time. A little sieved flour may be added between each addition of egg if liked.

3. Fold in the remainder of the flour using a metal spoon, adding a little water if necessary to make to a dropping consistency. Add the baking powder mixed with the last addition of flour. Baking powder is not required when using an electric mixer.

4. Turn into a greased 5-inch pudding-bowl, cover with greased paper. Steam for about 1½ hours.

5. Serve on a d'oyley on a hot dish, dredge castor sugar on top

CASTLE PUDDINGS

2 ozs. butter or margarine	About 1 dessertspoonful water
2 ozs. castor sugar	Vanilla essence
3 ozs. flour	$\frac{1}{4}$ teasp. baking powder
1 egg	

To serve:—Jam Sauce (page 154).

1. Make as for Canary Pudding (page 131).
2. Grease 5 dariole moulds and put the mixture into these, having them two-thirds full.
3. Bake in a moderate oven until cooked—about 15–20 mins.
4. Turn on to a hot dish and serve.

ORANGE SPONGE PUDDING

4 ozs. butter or margarine	Grated rind and juice of
4 ozs. castor sugar	$\frac{1}{2}$ orange
6 ozs. flour	$\frac{1}{2}$ teasp. baking powder
2 eggs	About 1 tablespoonful water

To serve:—Orange Sauce (page 155) or Custard Sauce (page 153).

Make as for Canary Pudding (page 131), adding rind and juice of orange after the eggs.

LEMON SPONGE PUDDING

4 ozs. butter or margarine	Grated rind of $\frac{1}{2}$ lemon
4 ozs. castor sugar	$\frac{1}{2}$ teasp. baking powder
6 ozs. flour	About 1 tablespoonful water
2 eggs	

To serve:—Lemon Sauce (page 155) or Custard Sauce (page 153).

Make as for Canary Pudding (page 131), adding the grated rind to the creamed butter and sugar.

CHOCOLATE SPONGE PUDDING

4 ozs. butter or margarine	$\frac{1}{2}$ oz. cocoa
5 ozs. castor sugar	$\frac{1}{2}$ teasp. Vanilla essence
6 ozs. flour	$\frac{1}{2}$ teasp. baking powder
2 eggs	About 1 tablespoonful water

To serve:—Chocolate Sauce (page 150).

Make as for Canary Pudding (page 131), sifting the cocoa with the flour.

RASPBERRY PUDDING

4 ozs. butter or margarine	About 1 tablespoonful water
4 ozs. castor sugar	Flavouring
6 ozs. flour	$\frac{1}{2}$ teasp. baking powder
2 eggs	2 tablesps. raspberry jam

To serve:—Jam Sauce (page 154), or Custard Sauce (p. 153).

1. Make as for Canary Pudding (page 131).
2. Grease a 5-inch pudding-bowl and put the raspberry jam in the bottom.
3. Put the mixture on top of the jam, cover with greased paper and steam for about 1½ hours.
4. Turn on to a hot dish and serve.

SULTANA SPONGE PUDDING

4 ozs. butter or margarine	A few drops of Vanilla essence
4 ozs. castor sugar	$\frac{1}{2}$ teasp. baking powder
6 ozs. flour	2 ozs. sultanas
2 eggs	About 1 tablespoonful water

To serve:—Custard Sauce (page 153).

Make as for Canary Pudding (page 131), folding in the cleaned sultanas after the flour.

EVE'S PUDDING

2 ozs. margarine	3 ozs. flour
2 ozs. castor sugar	$\frac{1}{4}$ teaspoonful baking powder
1 egg	A few drops Vanilla essence
About 1 dessertspoonful water	

1 lb. apples	About 2 ozs. sugar
2 cloves	

1. Peel, core and slice the apples and put them into a greased pie-dish with the sugar, cloves and a little water.
2. Make cake mixture as for Canary Pudding (page 131), spread over the apples and smooth with a knife. Bake in a very moderate oven for about 40–45 minutes until the mixture is quite cooked. Dredge castor sugar on top and serve.

Batters

A batter is a mixture of flour, eggs and a liquid, *e.g.*, milk, water and oil, which is well and smoothly mixed, then beaten to entrap as much cold air as possible.

VARIETIES OF BATTERS

KIND	PROPORTIONS	EXAMPLES OF USE
Plain or Pancake Batter.	4 ozs. flour. Pinch of salt. 1 egg. ½ pt. milk.	Pancakes. Yorkshire Pudding. Toad in the hole. Fruit in batter.
Simple Coating Batter.	4 ozs. flour. Pinch of salt. 1 egg. ¼ pt. milk.	Fritters. Fish in batter.
" Kromeski " or Rich Coating Batter.	2 ozs. flour. Pinch of salt. 1 dessertsp. oil. ⅛ pt. tepid water. 1 stiffly-whisked white of egg. This is made in the same way as other batters (page 135) adding the oil and water to mix. The white of egg is folded into the batter just before using.	Fritters. Kromeskies. Coating of fish.

MAKING OF BATTER

1. Sieve the flour and salt, make a well in the centre of the flour, drop the egg into it, add about 1 tablespoonful of the liquid, and mix with a wooden spoon, allowing the flour to fall in gradually from the sides.

2. Add half the liquid very gradually (keeping the batter thick at the beginning to make sure there are no lumps).

3. Beat for about 3 minutes, until the surface of the batter is covered with little bubbles.

4. Then mix in the remainder of the liquid; cover the bowl and leave to stand in a cold place for about an hour; by leaving the batter stand, the starch grains get time to absorb liquid and swell. Cook at a fairly high temperature, as otherwise the batter will become heavy and sodden.

To Season a Pan

Heat a little fat or oil in the pan. Leave to cool and heat again. Pour off the fat and wipe the pan with kitchen paper.

PANCAKES

4 ozs. flour	1 egg
Pinch of salt	½ pint milk

To fry:—Clarified fat or oil.

To serve:—Castor sugar, lemon juice and cut lemon.

1. Make batter as above. Leave to stand for at least an hour. Pour into a jug.

2. Melt the fat, grease a small hot **pan with it**. Pour in enough batter to cover the bottom thinly.

3. Fry quickly until set and a golden brown, shake it occasionally and loosen it round the edges to make sure it will turn easily.

4. Toss the pancake or turn with a knife, and fry the second side until golden brown.

5. Turn on to a paper dredged with castor sugar, sprinkle a little lemon juice and sugar over and roll up neatly.

6. Place on a plate which is being kept hot over a saucepan of boiling water (pancakes must always be kept hot by moist heat, otherwise they will become hard and dry) ; cover with a lid or plate cover.

7. Make the remainder of the pancakes in the same way.

8. Serve very hot on a d'oyley on a hot dish. Dredge the top with castor sugar. Garnish with cut lemon.

Fresh Fruit Puddings

PREPARATION OF FRUIT

FRUIT	PREPARATION
Apples .. Pears ..	Peel thinly, core and cut into quarters, eighths, or thin slices as required.
Plums .. Damsons ..	Remove stems and wash.
Gooseberries ..	Top and tail, then wash.
Rhubarb	Remove leaves and stump, wash, dry, and cut into 1 inch lengths.
Blackcurrants Redcurrants Whitecurrants	Remove stalks. Wash carefully in a colander if necessary.
Raspberries Loganberries Blackberries Strawberries	Pick carefully and remove hull. Wash carefully in a colander if necessary.
Oranges	Dip for half-minute in boiling water, roll around on the board. Remove rind and any pith. Divide into sections or cut as required.
Bananas	Remove skin and any threads from sides.
Cherries	Wash. Cut in half and remove the stones.

STEWED APPLES

1 lb. apples	Sugar to sweeten
¼ pint water	3 or 4 cloves

1. Put the sugar and water into a saucepan and allow to dissolve without boiling. Add cloves.

2. Bring to the boil and boil for 2 or 3 minutes.

3. Peel, core the apples and cut in quarters or eighths according to size.

4. Put into the syrup and cook gently until soft but unbroken.

5. Cool a little, then turn into a glass dish. Serve either hot or cold.

NOTE.—Stewed fruit may also be cooked in a casserole in the oven. Put prepared fruit into the casserole, pour the syrup over. Cover and cook in a moderate oven until soft. Serve as above.

STEWED DRIED FRUIT (Prunes, Apricots, etc.)

1 lb. dried fruit   About 2 ozs. sugar
Strip of lemon rind

1. Wash the fruit well and steep overnight in cold water.

2. Next day, put it into a saucepan with the covering liquid, add the sugar and lemon rind, bring to the boil and simmer until the fruit is soft.

3. Cool a little, then turn into a glass dish. Serve either hot or cold.

SWISS APPLE PUDDING

6 ozs. crumbs   2 or 3 apples
1½ ozs. melted butter   1 oz. sugar
1 oz. brown sugar   1 tablesp. water
Grated rind of ½ lemon   Browned crumbs

To serve:—Custard Sauce (page 153). Vanilla Sauce (page 149), or Syrup Sauce (page 155).

1. Grease a 5-inch cake tin and line it with browned crumbs.

2. Put the breadcrumbs, butter and sugar into a bowl, add lemon rind and mix all well together.

3. Stew the apples to a thick pulp with the sugar and water.

4. Put a layer of crumb mixture in the bottom of the tin, then a layer of apples, keeping them about ½ inch from edge of tin.

5. Continue in layers, finishing with a layer of breadcrumbs. Bake in a moderate oven for about half an hour.

6. Turn out on to a hot dish.

NOTE.—(1) 1½ ozs. finely-chopped suet may be used instead of butter or margarine. In this case 1 hour is required for baking.

(2) This pudding may be made in a pie-dish if liked, then omit the lining with browned crumbs and do not turn out.

BAKED APPLES

4 apples (even-sized)   1 oz. sugar
½ oz. butter or margarine   A little grated lemon rind *or*
                                       ground cinnamon

1. Wash the apples well and remove the cores.

2. Make a cut in the skin all the way round the centre of the apples.

3. Mix the butter, sugar and lemon rind or cinnamon in a small bowl. Fill the hole in the centre of the apples with this mixture.

4. Place in a fireproof dish, pour a little water around. Bake in a moderate oven until soft—about 30 minutes.

5. Remove skin from the upper halves of apples, and serve.

NOTE.—If liked, 2 or 3 cloves may be stuck in the skin of each apple.

APPLE SNOW

2 lbs. apples	Grated rind of half a lemon
A little water	2 whites of eggs
4–6 ozs. sugar	1 or 2 tablespoonfuls cream

1. Peel, core and slice the apples.
2. Stew to a thick pulp with a little water and lemon rind.
3. Beat out all lumps with a spoon or put through a sieve. Add sugar and leave until cold.
4. Beat the whites of eggs stiffly, fold them lightly into the apple purée.
5. Stir in cream at the end and pile roughly in a glass dish.

GOOSEBERRY FOOL

2 lbs. gooseberries	¼ pint cream
½ lb. sugar	¼ pint milk ⎱ Custard (see
¼ pint water	1 egg ⎰ page 153)

To serve:—¼ pint whipped cream.

1. Top and tail the gooseberries. Wash them and put them into the saucepan with the water and sugar.
2. Cook until they are quite soft, then rub them through a fine sieve or use a liquidiser.
3. Half-whip the cream and add it with the cold custard to the gooseberry purée. Mix well.
4. Pour into individual glasses or into a large glass dish.
5. Serve whipped cream separately.

NOTE.—All cream or all custard may be used if liked. Other fruit purée may be used in the same way.

APPLE SOUFFLÉ PUDDING

1 lb. apples	2 cloves
2 ozs. sugar	A little water

Soufflé Mixture:—1 oz. butter or margarine	¼ pint milk
1 oz. flour	1 egg
½ oz. sugar	

1. Stew the apples as on page 136. Cook until they are nearly soft. Put them into a greased pie-dish.
2. Melt the butter, mix in the flour and cook for a few minutes. Cool a little and add the milk. Bring to the boil and cook for 3 minutes.
3. Separate the yolk from the white of the egg, add the sugar and yolk to the sauce. Beat the white stiffly and fold into the mixture.
4. Pour over the fruit in the pie-dish and bake in a very moderate oven until well risen and nicely browned—about 40 minutes.
5. Dust with castor sugar and serve.

PUFFED SWEET OMELET

2 eggs	Vanilla essence
1 tablespoonful water	$3/_4$ oz. butter
$1/_2$ oz. castor sugar	1 tablespoonful jam

1. Put the jam in a warm place to heat.

2. Beat the yolks of eggs and sugar until creamy. Add water and vanilla essence.

3. Beat the whites of eggs stiffly, pour the yolks over, and fold lightly through.

4. Put the butter on a seasoned omelet pan (page 135) and allow to become sizzling hot.

5. Pour on the omelet mixture. Cook until lightly browned underneath.

6. Brown the top of the omelet under a griller, in front of a radiant fire, or put in the oven for a few minutes.

7. Turn on to a hot dish or plate, allowing half of the omelet to rest on the palm of the left hand. Crease the centre with a knife.

8. Spread the hot jam over one half of the omelet, and fold the other half over.

9. Dredge the top with castor sugar and serve immediately.

Pastry Dishes

APPLE PIE

4 ozs. short pastry (page 174)
Filling:—1 lb. apples. 2 cloves. Sugar to sweeten.
To frost pastry:—White of egg. A little castor sugar.
To serve:—Custard Sauce (page 153).

1. Roll out pastry a little larger than pie-dish. Leave in a cold place while preparing the filling.

2. Peel, core and slice the apples. Put into the pie-dish, sprinkle cloves and sugar in between. Add a little water.

3. Cut a strip of pastry about $\frac{1}{2}$ inch wide. Damp round the edge of the pie-dish. Place the strip on edge of pie-dish with the cut edge to the outside.

4. Brush the strip with cold water. Place the remainder of pastry on top of pie-dish, easing it over the top of the apples.

5. Press edges well together. Trim with a sharp knife. Flake and decorate the edge.

6. Stand pie-dish on a tin, and bake in a hot oven for the first 8–10 minutes. Reduce the heat until the pie is cooked—about $\frac{1}{2}$ hour.

7. Brush over the top with slightly-beaten white of egg. Dredge with castor sugar. Return to the oven for a few minutes until nicely browned.

8. Dust with castor sugar and serve.

GOOSEBERRY PIE ⎫
RHUBARB PIE   ⎬ Make as for APPLE PIE.
CHERRY PIE   ⎭

APPLE TART OR CAKE

6 ozs. short pastry (page 174)

Filling:

¾ lb. apples   2 or 3 cloves

A little sugar

1. Cut pastry into two pieces. Roll each out until large enough to cover a tart plate.
2. Grease the plate and place one round of pastry on it. Trim the edges.
3. Peel, core and slice the apples. Place them on the pastry, sprinkle cloves and sugar between.
4. Damp the edge of this round of pastry. Cover with the second round of pastry, easing it over the fruit. Press edges well together.
5. Trim the edges, flake and decorate them.
6. Put on a tin. Place in a hot oven for the first 5 minutes, then reduce the heat until the cake is cooked—about 30 minutes.
7. Dredge castor sugar on top and serve.

BLACKCURRANT TART ⎫
GOOSEBERRY TART   ⎪
RHUBARB TART   ⎬ Make as for APPLE TART
CHERRY TART   ⎭

OPEN JAM TART

5 ozs. short pastry (page 174)   3–4 tablesps. jam

1. Grease a tart plate about 8 ins. in diameter.
2. Roll the pastry into a round shape a little larger than the plate.
3. Cut a strip ½ inch wide off the pastry and put round the edge of the plate with the cut edge outwards.
4. Damp this strip of pastry and line the plate with the remainder of the pastry. Trim the edges, flake and decorate them. Prick pastry with a fork.
5. Spread the centre of the plate with jam, having it about ¼ inch thick.
6. Roll out the trimmings and cut into 8 strips about ½ inch wide. Put these trellis-wise on top of jam.
7. Put the plate on a tin and bake in a hot oven for the first 8–10 minutes, then reduce heat until the pastry is cooked—about 30 minutes.
8. Serve the tart on a d'oyley on a plate.

LEMON TART

4 ozs. short pastry (page 174)

Filling:

2 lemons	½ pint water
4 ozs. sugar	1½ ozs. cornflour

2 yolks of eggs

Meringue: 2 whites of eggs.   4 ozs. castor sugar.

1. Roll pastry out and line a greased tart plate with it.
2. Flake and decorate the edges, prick centre with a fork and cover with a round of greased paper Place some beans on it to prevent the pastry from rising.
3. Bake in a hot oven for the first 10 minutes, then reduce heat until pastry is cooked—about 25 minutes. Remove beans and paper and put back in the oven for a further five minutes to allow the pastry to dry out.
4. For the filling, infuse the lemon rind in the water, blend the cornflour with the lemon juice, and strain the hot liquid on to it. Return the mixture to the saucepan, bring to the boil and boil for 5 minutes.
5. Remove from the heat. Cream the yolks of eggs with the sugar, pour the hot lemon mixture on to them. Stir quickly to mix well. Pour into the cooked pastry case.
6. Beat whites of eggs stiffly and fold in the castor sugar. Pile roughly on top of the filling, and decorate with a few cut cherries.
7. Put into a cool oven until the meringue is set and very lightly browned, about 30 minutes.
8. Serve on a d'oyley on a plate.

BAKEWELL TART

4 ozs. short pastry (page 174)
2 tablespoonfuls jam

Filling:

2 ozs. butter or margarine	2 ozs. castor sugar
3 ozs. flour	1 egg
A little grated lemon rind	¼ teaspoonful baking powder
A little water	

To serve:—Jam Sauce (page 154).

1. Line a greased tart plate with the pastry as for Open Jam Tart (page 140).
2. Spread the centre with jam.
3. Make cake mixture as for Canary Pudding (page 131) and spread on top of the jam.
4. Roll out any trimmings of pastry, cut in strips half-inch wide and lay trellis-fashion across pudding.
5. Bake in a fairly moderate oven for about 30 minutes until brown and thoroughly cooked.
6. Dredge with sugar and serve on a d'oyley on a plate.

APPLE AMBER TART

4 ozs. short pastry (page 174)

Filling:

3 or 4 apples	Sugar to sweeten
Grated rind of ½ lemon	1 oz. butter or margarine

2 yolks of eggs

Meringue: 2 whites of eggs.   4 ozs. castor sugar.

1. Line a pie-plate with the pastry as for Lemon Tart, and bake.
2. Peel, core and slice the apples. Put them into a saucepan with the butter and grated lemon rind and cook until reduced to a pulp. Beat until smooth with a wooden spoon.
3. Cream the yolks of eggs and sugar, pour the apple mixture on to them. Mix well and pour into the pastry case.
4. Beat the whites of eggs until stiff, fold in the castor sugar and pile roughly on top of apple mixture.
5. Put into a cool oven until the meringue is set and lightly browned, about 30 minutes. Serve on a d'oyley on a dish.

APPLE PUFFS

6 ozs. short pastry (page 174)

4 apples	¾ oz. butter or margarine
1 oz. sugar	Grated rind of ½ lemon

To frost pastry:—White of egg.   Castor sugar.

1. Roll pastry out thinly and cut into four 6–inch squares.
2. Mix the butter, sugar and lemon rind well together.
3. Peel and core the apples, place one apple on each square of pastry, fill the centres with the butter mixture.
4. Damp the edges of the pastry, draw up the pastry so that the corners meet on top of each apple, press the edges together.
5. Place on a greased tin, bake in a hot oven for the first ten minutes, then reduce the heat to finish cooking, about ½ hour.
6. Brush over with slightly-beaten white of egg and then dredge with castor sugar. Return to the oven until nicely browned.
7. Serve Puffs on a d'oyley on a hot dish.

GOLDEN SYRUP TART

5 ozs. short pastry (page 174)

Filling:

2 tablespoonfuls golden syrup	Juice of ½ lemon
2 tablespoonfuls breadcrumbs	1 egg

1. Mix syrup, crumbs and lemon juice well together in a small bowl. Add the beaten egg.
2. Make as for Open Jam Tart (page 140) using syrup mixture instead of jam.
3. Put 8 thin strips of pastry trellis-wise across syrup mixture.
4. Bake and serve as for Open Jam Tart.

Cold Puddings and Sweets

TRIFLE

6 small sponge cakes, or one 7- or 8-inch sponge cake
Raspberry jam

2 tablesps. sugar
2 tablesps. water
1 glass sherry

Custard:
½ pt. milk
2 eggs

1 level tablespoonful sugar
Flavouring

To decorate:—½ pint whipped and sweetened cream.
Cherries, angelica and shredded almonds.

1. Split the sponge cakes, spread jam between, prick with a fork and cut into three or four pieces, arrange in a glass dish.
2. Put sugar and water into a saucepan, bring to the boil, boil for 2 minutes. Cool and add sherry.
3. Pour this syrup over the sponge cakes, and leave soaking for about 20 minutes.
4. Make the custard as on page 153. Allow to cool, and pour over the sponge cakes.
5. When cold, pipe roses of cream on top.
6. Decorate with cut cherries, angelica and shredded almonds.

FRUIT TRIFLE

Make as for Trifle (page 143) using tinned or stewed fruit. The juice from the fruit is used to soak the sponge cakes. Arrange the fruit on top of the sponge cakes before masking with custard. A little fruit may be kept back for decoration.

MOSS CREAMS

1 pint milk
½ oz. carrageen
1 tablesp. powdered chocolate

1 oz. sugar
½ pint cream
¼ teaspoonful Vanilla essence

1. Steep the carrageen in cold water for 10–15 minutes. Rinse well in cold water. Put it with the milk into a saucepan and cook until it coats the back of a wooden spoon.
2. Strain into a bowl, add chocolate, vanilla, sugar and mix well. Leave until beginning to set. Whisk for a few minutes.
3. Half-whip the cream and add half of it to the carrageen. Whisk for a few minutes longer.
4. Pour into individual glasses and leave until set.
5. Whip the remainder of the cream and put a rose of cream on top of each sweet.

CARRAGEEN SOUFFLÉ

1 pint milk	1 egg (separated)
½ oz. carrageen	¼ pint cream
1 oz. sugar	1 tablespoonful sherry

To decorate:—Chopped nuts; whipped and sweetened cream.

1. Prepare a soufflé mould by tying a band of doubled paper around the outside of the mould. The paper should come about 2 inches above the top of the mould.
2. Steep the carrageen in cold water for 10–15 minutes. Rinse well in cold water. Put it with the milk into a saucepan, and cook until it coats the back of a wooden spoon.
3. Beat the yolk of egg with the sugar and flavouring and strain the carrageen on to it. Whisk well until it begins to set.
4. Fold in half-whipped cream and the stiffly-beaten white of egg. Put into the prepared soufflé mould, or into individual glasses.
5. Leave until set, and carefully remove the paper. Decorate with roses of cream, and sprinkle chopped nuts over.

LEMON CHIFFON PIE

To make Pie-shell:—1½ cups cornflakes
2 ozs. melted butter or margarine
2 ozs. sugar

Filling:—¼ oz. powdered gelatine	2 lemons
2 eggs	4 ozs. castor sugar
A pinch of salt	

To serve:—Whipped Cream.

1. Break the cornflakes into pieces. Mix with the sugar and bind with the melted butter. Line a pie-plate with the mixture by pressing firmly against sides and bottom of the plate. Put in a cool place to set.
2. Separate the yolks from the whites of eggs and put them with salt, 2 ozs. sugar, grated rind and juice of lemons into a bowl. Beat over a saucepan of boiling water until thick.
3. Add 2 tablespoonfuls of cold water to the gelatine, leave for a few minutes until it has absorbed the water, add to the egg mixture. Stir until it is dissolved. Remove from the saucepan and leave to cool.
4. Beat the whites of eggs stiffly, add the sugar and continue to beat until the mixture stands in points.
5. When the yolk mixture begins to thicken fold in the stiffly-beaten whites. Fill into the prepared shell and leave aside until set.
6. Decorate with cream.

LEMON SPONGE

2 lemons	$\frac{1}{2}$ oz. powdered gelatine
2 ozs. sugar	$\frac{1}{2}$ pint water
2 whites of eggs	1 tablespoonful sherry

To decorate:—Angelica.

1. Wipe the lemons with a damp cloth and peel the rind off as thinly as possible.

2. Put the rind into a saucepan with the sugar and water. Allow to dissolve slowly over the heat. Bring to the boil.

3. Add 3 tablespoonfuls of cold water to the gelatine, leave for a few minutes until it has absorbed the water. Add to the hot lemon syrup and stir until dissolved. Strain into a bowl, add strained lemon juice and the sherry. Leave in a cold place until beginning to set. Add the stiffly-beaten egg whites and whisk all together until white and frothy.

4. Pile in a glass dish or in individual glasses. Decorate with small pieces of angelica.

LEMON CREAM

2 lemons	2 eggs
1 pint water	6 ozs. sugar
$1\frac{1}{2}$ ozs. cornflour	

To decorate :—Cherries and Angelica.

1. Wash and dry the lemons. Peel off the rind as thinly as possible. Put it into a saucepan with the water, and bring slowly to the boil.

2. Blend the cornflour with the juice from the lemons. Strain the hot liquid on to it, stirring well.

3. Return to the saucepan and cook for about 7 minutes.

4. Cream the yolks of eggs with the sugar and pour the hot lemon mixture on to them. Put back on the fire for a few mins. to cook the eggs, do not allow to boil. Stir all the time.

5. Beat the whites of eggs stiffly and fold into the lemon mixture.

6. Pour into a wet mould and leave until set.

7. Loosen round the edges and give it a few gentle shakes to make sure the cream is loose.

8. Turn out on a glass dish and decorate with cherries and angelica.

RHUBARB WHIP

1 lb. rhubarb	2–3 tablespoonfuls water
2–3 ozs. sugar	{ 1 square red jelly
¼ pint cream	{ ¼ pint water

To decorate:—Whipped and sweetened cream; chopped nuts.

1. Prepare the rhubarb as on page 136.
2. Stew it with water until soft and pulpy. Add sugar and put pulp through a sieve, or use a liquidiser.
3. Measure the pulp and, if necessary, make up to ¾ pint by adding a little water.
4. Dissolve jelly in hot water, add to pulp, leave until cold. Whip until frothy.
5. Add half-whipped cream and continue whipping until beginning to set. Pour into individual glasses and leave until set.
6. Decorate each with a rose of cream, sprinkle chopped nuts over.

PEAR CONDÉ

1 pint milk	1 oz. butter
2 ozs. rice (shortgrained)	1 egg
2 ozs. sugar	Flavouring

3 pears (cut in halves and cooked)

Jam Glaze:—2 tablesps. apricot jam, 1 tablesp. water, 1 tablesp. sugar.

To decorate:—A little whipped and sweetened cream, cherries and angelica.

1. Wash the rice, bring the milk to the boil, sprinkle in the rice, bring back to the boil, stirring all the time. Cover with a lid, place over a low heat (when using a gas cooker place an asbestos mat under the saucepan) and cook gently until the grains swell and become soft, thus absorbing a lot of the milk. Stir occasionally. Time—about 30 minutes.
2. Cream the butter and sugar, add the egg and flavouring and beat well.
3. Pour the cooked rice on to this and mix well. Return to the heat and stir for a few minutes to cook the egg. Leave aside until cold.
4. Put a large spoonful into six individual glasses, put a half pear on top with the curved side uppermost.
5. Put the jam, sugar and water into a saucepan, bring to the boil and simmer until thick enough to mask the back of the spoon. Leave until cool.

6. Mask each pear with this apricot glaze.

7. Pipe a rosette of cream on each and decorate with half a cherry and a few pieces of angelica.

NOTE.—Any suitable fruit may be used instead of pears or any tinned fruit.

LOGANBERRY DELIGHT

2 ozs. sago	4 ozs. loganberries
1 pint water	6 ozs. sugar

To serve:—Whipped cream.

1. Wash the sago and put it into a saucepan with the water.

2. Bring to the boil, simmer until the grains of the sago become clear. Stir all the time.

3. Add the loganberries and cook until soft. Put in the sugar and stir until dissolved.

4. Allow to cool, pour into a glass dish and leave until cold.

NOTE.—Other fruits may be used, *e.g.*, apples, raspberries, rhubarb, etc., prepare as on page 136.

SAUCE-MAKING

THE simplest and plainest food can be given a greater finish by the accompaniment of a well-prepared sauce, whereas a badly-prepared sauce takes from the most creditable product.

A sauce may be used to add to the richness of food to improve the flavour, to increase the food value, or, even in some cases, to counteract the richness of a particular food, *e.g.*, apple sauce with roast pork, duck or goose. Each sauce should be suitable to the food with which it is served, *e.g.*, with a food lacking in flavour serve a highly-flavoured or well-seasoned sauce, while a food which has a very delicate flavour of its own requires a milder sauce.

Sauce-making is comparatively simple if the few basic rules are borne in mind. Nearly all sauces, which may be defined as liquid flavourings thickened by various means, fall into five classes, and if this is remembered, sauce-making becomes greatly simplified. These categories are :—

1. Sauces made with roux (flour and melted fat blended and cooked for 3 minutes) and liquid. These owe their thickness to the cooked flour in them, *e.g.*, White Sauce, Brown Sauce, and the variations of each.

2. All types of custard sauces, or sauces which owe their thickening properties to the cooking of the eggs in them, *e.g.*, Custard Sauce.

3. Cold Sauces divided into :—

    (*a*) Those made by combining egg yolk and oil without cooking, *e.g.*, Mayonnaise, Tartare Sauce ;

    (*b*) Those used as dressings for various salads.

4. Syrup Sauces and Fruit Sauces. These are often thickened by the addition of a blended farinaceous substance, *e.g.*, Apple Syrup Sauce.

5. Miscellaneous Sauces, *e.g.*, Bread Sauce, Mint Sauce, Tomato Sauce, Horseradish Sauce, etc.

Sauces made with Roux

A **Roux** is a mixture of fat and flour cooked together. When a white roux is required (as in the case of a white sauce) it is cooked until dry and sandy. For a fawn roux the mixture is allowed to colour slightly. For a brown sauce the roux is cooked until brown.

The proportion of liquid added to the roux varies according to the consistency required.

WHITE POURING SAUCE

1 oz. butter or margarine   1 pint milk
1 oz. flour

(Served as an accompaniment.)

1. Melt the fat, draw aside and add the flour. Stir well and cook until dry and sandy.
2. Remove the saucepan to the side of the cooker or to the table and allow to cool for a few minutes. Add the milk slowly, stirring all the time and making sure to blend out all the lumps.
3. Return to the heat and bring to the boil, stirring all the time. Boil for 5 minutes. If a savoury sauce is required, season with salt and pepper. Add sugar and suitable flavouring if serving with a sweet pudding.

NOTE.—All the ingredients may be mixed in a liquidiser and then cooked.

WHITE STEWING SAUCE

1 oz. butter or margarine   ³⁄₄ pint milk
1 oz. flour

(Used when stewing.)
Make as above.

WHITE COATING SAUCE

1 oz. butter or margarine   ½ pint milk
1 oz. flour

(Used to coat meat, vegetables, etc.)
Make as above.

WHITE BINDING SAUCE

1 oz. butter or margarine   ¼ pint milk
1 oz. flour

(Used to bind mixtures together and as a foundation for Scufflés.)
Make as above.

VANILLA SAUCE

½ oz. butter or margarine   1 teaspoonful sugar
½ oz. flour   ½ pint milk
A few drops of Vanilla essence   Carmine (if liked)

Make White Pouring Sauce (above,) add sugar, vanilla essence and a little colouring if liked.

NOTE.—Other flavourings which may be used : Almond, Laurel, Lemon.

CHOCOLATE SAUCE

½ pt. White Pouring Sauce (p. 149)   1 tablesp. milk or water
½ oz. cocoa   1 oz. sugar
Vanilla essence

Blend the cocoa with the milk or water. Add it to the sauce with the sugar and a few drops of vanilla essence. Stir well, bring to the boil, cook for a few minutes and serve.

ANCHOVY SAUCE

White Pouring Sauce (page 149) to which 1 tablespoonful of anchovy essence and a few drops of lemon juice are added. Season to taste.

CAPER SAUCE

White Pouring Sauce (page 149) to which 1 tablespoonful of chopped capers is added. Season to taste.

CHEESE SAUCE

White Pouring Sauce (page 149) to which 2 ozs. grated cheese is added. Season to taste. Do not boil after adding the cheese.

EGG SAUCE

White Pouring Sauce (page 149) to which a chopped hard-boiled egg is added. Season to taste.

MUSTARD SAUCE

White Pouring Sauce (page 149) to which 1 dessertspoonful made mustard and 1 tablespoonful vinegar is added. Season to taste.

PARSLEY SAUCE

White Sauce (page 149) to which 1 dessertspoonful finely-chopped parsley is added. Season to taste.

ONION SAUCE

4 ozs. chopped onion   ½ pt. White Pouring Sauce (p. 149)
½ oz. butter or margarine   Pinch of nutmeg
Salt and pepper

1. Melt the butter in a saucepan, put in the onion, cover with a round of greaseproof paper. Put the lid on the saucepan and cook without colouring over a very low heat for about 15 minutes until the onion is cooked.

2. Add the onion, nutmeg, salt and pepper to the White Pouring Sauce, stir well, bring to the boil, and serve.

DUTCH SAUCE

½ pt. White Pouring Sauce (page 149)   ¼ teasp. made mustard
Salt and pepper   1 egg or egg yolk
                    1 tablesp. white vinegar

1. Add mustard and seasoning to the sauce. Cool a little.

2. Beat the egg and pour the sauce on to it, stirring all the time. If sauce is too hot the egg may curdle.

3. Put back on the fire and cook for a few minutes, but do not let it boil. Stir while cooking.

4. Add vinegar gradually and mix well through the sauce.

NOTE.—This sauce may be served cold as a salad dressing.

BÉCHAMEL SAUCE

½ pint of milk   1 oz. butter or margarine
1 blade of mace   1 oz. flour
1 bay leaf   Salt and pepper
½ small onion   1 tablespoonful of cream (if liked)
2 cloves

1. Put the milk, mace, washed bay leaf, and onion stuck with the cloves, into a saucepan. Cover and infuse for 20 minutes. Bring to the boil and strain.

2. Make the White Coating Sauce as on page 149, using flavoured milk. Season with pepper and salt.

3. Just before serving add cream. Do not re-boil.

BROWN STEWING SAUCE

1 oz. fat   2 ozs. chopped onion
1 oz. flour   ¾ pint stock
                Salt and pepper

1. Melt the fat, add the onion and cook until beginning to brown.

2. Add salt and pepper to the flour, put into the saucepan, cook over a moderate heat until brown in colour, stirring to prevent burning.

3. Draw the saucepan to the side of the cooker or remove to the table, cool and add stock slowly, stirring to blend out all the lumps. Return to the heat, bring to the boil and boil for 5 mins.

BROWN BINDING SAUCE

1 oz. fat   1 oz. flour
1 oz. chopped onion   ¼ pint stock
                Salt and pepper

Make as for Brown Stewing Sauce.

ESPAGNOLE SAUCE

1 oz. fat	1 oz. chopped onion
1 oz. flour	2–3 soft tomatoes
1 pint brown stock	Bouquet garni
½ oz. bacon rinds	4 peppercorns
1 oz. chopped carrot	Salt

1. Extract fat from bacon rinds without colouring.
2. Add fat and prepared vegetables and fry until lightly browned.
3. Put in the flour and cook over a low heat until brown.
4. Stir in the stock gradually, bring to the boil and skim.
5. Add the chopped tomatoes, bouquet garni, peppercorns and salt. Simmer for about ¾ hour.
6. Strain, correct seasoning and consistency. Bring to the boil and serve.

CURRY SAUCE

1 oz. fat	½ apple
1 oz. chopped onion	¾ pint stock
1 oz. flour	1 dessertsp. chutney
1 teaspoonful curry powder	1 soft tomato
Salt	

1. Melt the fat and fry the onion until golden brown.
2. Put in the flour and curry powder and cook all together for a few minutes. Remove from the heat and cool slightly.
3. Add the stock gradually, stirring all the time. Bring to the boil and skim.
4. Add the chutney, chopped apple, tomato and salt. Mix well together, cover and simmer for about ¾ hour, stirring frequently.
5. Strain and use as required.

TOMATO SAUCE

½ lb. sliced tomatoes *or*	2 ozs. chopped carrot
1 tablesp. tomato purée	1 oz. fat
¾ pint stock or water	1 oz. flour
1 oz. chopped onion	Salt and pepper
Bouquet garni	

1. Heat the fat, add the onion and carrot, fry until lightly browned.
2. Add the flour and cook over a low heat for about 5 minutes.
3. Add the sliced tomatoes or tomato purée, cook for a few minutes. Add the stock, bouquet garni and salt, bring to the boil, skim and simmer for about 15 minutes.
4. Strain, correct seasoning and consistency. Bring to the boil and serve.

Custard Sauces

In the making of Custard and other sauces thickened with eggs, it is important to cook them at a low temperature.

For this reason a bain-marie or double saucepan may be used.

CUSTARD SAUCE

1 egg	½ pint milk (a little less)
Flavouring	1 teaspoonful sugar

1. Beat the egg with the sugar and flavouring.
2. Heat the milk, add it to the egg.
3. Put into a heavy saucepan and stir over a gentle heat until the custard coats the back of the wooden spoon.

CORNFLOUR CUSTARD SAUCE

½ pint of milk	1 egg
½ teaspoonful cornflour	Flavouring
1 teaspoonful sugar	

1. Blend the cornflour with about 1 tablespoonful of milk.
2. Boil the remainder of the milk. Pour on to blended cornflour stirring all the time to prevent lumping.
3. Return to the saucepan, bring to the boil and boil for 7 minutes.
4. Add sugar and flavouring. Cool for a few minutes. Beat the egg.
5. Pour the cornflour mixture slowly on to the beaten egg, stirring all the time to prevent lumping. If the cornflour is too hot the egg will curdle.
6. Return to the saucepan and re-heat for a few minutes to cook the egg, but do not re-boil.

Salad Dressings

VINAIGRETTE or FRENCH DRESSING

4 tablespoonfuls salad oil	Pinch of pepper, salt,
2 tablespoonfuls vinegar	and mustard

Mix the seasonings, add oil and vinegar. Put into a bottle with a tightly-fitting stopper and shake well before use.

SALAD DRESSING

1 teaspoonful mustard	Pinch pepper
1 tablespoonful flour	$\frac{3}{4}$ cup vinegar
1 tablespoonful sugar	2 eggs
$\frac{1}{2}$ teaspoonful salt	$\frac{1}{4}$ pint milk

1. Mix the dry ingredients together. Add beaten eggs and vinegar.

2. Cook over a slow heat as for custard.

3. Cool and stir in the milk until the right consistency is obtained.

DUTCH SAUCE (page 151)

May be used cold as Salad Dressing.

Syrup and Fruit Sauces

GOLDEN SYRUP SAUCE

$\frac{1}{4}$ pint water	1 dessertsp. lemon juice
2 tablespoonfuls golden syrup	

Put water, syrup and lemon juice into a saucepan. Bring to the boil and boil for 5 minutes. A little blended cornflour may be used to thicken the sauce if liked.

JAM SAUCE

$\frac{1}{2}$ pint water	Strip of lemon rind
2 tablespoonfuls jam	1 dessertsp. lemon juice
1 teaspoonful sugar	1 teaspoonful cornflour

1. Put water, lemon rind and jam into a saucepan.

2. Infuse for 15 minutes and then bring slowly to the boil, and boil for 5 minutes.

3. Strain and pour on to cornflour, which has been blended with a little water, stirring to prevent lumping.

4. Put back on the heat and bring to the boil, still stirring, and boil gently for 5 minutes. Add lemon juice and sugar.

NOTE.—If red jam is used, a few drops of carmine may be required to improve the colour.

MARMALADE SAUCE

½ pint water
2 tablesps. marmalade

1 teasp. cornflour
1 tablesp. sugar

Make as for Jam Sauce (page 154) omiting lemon rind and juice. Do not strain.

ORANGE SAUCE

½ pint water
1 orange

1 oz. sugar
1 teasp. cornflour

1. Grate the rind from the orange, put it with the juice and the water into a saucepan. Infuse for about 15 minutes. Boil for 5 minutes.
2. Blend the cornflour with a little water, pour the hot liquid on to it, stirring to prevent lumping.
3. Put back on the heat, bring to the boil and boil gently for 5 minutes. Add sugar, and use.

LEMON SAUCE

½ pint water
Grated rind and juice of ½ lemon

1 oz. sugar
1 teasp. cornflour

Make as for Orange Sauce.

APPLE SYRUP SAUCE

Peels and cores of 3–4 apples
Water
3 cloves

1 dessertspoonful sugar
1 teaspoonful cornflour to
½ pt. fruit liquid
A few drops of carmine

1. Wash apples before peeling. Put peels, cloves and cores into a saucepan, cover with water, bring to the boil, and simmer for half hour.
2. Strain off liquid and measure it. If necessary, make up to half pint by the addition of more water.
3. Blend cornflour with 1 tablespoonful cold water.
4. Pour on the fruit liquid, stirring all the time to prevent lumping.
5. Bring to the boil, still stirring, and boil gently for 7 mins.
6. Add a few drops of carmine. Put in sugar, stir until dissolved.

APPLE SAUCE

2 apples	1–2 teaspoonfuls brown sugar
2 tablespoonfuls water	Pinch of nutmeg
1 oz. butter or margarine	

1. Peel, core and slice the apples.
2. Put them into a saucepan with water, sugar and nutmeg. Stew all together until soft.
3. Bruise out all lumps with back of wooden spoon or put through a sieve.
4. Add butter, and mix well. Re-heat.

Miscellaneous Sauces

BREAD SAUCE

½ pint milk	2 cloves
1½ ozs. breadcrumbs	1 bay leaf
½ oz. butter	Blade of mace
1 small onion	4 peppercorns
Salt	

1. Peel the onion and stick the cloves into it.
2. Put milk, prepared onion, peppercorns, bay leaf and mace into a saucepan.
3. Cover and infuse for 30 minutes, then bring slowly to the boil.
4. Strain, and return milk to saucepan.
5. Add breadcrumbs and stir well. Leave over a gentle heat until the breadcrumbs swell and thicken the sauce, stirring occasionally.
6. Add butter, season, and serve.

MINT SAUCE

2 tablespoonfuls chopped mint	2 tablespoonfuls boiling water
1 teaspoonful brown sugar	¼ pint brown vinegar

1. Put the mint into a small bowl with the sugar.
2. Pour the boiling water over and leave until the sugar is dissolved.
3. Add vinegar, and mix all well together.
4. Leave to stand for 1–2 hours before serving.

HORSERADISH SAUCE

1 tablesp. grated horseradish	½ teaspoonful made mustard
1 tablespoonful vinegar	¼ pt. cream (if cream is unobtainable,
1 teaspoonful castor sugar	use 2 tablesps. milk and 1 tablesp.
Good pinch of salt	very fine breadcrumbs mixed)

1. Wash the horseradish, scrape it, grate or shred it in a liquidiser.
2. Put into a bowl, add flavouring and mix well.
3. Beat the cream slightly and mix very lightly into ingredients.
Serve cold.

BRANDY BUTTER

2 ozs. butter	1–2 tablespoonfuls brandy
4 ozs. castor or icing sugar	

1. Cream the butter in a bowl or in an electric mixer.
2. Add the sieved sugar very gradually to the butter and continue beating until white and creamy. Add the brandy and a little colouring if liked.
3. Pile in a dish and serve or make into flat pats and serve on a small plate. Keep in a cold place until required.

MAÎTRE D'HÔTEL BUTTER

1 oz. butter	1 teaspoonful lemon juice
1 teaspoonful finely-chopped parsley	Pepper and salt

1. Cream the butter in a small bowl.
2. Add parsley, lemon juice and seasoning, and mix all well together.
3. Set on ice or in a cool place until required.
4. Form into neat pats and serve on grilled meat, etc.

BREAKFAST AND SAVOURY DISHES

THE breakfast menu is usually compiled from :—

    (a) Fruit or fruit juice.
    (b) Cereal.
    (c) Fish.
    (d) Meat or Egg Dish.
    (e) Bread, butter and preserves.
    (f) Beverage.

Fruit :

Grapefruit ; Orange or Orange Juice ; Melon or other fresh fruits ; Dried Fruits, *e.g.*, Stewed Prunes or Figs.

Cereal :

Porridge, Cornflakes, etc.

Fish :

Kipper ; Smoked Haddock ; Fried Plaice ; Sole or Trout.

Meat :

Bacon with :—Egg ; Liver ; Sausage ; Black and White Pudding.

Egg Dishes :

Boiled ; Poached ; Scrambled ; Fried ; Omelets.

Bread :

Toast ; Rolls ; Breakfast Scones ; Brown or White Bread.

Beverages :

Tea ; Coffee ; Cocoa ; Chocolate.

TEA

1. Fill the kettle with freshly-drawn water and bring to the boil.
2. Heat the tea-pot with boiling water and drain out well.
3. Put in the required amount of tea, allowing 1 teaspoonful per person, or according to taste.
4. Pour on the freshly-boiled water, leave in a warm place 5 or 6 minutes to infuse. Serve.

COFFEE

½ oz. ground coffee   ½ pint freshly-boiled water

1. Put the coffee into a saucepan and warm it slightly.
2. Pour the boiling water over, stir, put over a very gentle heat and leave it for 5 minutes.
3. Strain through a fine strainer into a hot coffee-pot and serve black or with hot milk or cream.

NOTE.—Coffee may be made in a percolator, following the directions with it.

COFFEE ESSENCE

½ lb. ground coffee   1 qt. hot water

Syrup: 2 lbs. sugar   ½ pint water

1. To make the syrup, put the sugar and water into a saucepan, stir until the sugar is dissolved, then boil until a dark brown colour.
2. Add the hot water and stir over the heat until well mixed together.
3. Bring to the boil, add the coffee and simmer for ½ hour. Pour into a jug and leave overnight.
4. Strain next day, bottle, label and store.
5. When required, heat the milk or a mixture of milk and water and add the coffee essence in the proportion of 1 teaspoonful per cup.

COCOA

1 teaspoonful cocoa   1 breakfastcupful milk, water
Sugar to taste   or milk and water

1. Mix the cocoa to a smooth paste with a little of the milk.
2. Bring the rest of the milk to boiling-point and stir this into the cocoa paste.
3. Return to the saucepan and boil for 1 minute. Sweeten to taste.

GRAPEFRUIT

1. Wash the grapefruit, cut it across in halves and remove the centre core.
2. Cut between the sections and loosen from the skin, using a grapefruit knife if available.
3. Sweeten with castor sugar and serve on a small plate.

PORRIDGE

2 ozs. flakemeal   1 pint water

$^1/_4$ teaspoonful salt

To serve:—Milk. Sugar (if liked).

1. Add the salt to the boiling water in the saucepan and sprinkle in the flakemeal. Stir for a few minutes.
2. Put the lid on the saucepan and cook gently until the porridge thickens, stirring frequently. Time, about ½ hour.
3. Serve very hot with milk or cream.

NOTE.—Pin-head oatmeal may be used instead of flakemeal. In this case, pour boiling water over the meal and steep overnight. Cook for 1½ hours.

TOAST

1. Cut the bread into slices of even thickness and toast until golden brown on both sides, before a radiant heat.
2. Trim off the crusts and serve the toast in a toast-rack. Never place it down flat as it would become sodden.

FRIED BACON AND EGG

2 rashers of bacon   1 egg

To garnish:—Parsley.

1. Remove rind and bone from the bacon.
2. Put the rashers on a frying pan and cook until the fat is transparent and the lean cooked, turning frequently. Lift on to a hot dish.
3. Cool the fat a little. Break the egg into a cup. Tilt the pan and slip the egg into the fat.
4. Fry slowly, basting with the hot fat until lightly set. Lift out with an egg slice and serve with the rashers on a hot dish or plate. Garnish with parsley.

BOILED EGG

1 egg   Cold water

Put the egg into cold water and bring to boiling-point. Boil gently for 2–3 minutes according to taste, or put the egg into boiling water and boil gently for four minutes. Lift out and serve.

HARD-BOILED EGG

1 egg   Cold water

1. Shake the egg gently to get the yolk in the centre. Put it into cold water and bring it to boiling-point.
2. Simmer for 10 minutes. Lift out, put into cold water.
3. Tap the shell all around and remove it carefully without damaging the white.

POACHED EGG

1 egg   ¼ teaspoonful salt
Boiling water   1 square or round of
                                                  buttered toast

To garnish:—Parsley.

1. Have about two inches of boiling water in a deep pan or saucepan. Add the salt.
2. Stir around with a spoon to make a little whirlpool. Drop in the egg and cook gently until the white is set.
3. Lift out the egg with a perforated spoon and drain well. Serve on the toast and garnish with parsley.

SCRAMBLED EGG

1 egg   Pepper and salt
½ oz. butter or margarine   1 square or round of
1 tablespoonful milk   buttered toast

To garnish:—Parsley.

1. Beat the egg and add pepper and salt.
2. Heat the butter and milk in a saucepan and pour in the egg. Cook over a moderate heat, stirring all the time until the mixture becomes thick and creamy.
3. Pile on the toast, garnish with parsley and serve.

EGGS WITH YOGHURT

2 rashers of streaky bacon   5 ozs. yoghurt
½ teaspoonful curry powder   5 eggs
¼ teaspoonful salt   4 rounds buttered toast
                        Chopped parsley

1. Cut the rashers into pieces and fry in a heavy saucepan, drain off the fat.
2. Add the curry powder and salt to the yoghurt, mix in the beaten eggs. Pour on to the cooked rashers and stir over the heat until thick.
3. Serve on rounds of buttered toast and garnish with parsley.

SCALLOPED EGGS

4 eggs	1 oz. chopped cooked ham *or*
½ pint white coating sauce	1 oz. sieved cheese
Pepper and salt	Breadcrumbs

To garnish:—Parsley.

1. Break each egg into a greased scallop shell or individual fireproof dish.

2. Mix the ham or three-quarters of the cheese with the sauce, season and pour a little over each egg.

3. Sprinkle the remainder of the cheese on top or sprinkle fine breadcrumbs on top if using ham.

4. Bake in a moderate oven for about 15 minutes. Garnish and serve.

BAKED EGGS

4 eggs	1 oz. butter or margarine
Pepper and salt	4 tablesps. cream

To garnish:—Parsley.

1. Break each egg into a greased individual fireproof dish.

2. Dot each egg with small pieces of butter and sprinkle them with pepper and salt. Pour 1 tablesp. cream over each egg.

3. Bake in a moderate oven 15–20 minutes. Garnish with parsley and serve.

SCOTCH EGGS

2 hard-boiled eggs	2 sausages

To coat:—Beaten egg and breadcrumbs.
To fry:—Bath of fat.
To serve:—4 slices of toast or fried bread.

1. Skin the sausages and flatten each out on a lightly-floured board.

2. Remove the shells from the eggs, dry them, and dust lightly with flour. Cover each egg evenly with the sausage-meat.

3. Coat with egg and breadcrumbs, and fry in hot fat until golden brown in colour and sausage-meat is well cooked. Drain on kitchen paper.

4. Cut each egg in half on the length and place on the slices of toast, cut side up.

5. Garnish with parsley and serve.

WELSH RAREBIT

1 oz. butter or margarine	4 ozs. Cheddar Cheese
1 oz. flour	$\frac{1}{4}$ teaspoonful made mustard
$\frac{1}{4}$ pint milk	Salt and pepper

4 slices of buttered toast

To garnish:—Parsley.

1. Melt the butter in a small saucepan. Add the flour, stirring over the heat for a few minutes. Add the milk and cook.

2. Add mustard, pepper, salt, and the sieved cheese and mix together.

3. Spread on the toast. Brown under the griller. Garnish with parsley, and serve.

CORNISH PASTIES

$\frac{1}{4}$ lb. short pastry (page 174)

Filling:	$\frac{1}{4}$ lb. lean mutton	2 ozs. potato
	1 teaspoonful chopped onion	Pepper and salt

To garnish:—Parsley.

1. Cut the mutton and potato into small cubes and mix with the onion, pepper and salt.

2. Roll the pastry into a square shape. Trim the edges and cut in four squares.

3. Put a quarter of the filling into each square.

4. Damp the edges, take two opposite corners together, press along the edges and crimp them, leaving a small opening in the centre.

5. Place on a tin, brush over with beaten egg. Bake in a fairly hot oven for about $\frac{3}{4}$ hour. Garnish with parsley, and serve.

SMOKED FISH SAVOURY

1 oz. butter or margarine	1 tablespoonful milk
1 egg	$\frac{1}{4}$ lb. cooked finnan haddock, *or*
Pepper	other smoked fish
4 rounds buttered toast or fried bread	1 teasp. finely-chopped parsley

To garnish:—Parsley.

1. Heat butter and milk together in a saucepan.

2. Add the shredded fish, parsley, pepper, and beaten egg.

3. Cook over a gentle heat until the mixture becomes thick and creamy. Pile on hot toast or fried bread, garnish with parsley, and serve.

POTATO APPLE CAKES

Potato cake mixture (page 187)　　　　2 apples

To fry:—Fat.

1. Peel and core the apples and cut into ¼ inch slices.
2. Roll out the potato-cake mixture and cut into rounds a little larger than the apple slices.
3. Damp round the edges of half of the rounds, place a slice of apple on these, and put a second round on top. Press the edges well together.
4. Fry in very little hot fat until golden brown on both sides and well cooked through.
5. Serve hot, garnish with parsley.

EGG CUTLETS

¼ pt. white binding sauce (page 149)　　Pepper and salt
1 oz. breadcrumbs　　　　2 hard-boiled eggs
½ teaspoonful lemon juice　　Pinch of ground mace
1 stick of macaroni

To coat:—Egg and crumbs.
To fry:—Bath of fat.
To garnish:—Parsley.

1. Chop eggs. Add to the sauce with the breadcrumbs, lemon juice, mace and seasonings.
2. Finish as for Durham Cutlets (page 82).

MACARONI CHEESE

3 ozs. cooked macaroni　　　　¾ pint white stewing sauce
(page 217)　　　　(page 149)
3 ozs. sieved cheese　　　　½ teasp. made mustard
Salt and cayenne pepper

To garnish:—Parsley.

1. Add the macaroni, mustard, seasoning, and three-quarters of the sieved cheese to the white sauce, and mix well.
2. Pour into a greased pie-dish and sprinkle the rest of the sieved cheese on top.
3. Bake in a moderate oven until hot and brown on top. Garnish with parsley, and serve.
   NOTE.—A variation can be made in this dish by using Tomato Sauce (page 152) instead of White Sauce.

CHEESE PUDDING

½ oz. butter or margarine	1 egg (separated)
½ pint of milk	1½ ozs. breadcrumbs
Pepper and salt	1 oz. sieved cheddar cheese
¼ teaspoonful made mustard	Slices of tomatoes

To garnish:—Parsley.

1. Heat the milk and butter, and add the seasonings and beaten egg yolk.
2. Mix the crumbs and cheese (reserving a little for the top) in a bowl. Pour the liquid over and mix well.
3. Allow to stand until the breadcrumbs swell, and then fold in the stiffly-beaten white of egg. Pour into a greased pie-dish. Sprinkle the remainder of the cheese on top.
4. Bake in a moderate oven until set and golden brown on top.
5. Five minutes before it is cooked, place slices of tomato on top and return to the oven.
6. Garnish with parsley, and serve.

VEGETABLE CHEESE

½ lb. mixed cooked diced vegetables, *e.g.*, carrots, potatoes, beet, peas, white turnip, artichoke, celery and onion	½ pint cheese sauce (page 150) ½ oz. sieved cheese

To garnish:—Parsley.

1. Place the vegetables in a greased pie-dish and pour the sauce over them, sprinkle the cheese on top and bake in a moderate oven until thoroughly heated and brown on top.
2. Garnish with parsley, and serve.

CHEESE AND POTATO PIE

1 lb. potatoes	Pepper and salt
½ onion (chopped finely)	1½ ozs. sieved cheese
½ pt. white pouring sauce (page 149)	Breadcrumbs

To garnish:—Parsley.

1. Half-cook the potatoes and dice them. Place them with the chopped onion in a greased pie-dish.
2. Add the seasonings and three-quarters of the cheese to the sauce and pour over the potatoes.
3. Mix the rest of the cheese with the breadcrumbs and sprinkle over the top.
4. Bake in a moderate oven for 25–30 minutes. Garnish with parsley, and serve.

SAUSAGE AND MASH

½ lb. sausages   1 lb. potato purée (page 111)
½ oz. fat

To garnish:—Parsley.

1. Separate the sausages and prick them.
2. Heat the fat a little and fry the sausages slowly until nicely browned all over and well cooked through.
3. Have the potato purée very hot, and form it into a bank down the centre of the hot dish.
4. Lift out the sausages, drain them well, and arrange them on top of the bank of potatoes. Garnish with parsley.

VEGETABLE PIE

¼ lb. short pastry (page 174)

Filling:—

1 cooked potato	1 cooked carrot
1 onion	3 sticks celery
2 tablespoonfuls cooked peas	1 teaspoonful chopped parsley

White Stewing Sauce—½ quantity on page 149

1. Dice or chop vegetables according to kind, and add to the sauce.
2. Put into a greased pie-dish, allow to cool and cover with the pastry. (See method for covering fruit pie, page 139.) Brush over with beaten egg.
3. Bake in a hot oven for the first 10 minutes, reduce the heat and bake in a moderate oven for ¾ of an hour.
4. Garnish with parsley, and serve hot.

SAVOURY RICE (RISOTTO)

½ lb. of rice (shortgrained)	1 pint of stock
2 ozs. chopped onion	Pepper and salt
1 oz. butter or margarine	Parmesan Cheese

To garnish:—Chopped parsley.

1. Melt the butter, put in the onion, cover with a round of greaseproof paper. Put the lid on the saucepan and place over a very slow heat for about 5 minutes.
2. Remove paper, add the rice and mix well to make sure that each grain of rice is coated with butter and onion.
3. Pour the boiling stock over, add the seasoning, put the round of greaseproof paper on top, replace the lid and put the saucepan into a moderate oven for about 25–30 minutes when the rice will have absorbed all the stock.
4. Work in some grated parmesan cheese with a skewer. Sprinkle generously with grated parmesan cheese. Garnish with parsley, and serve.

SAVOURY RICE WITH MUSHROOMS

½ lb. of rice (shortgrained)	1 pint of stock
2 ozs. chopped onion	Pepper and salt
1 oz. butter or margarine	4 ozs. mushrooms

To garnish:—Parsley.

1. Cook Savoury Rice (page 166).
2. Remove stalks from the mushrooms, skin if liked, and wash well. Cut into thin slices.
3. Heat a little butter or margarine in a saucepan, put in the mushrooms, cover tightly, and cook over a gentle heat for about 5 minutes.
4. Mix the mushrooms through the rice with a fork, pile into a heated entrée dish and garnish with parsley.

SAVOURY RICE WITH HAM

Make as for Savoury Rice with Mushrooms but substitute 2 ozs. chopped cooked ham for the mushrooms.

FRENCH TOAST

4 slices of bread	¼ pt. milk
1 egg	Pepper and salt

To garnish:—Parsley.

1. Beat the egg and mix in the milk and seasonings. Dip the slices of bread in it and fry them on both sides in hot fat until golden brown.
2. Serve on a hot dish garnished with parsley.
Note.—Fried Bacon, Tomato or Apple may be served with French Toast. It may also be served sweet by omitting pepper and salt and sprinkling with sugar.

SAUSAGES ON TOAST

½ lb. sausages	Slices of toast

To garnish:—Parsley.

1. Separate the sausages and prick them.
2. Place on a heated grill-pan and grill according to directions on page 77, allowing them 5–6 minutes and turning them often to have them evenly browned and cooked.
3. Serve two on each slice of toast and garnish with parsley.

SAUSAGE ROLLS

5 ozs. rough puff pastry (page 175)   ¼ lb. sausage-meat

To glaze:—Beaten egg.
To garnish:—Parsley.

1. Roll out the pastry into an oblong ¼″ in thickness and about 6″ in width. Cut in two on the length.
2. Divide the sausage-meat in two, put on to a floured board and form into two rolls the length of the pastry.
3. Put the sausage-meat on the pastry and brush the edges with cold water. Fold the pastry over the sausage-meat and press the edges together.
4. Make slits on top with a knife, brush over with beaten egg and cut into 3-inch pieces.
5. Put on to a tin, bake in a hot oven for the first 10 minutes. Reduce the heat and bake for a further 25–30 minutes.
6. Serve hot and garnish with parsley.

POTATO AND SAUSAGE ROLLS

½ lb. mashed potatoes   4 cooked sausages
Beaten egg   A little flour
Pepper and salt
To coat:—Egg and breadcrumbs.
To fry:—Bath of fat.
To garnish:—Parsley.

1. Add beaten egg, pepper and salt to the mashed potatoes and roll out on a lightly-floured board to about quarter inch in thickness.
2. Skin the sausages and cut into halves or quarters, according to size. Cut the potato mixture in strips a little wider than the pieces of sausages.
3. Roll each piece of sausage in potato mixture, seal the ends and coat with egg and crumbs.
4. Fry in hot fat until brown and crisp, and drain on kitchen paper. Garnish with parsley and serve hot.
NOTE.—These rolls may be brushed with beaten egg and baked in a hot oven till golden brown.

KIDNEYS ON TOAST

2 mutton kidneys   Pepper and salt

To fry:—Fat.
To serve:—Slice of toast. Parsley.

1. Skin and core the kidneys. Split, leaving on a hinge. Sprinkle with pepper and salt.

2. Heat some fat on a frying pan, put in the kidneys cut side downwards. When cooked, turn and cook on the other side. Time : 7–8 minutes.

3. Serve on hot buttered toast and garnish with parsley.

NOTE.—Kidneys may be grilled if liked (page 77).

FRIED KIDNEY AND BACON

Cook as for Kidneys on Toast (page 168) and serve with fried rashers of bacon.

POTATO ROSES WITH KIDNEY

1/4 lb. kidney	1/2 oz. flour
1 oz. butter or margarine	1/4 pt. stock
1 oz. chopped onion	1 teasp. Tomato Sauce

Pepper and salt

To serve:—Potato Roses (page 113).

1. Skin and core the kidney and cut into 1/2 inch dice. Soak in cold water for 15 minutes. Dry.

2. Heat the butter, add the onion and kidney and fry until brown.

3. Add the flour, cook until brown, then add the stock and Tomato Sauce and stir until it boils. Skim.

4. Simmer for 20 minutes. Season.

5. Fill into the Potato Roses and serve very hot.

TOAD IN THE HOLE

1/2 lb. sausages

Batter:

4 ozs. flour	1 egg
1/2 teasp. salt	1/2 pt. milk

To garnish:—Parsley.

1. Make the batter as on page 135 and leave aside for about one hour.

2. Prick the sausages, put into a greased pie-dish and bake in a moderately hot oven for about 10 minutes. Drain off most of the fat.

3. Pour the batter over the sausages and bake in a moderately hot oven until well risen and set—about 25 minutes.

4. Garnish with parsley and serve hot.

BAKED STUFFED TOMATOES

6 medium-sized tomatoes

Filling:

1 oz. breadcrumbs	1 oz. cooked ham *or* rasher, *or*
1 oz. butter	1 oz. sieved cheese
1 slice onion (chopped)	½ teasp. parsley (chopped)

Pepper and salt

1. Wash the tomatoes, cut a slice off the rounded end of each. Scoop out the pulp, remove the hard part.

2. Melt the butter, add tomato pulp, onion, chopped ham, breadcrumbs, parsley, pepper and salt. Mix well

3. Fill the tomatoes with this mixture. Replace caps. Put on to a greased baking tin, cover with a sheet of greased paper. Bake in a very moderate oven 15–20 minutes.

4. Garnish with parsley and serve hot. They may also be served on rounds of fried bread or buttered toast.

STUFFED ONIONS

5 or 6 Spanish onions	2 ozs. cooked meat
2 ozs. breadcrumbs	1 teaspoonful chopped parsley
Salt and pepper	4 or 5 button mushrooms
Pinch of nutmeg	2 tablespoonfuls Tomato Sauce or
1 oz. butter or margarine.	Brown Sauce

¼ pt. stock

1. Choose onions of even size, peel off the brown skin and blanch them (page 217). When cold remove the centres.

2. Prepare the stuffing by mixing the finely-chopped meat, breadcrumbs, parsley, chopped mushrooms, salt, pepper and nutmeg together. Moisten with Tomato or Brown Sauce.

3. Fill the onion cases with the stuffing. Put them into a fireproof dish.

4. Chop the centres of the onions finely. Melt the fat in a saucepan, add the chopped onion, cover with a round of greaseproof paper, put on the lid and cook over a gentle heat for about 5 minutes, add the stock and seasoning.

5. Pour this mixture round the onions, cover with greased paper, put the lid on the dish and bake in a moderate oven until the onions are tender—about 1–1½ hours.

6. Remove the lid and paper and serve the onions garnished with parsley.

BRAIN CAKES

Calf's or sheep's brains	3 ozs. breadcrumbs
Lemon juice or vinegar	1 teaspoonful chopped onion
Beaten egg to bind	Pinch mixed herbs

Pepper and salt

To coat:—Egg and breadcrumbs.
To fry:—Bath of fat.
To garnish:—Parsley and lemon.
To serve:—Tomato Sauce.

1. Steep the brains in cold water and vinegar for about 1 hour.

2. Wash the brains well, changing the water several times. Blanch. Put into a saucepan, cover them with cold water, add a little salt and vinegar. Bring to the boil, skim and cook for 10–12 minutes. Drain well.

3. Mince, mix with the breadcrumbs, onion, herbs and seasonings. Bind with beaten egg, form into a roll on a floured board and cut into even-sized pieces.

4. Form into flat cakes, coat with egg and breadcrumbs and fry in hot fat.

5. Drain on kitchen paper and serve garnished with lemon and parsley.

FRENCH SAVOURY OMELET

2 eggs	1 slice onion, finely-chopped
Pepper and salt	(if liked)
1 teasp. finely-chopped parsley	1 tablesp. water
$\frac{1}{4}$ teasp. mixed fresh herbs (chopped)	$\frac{1}{2}$ oz. butter

To fry:—$\frac{3}{4}$ oz. butter.

1. Beat the eggs just sufficiently to mix yolks and whites together. Add the seasonings, flavourings and water, and mix. Add the butter, cut in small pieces.

2. Heat the $\frac{3}{4}$ oz. butter in an omelet pan. When sizzling hot, pour in the omelet mixture. Cook the omelet in layers by tilting the pan from side to side. Use a palette knife or spoon to fold the layers towards the centre. Do not overcook, it should be moist and creamy.

3. When cooked turn each side of the omelet in towards the centre and then fold in two. Turn on to a hot dish.

4. Serve immediately garnished with parsley.

PUFFED SAVOURY OMELET

2 eggs
Pepper and salt
1 teasp. finely-chopped parsley

¼ teasp. mixed fresh herbs (chopped)
1 slice of onion, finely-chopped
1 tablespoonful water

To fry:—1 oz. butter.
To garnish:—Parsley.

1. Separate the yolks from the whites of the eggs. Beat the yolks and add the water, seasonings and flavourings, and mix until creamy.
2. Whisk the whites stiffly, and gently fold in the yolk mixture.
3. Cook as for Puffed Sweet Omelet (page 139). Turn on to a hot dish, fold over and garnish with parsley.

CHEESE SOUFFLÉ

2 ozs. grated cheese
¼ pt. White Binding Sauce (page 149).
¼ teaspoonful made mustard

Salt and Cayenne pepper
3 eggs
Parsley

1. Make the sauce, add the mustard, salt, pepper and nearly all the cheese.
2. Add the yolks of eggs, one at a time and beat well. Beat the whites of eggs stiffly and mix one tablespoonful into the sauce, then fold in the remainder.
3. Use a fireproof dish large enough to hold the mixture and still leave sufficient room for the soufflé to rise to double its original size. Grease the dish, put in the mixture, sprinkle the remainder of the cheese on top. Cover with a piece of greased paper.
4. Put the dish on a baking tin, place over a slow heat (with a gas stove use an asbestos mat) for about 10–15 minutes until the bottom of the soufflé begins to set. Then place in a moderate oven for about 40 minutes, until well risen and set.

PASTRY-MAKING

PASTRY is a mixture of flour and fat bound together with water.

The quality most desired in pastry is lightness, and this depends almost entirely on the amount of cold air which has been introduced into the pastry before baking. The raising of pastry is effected by the expansion of cold air when heated, hence the best pastry is that which contains the greatest amount of cold air before cooking.

The usual ingredients used in pastry-making are :—

(1) *Flour*, which must be of a good quality, dry, with no lumps. If damp, put to dry in a warm place, but have perfectly cold before using. Fine starchy flour makes the best pastry. Further Notes on Flour (page 176).

(2) *Shortening* is the collective term which comprises the various types of fats used in pastry-making. They are butter, margarine, lard, vegetable fats or oils, or suet. A mixture of butter or margarine and lard makes an excellent pastry. All fats used must be of good quality and fresh.

(3) *Water*.

(4) *Lemon juice* is added to make the pastry light, and also to counteract the excessive richness of puff pastry.

(5) *Eggs* are sometimes added to make pastry richer.

Rules to be observed in Pastry-making

1. Have all utensils clean, because pastry readily absorbs flavours.

2. Use correct proportions. Sieve flour before use.

3. Have everything as cold as possible. Use a knife to mix the pastry.

4. Handle the pastry as little and as lightly as possible. To lift pastry place it over the rolling-pin.

5. Roll pastry with light even strokes.

6. Leave Puff, Rough Puff, and Flaky pastries in a cold, airy place between the rollings, and before placing in the oven.

7. Bake in a very hot oven at the beginning to burst the starch cells in the flour and so enable them to absorb the fat as soon as it melts. Then reduce the heat or move to a cooler part of the oven until cooking is completed.

Varieties of Pastry

1. Short pastry
2. Cheese pastry.
3. Suet pastry.
4. Rough Puff pastry.
5. Flaky pastry.

6. Puff pastry.
7. Biscuit pastry.
8. Choux pastry.
9. Raised Pie Crust.

SHORT PASTRY

4 ozs. flour
2–3 ozs. butter or margarine

Pinch of salt
Cold water

1. Sift the flour and salt into a bowl.
2. Put in butter and cut it into small lumps with a knife, mixing lumps and flour in the process.
3. Rub the fat into the flour with the tips of the fingers until the mixture looks like fine breadcrumbs. Lift the hands high so as to introduce as much cold air as possible into the flour. Care must be taken not to let the fat melt or the pastry will be oily and heavy.
4. Add the water gradually and mix to a stiff paste with a knife. When paste is wet enough it should stick together, but not to the bowl or hands.
5. Turn out on a lightly-floured board and knead lightly with the tips of the fingers.
6. Press out a little with the rolling-pin, and then, with light, even strokes roll into the required shape.

NOTE.—If the pastry sticks to the rolling-pin or board, scrape off the part that has stuck with the back of a knife, wipe with a cloth, flour the rolling-pin and board and continue rolling. Avoid the use of too much flour when rolling pastry.

CHEESE PASTRY

4 ozs. flour
2 ozs. butter or margarine
1/8 teaspoonful salt

Pinch cayenne pepper
1 oz. hard cheese
1 yolk of egg

A little water

1. Sift flour and salt into a bowl.
2. Rub in the butter with the tips of the fingers until the mixture looks like fine breadcrumbs.
3. Rub cheese through a sieve. Add it with the pepper to the flour and butter. Mix well.
4. Beat the yolk of egg with 1 tablespoonful cold water.
5. Add this to the dry ingredients in the bowl and mix all to a stiff paste, using a little more water if necessary.
6. Turn on to a lightly-floured board. Knead lightly until smooth. Roll into required shape. Use for small cheese biscuits, flans, or for any savoury dish.

SUET PASTRY

6 ozs. flour	½ teaspoonful baking powder
2 ozs. beef suet	¼ teaspoonful salt

Cold water

1. Sift flour, salt and baking powder into a bowl.
2. Chop the suet finely, using a little of the weighed flour. Add to the dry ingredients.
3. Mix to a fairly stiff paste with cold water, using a knife for mixing.
4. Turn out on to a lightly-floured board. Knead with the tips of the fingers until smooth. Roll into the required shape and use.

ROUGH PUFF PASTRY

5 ozs. flour	1 teaspoonful lemon juice
4 ozs. butter or margarine	Cold water

Good pinch salt

1. Sift flour and salt into a bowl.
2. Put in butter and cut into pieces about the size of a walnut. Mix with the flour.
3. Mix to a stiff paste with cold water and lemon juice.
4. Turn out on a lightly-floured board. Roll into a long strip with a floured rolling-pin.
5. Fold evenly in three and turn the fold to the left-hand side. Press edges of the pastry lightly with the rolling-pin.
6. Roll again into a long strip and repeat 4 times. Leave aside in a cool, airy place after the third rolling.
7. Roll into the required shape. Leave in a cool place before putting in the oven. Bake in a hot oven for first 5–10 minutes, then reduce the heat for remainder of cooking.

BISCUIT PASTRY

4 ozs. flour	Pinch of salt
2 ozs. butter or margarine	1 yolk of egg
1 oz. castor sugar	Cold water

1. Sift the flour and salt into a bowl.
2. Rub in the butter with the tips of the fingers until the mixture looks like fine breadcrumbs.
3. Add the sugar and mix well.
4. Beat the yolk of egg with a little water. Add to the dry ingredients and mix to a stiff dough, using a little more water if necessary.
5. Turn on to a floured board. Knead lightly until smooth. Roll into the required shape and use.

BREAD AND CAKES

BREAD-MAKING is an art of which it may be said : " Practice makes perfect ", because it is only after much practice that one knows the exact consistency of the perfect loaf and that kneading is light but sufficient.

Unfortunately, little bread- or cake-making is now done in the home ; the shop product is so easily obtained, but it lacks the excellent flavour, purity of ingredients and high nutrient qualities of a well-made, properly baked home-made cake.

Choice of Ingredients used in Bread- and Cake-Making

All ingredients must be of the highest quality, and fresh, if the finished product is to be a success.

Flour may be obtained from any grain, but that obtained from the wheat grain is used because it contains gluten.

The Wheat Grain may be divided into three parts :—

I.—*The Germ* is the young plant. It is very rich in protein, in the form of gluten. It also contains oil and Vitamin B.

II.—*The Endosperm*, comprising about 85 per cent of the grain, consists mainly of starch with a small amount of protein, iron and Vitamin.

III.—*The Bran*, or outer covering, contains protein and mineral matter.

There are two kinds of flour obtained from the wheat grain :—

(*a*) *White Flour* contains the endosperm and part of the germ, but the part of the germ eliminated in the various processes of sifting lessens the nutrient value of this particular type of flour. Further sifting lessens the gluten content of pastry flour, by removing more of the germ and leaving this kind of flour whiter and richer in starch by comparison with household flour.

(*b*) *Wheatmeal Flour*, in which practically all the grain is retained. On account of this the nutrient quality is much higher than in white flour.

Flour obtained from the Wheat grain is the most suitable for bread- and cake-making because it is the only kind of flour which contains gluten. When using other flours in bread- or cake-making it is also necessary to use flour from the wheat grain because of the lack of gluten in the former.

Gluten is a protein substance which becomes sticky when moistened, and it is the presence of this gluten in the flour that

176

gives the very necessary tenacious and elastic properties to the dough.

This cohesive dough is capable of encasing the gas produced by the raising agent used, and as the gas expands on heating, the dough also expands and is puffed up, *i.e.*, rises. At a certain temperature a crust forms and prevents further expansion or deflation of the dough.

The consistency of the dough is also important because the gas produced by the raising agent would be unable to push up a heavy stiff dough. Finding it impossible to push up the non-elastic dough the gas would burst through it, and escape, leaving a flat, heavy, unrisen bread.

Cooking Fats

I. *Butter.*—Very expensive but best for all purposes. It is a pure animal fat produced by the churning of cream.

II. *Margarine.*—A mixture of vegetable and animal fats churned with a little milk to give flavour and coloured to resemble butter. Most of the margarine is fortified with Vitamins A and D.

III. *Vegetable Fats.*—Produced by emulsifying a mixture of vegetable fats to resemble texture of butter.

IV. *Lard.*—Is the fat of the pig which has been rendered. It is used for pastry-making, but is too heavy for cake-mixtures.

Eggs

Fresh hen eggs are best ; preserved eggs may also be used. Eggs should be broken separately to make sure they are fresh.

Sugar

The different kinds of sugar used in cooking are Castor, Granulated, Brown and Icing.

Castor sugar is very fine and suitable for cake mixtures, scones, etc. It should be free from lumps.

Granulated sugar is coarse sugar, it is mainly used in cooking for sweetening fruit in pies and for stewing fruit.

Brown sugar is used for gingerbread, dark fruit cakes, plum puddings, etc.

Icing or Confectioners' Sugar is a powdered sugar. It must be sieved before using for icing cakes, etc.

Chocolate

1. Chocolate Powder is best, it is dissolved in very little warm water.

2. A bar of Dark Chocolate may also be used, it should be put on a plate in a very cool oven until soft.

3. Cocoa may be substituted for chocolate in most recipes, using half the amount stated for chocolate, but sugar and vanilla

must be added. Put the cocoa with a little water into a saucepan, bring to the boil, add sugar and vanilla essence. Boil for 1 minute, cool and use.

Preparation of Dried Fruits and Nuts

Sultanas and Seedless Raisins are sold in packets, clean and ready for use.

Currants and inferior quality *Sultanas.*—Wash in warm water, drain well and leave to dry. Pick over carefully.

Valencia Raisins.—Dip fingers in a bowl of warm water and remove stones. Leave the raisins until dry, then chop if liked.

Candied Peel.—Remove sugar from the centre and outside Slice thinly and chop.

Angelica.—Soak in hot water for a few minutes to remove sugar before cutting.

Lemon or Orange Rind and Juice.—Grate rind finely, removing only the yellow part. The white pith will cause a bitter flavour. Next roll lemon or orange lightly on the table to soften, cut in two, squeeze out juice on a lemon squeezer and strain.

Almonds.—To blanch : put into cold water, bring to the boil, pour off the water and cover with cold water and leave for a few minutes. Skin.

Walnuts.—Remove the nut from the shell and chop as required.

Pistachio Nuts.—As almonds.

Prunes : Wash and steam until soft, about 10 minutes. Cut into small pieces removing the stones.

Dates.—Remove stones and cut into small pieces.

Raising Agents

A raising agent is something which introduces gas into a dough or cake mixture. This gas may be introduced by using some chemical or chemicals the action of which produces a gas, or in some cases air may be introduced into the mixture. When an acid acts on a carbonate, carbon dioxide and a salt are produced, and it is on this principle that much bread- and cake-raising is based. Whether air has been introduced or gas produced, expansion takes place when heat is applied, pushing up the dough or cake mixture, thereby making it light and spongy in texture. Therefore we may say that the lightness of the dough or cake mixture depends on the expansion of gases. The agents for producing these gases are introduced into the mixture before cooking.

Raising agents commonly used :—
1. Air—as in Sponge Cakes.
2. Yeast.
3. Baking Powder.
4. Bread Soda (bicarbonate of soda) and Acid (usually sour milk or buttermilk).

Yeast

Yeast is a living one-celled organism of the fungi family, which grows and multiplies in suitable conditions *i.e.*, when warmth, food and moisture are present. During this growth it produces CO_2 and Alcohol. This gas forms bubbles in the dough and makes it rise. Yeast may be obtained fresh or in dried form.

Fresh Yeast

Fresh yeast keeps about 4 days tied loosely in a polythene bag. It should form a moist cake and be greyish putty colour. If it is very crumbly or dark in colour with a sticky consistency and an unpleasant odour it should not be used.

To use :—Dissolve the salt and any sugar in the hot water. Add the margarine, if used, and stir until melted. (The margarine may be rubbed into the flour if liked.) Cool and blend in the yeast. If there is any doubt of the freshness of the yeast leave until it rises to a froth.

Dried Yeast

Dried yeast keeps for at least six months in a small tin with very little air space.

To use :—Dissolve the salt and any sugar in the hot water. Add the margarine, if used, and stir until melted or rub the margarine into the flour if liked. Cool, (the water should be slightly warmer than for fresh yeast). Sprinkle in the yeast, mix and allow to stand until frothy, about 15 minutes.

NOTE.—Use twice the amount of fresh yeast to dried yeast *i.e.*, 1 oz. fresh yeast = ½ oz. dried yeast (1 level tablespoonful).

Points to remember when using Yeast

1. Lack of heat retards growth, too much heat kills yeast.

2. Slow rising is essential. Rising should be done in a warm place at 78–80°F. in 1–1½ hours. A higher temperature will leave a taste of yeast. At room temperature about 2 hours will be required to rise the dough, in a cold place 8–12 hours, in a refrigerator 12–14 hours. A yeast dough may be kept in a refrigerator for 5-6 days.

3. Water is best for blending yeast, it should be 80–90°F., slightly warmer for dried yeast but never higher than 115°F.

4. When milk is used in a yeast recipe it should be scalded before use. Even though milk is pasteurized it needs to be scalded because bacteria left in the milk will grow during fermentation and may cause an off-flavour in the bread. Heat the milk to 190°F. Cool before use.

5. A loose dough is required for yeast mixtures.

6. The dough may be put to rise in a greased polythene bag or in a bowl covered with polythene or a damp cloth.

7. Yeast enzymes soften dough gluten which has to be strengthened again. This is done by knocking-back or kneading which also aerates the dough and distributes the gas cells evenly and therefore evens the texture of the bread. Kneading may be done in an electric mixer at lowest speed for 2–3 minutes. Relax the dough (leave to rest) for 10 minutes before shaping.

8. Nearly all rising or proving is done out of the oven. Finally the dough is baked. This kills the yeast, stops any more fermentation, evaporates the alcohol, some of which remains to flavour the bread. The heat of the oven makes the bubbles of gas expand and the dough rises.

9. For bread-making the amount of yeast used varies with the quantity of flour. To rise 1 lb. flour or any quantity below that use ½ oz. fresh yeast or ¼ oz. (1 level dessertspoonful) of dried yeast. To rise 3 lbs. of white flour use 1 oz. of fresh yeast or ½ oz. (1 level tablespoonful) of dried yeast. Double the amount of yeast is required to rise wholemeal.

Baking Powder

Baking powder contains an acid and an alkali in correct proportion. A third ingredient is added—usually rice flour or cornflour—to give bulk and to absorb moisture, thus preventing the baking powder from becoming lumpy. When moistened, the acid acts on the carbonate, producing CO_2 and forming a salt. Since the action between the acid and carbonate takes place immediately the mixture is moistened, it is important that the baking powder is not added until last, and the cake put into the oven at the correct temperature without delay.

Baking powder should be used in the correct proportion, since an excess of it makes cakes dry, and may also blow up the mixture too rapidly, making it more liable to fall.

BAKING POWDER

6 ozs. rice flour or cornflour　　　　2 ozs. bread soda
4 ozs. cream of tartar *or* 2 ozs. tartaric acid.

1. Mix all ingredients together.
2. Sieve three or four times. Store in an air-tight tin. Use two teaspoonfuls of this baking powder to 1 lb. flour.

Bread Soda with Buttermilk or Sour Milk

Excellent for bread and scones. The lactic acid in the milk acts on the bicarbonate of soda in a similar way to that described under Baking Powder, the same gas is produced and the dough or cake rises in the same way. Where the milk is not very sour or the buttermilk is of a poor quality use ½ teasp. cream of tartar (acid) with the bread soda to each pound of flour. If sour milk is not available sweet milk may be used. In this case add 1 teasp. cream of tartar with the bread soda to each pound of flour.

Classification of Cake Mixtures

1. *Plain Cakes* in which the fat is rubbed into the flour, the other dry ingredients are then added and all mixed with the beaten eggs and milk.

2. *Rich Cakes* in which the butter and sugar are creamed together, the eggs beaten into the mixture and then the flour and other ingredients mixed through.

3. *Sponge Cakes* which may be :

 (*a*) Eggs and sugar whisked together and the flour folded through.

 (*b*) Yolks of eggs and sugar whisked together, the flour folded through, and lastly the stiffly-beaten whites.

 (*c*) Whites of eggs stiffly beaten, castor sugar and yolks of eggs whisked in, and lastly the flour folded through.

 (*d*) A hot syrup of sugar and water whisked on to the beaten egg, and the flour and flavouring folded through.

YEAST BREAD

1 lb. flour	½ teaspoonful salt
½ teaspoonful sugar	About ½ pt. hot water

½ oz. fresh yeast or 1 level dessertspoonful dried yeast (p. **179**)

1. Dissolve the sugar and salt in the hot water, cool, add the yeast and mix well together.

2. Sieve the flour into a bowl. Make a well in the centre and pour in the liquid. Mix to a loose dough, cover and leave to relax for about 10 minutes.

3. Flour the hands and knead for about 7 minutes.

4. Dredge a little flour under the dough in the bowl, cover with oiled polythene or a damp cloth and set to rise in a warm place until double in size 1–1½ hours.

5. Turn the dough on to a lightly-floured board. Knock-back and leave to relax for 10 minutes.

6. Put into a warm greased loaf tin, cover and put to prove for about ½ hour until double in size.

7. Brush over with milk and bake in a fairly hot oven for about ¾ hour.

SODA BREAD

1 lb. flour	½ teaspoonful salt
½ teaspoonful bread soda	About ½ pt. of sour milk or buttermilk

1. Put bread soda into the palm of the hand and press out lumps with the fingers. Sieve flour, soda and salt into a bowl.

2. Make a well in the centre of the flour, pour in nearly all the milk. Mix to a loose dough, adding more milk if necessary.

3. Turn on to a floured board and knead lightly. Turn the smooth side up, flatten out. Cut a cross on top with a floured knife.

4. Place on a lightly-floured tin. Bake in a fairly hot oven for about three-quarters of an hour.

SULTANA BREAD

Make and bake as for White Soda Bread, adding 4 ozs. prepared sultanas or currants and 1 teaspoonful sugar to the flour.

BROWN SODA BREAD I

10 ozs. wheatmeal	6 ozs. flour
½ teaspoonful salt	¾ teaspoonful bread soda
About ½ pint sour milk or buttermilk	

Make as for White Soda Bread, but do not sieve the wheatmeal. Add it to the sieved flour, salt and soda. If liked, a little bacon fat or butter may be rubbed into the flour.

BROWN SODA BREAD II

12 ozs. wheatmeal	½ teaspoonful salt
4 ozs. flour	1 teaspoonful castor sugar
¾ teaspoonful bread soda	1 oz. margarine
½ teaspoonful Cream of Tartar	11 ozs. sour milk

1. Press out all the lumps from the bread soda, sieve the flour, bread soda, salt and sugar into a bowl. Add the wheatmeal and mix well together.

2. Rub in the margarine. Make a well in the centre, pour in the milk and mix to a stiff batter.

3. Put into a greased tin. Smooth the top with a knife dipped in milk. Cut a cross on top.

4. Bake in a hot oven at first, reduce the heat and bake for about 1 hour.

OATMEAL BREAD

7 ozs pinhead oatmeal	9 ozs. flour
$\frac{1}{2}$ teaspoonful salt	$\frac{1}{2}$ teaspoonful bread soda
1 oz. butter	About $\frac{1}{2}$ pt. buttermilk or sour milk

1. Put oatmeal and salt into a bowl, add nearly $\frac{1}{2}$ pt. of buttermilk, and steep overnight.

2. Remove lumps from bread soda and sieve with flour. Rub butter into flour.

3. Add steeped oatmeal and mix to a very loose dough, adding a little more milk if necessary.

4. Turn into a greased loaf tin. Bake in a fairly hot oven for about 1 hour.

WHITE SODA SCONES

8 ozs. flour	$\frac{1}{4}$ teaspoonful bread soda
1 oz. butter or margarine	$\frac{1}{2}$ oz. castor sugar (if liked)
$\frac{1}{4}$ teaspoonful salt	About $\frac{1}{4}$ pt. buttermilk or sour milk

1. Sieve flour and salt into a bowl.

2. Add the butter, cut into small pieces and rub into the flour.

3. Add the sugar and bread soda free from lumps and mix well together.

4. Mix to a loose dough, turn on to a floured board, knead lightly, flatten out with the hand into a circle about half-inch in thickness.

5. Cut in halves, quarters and then in eighths, forming triangles.

6. Place on a greased tin, brush the top with milk and bake in a fairly hot oven for about 20 minutes.

TEA SCONES

8 ozs. flour	$\frac{1}{4}$ teaspoonful salt
2 ozs. butter or margarine	1 teaspoonful baking powder
1 oz. castor sugar	1 egg
About $\frac{1}{4}$ pt. milk	

1. Make as for White Soda Scones, using the beaten egg and fresh milk to mix.

2. Flatten out with the hand and cut into shape with a small round cutter.

3. Place on a greased tin, brush with a little beaten egg and bake in a fairly hot oven for about 15 minutes.

GRIDDLE SCONES

8 ozs. flour	¼ teaspoonful salt
¼ teaspoonful bread soda	About ¼ pint buttermilk
1 oz. butter	

1. Make and shape as for White Soda Scones.
2. Cook on a heated, greased heavy iron pan until well risen and browned underneath. Turn and cook on the second side. Cook well.

BROWN BREAKFAST SCONES

4 ozs. wheatmeal	¼ teaspoonful salt
4 ozs. flour	¼ teaspoonful bread soda
1 oz. butter or margarine	About ¼ pt. buttermilk or sour milk

Make and bake as for White Soda Scones, but do not sieve the wheatmeal.

SULTANA SCONES

8 ozs. flour	¼ teaspoonful bread soda
2 ozs. butter or margarine	2 ozs. sultanas
1 oz. castor sugar	1 egg
¼ teaspoonful salt	About ¼ pt. buttermilk or sour milk

Make, shape and bake as for White Soda Scones, adding the prepared sultanas and mixing with the beaten egg and sour milk.

MILK ROLLS

8 ozs. flour	1½ ozs. castor sugar (if liked)
Pinch of salt	1 egg
1½ ozs. butter or margarine	A little fresh milk
1 teaspoonful baking powder	

1. Sieve flour and salt into a bowl. Rub in the butter, add sugar and baking powder. Mix well.
2. Add beaten egg and sufficient milk to mix to a loose dough.
3. Turn on to a lightly-floured board, cut into two pieces. Knead each piece lightly.
4. Roll out into a round, one-quarter inch in thickness. Cut each round into six or eight pieces, triangular in shape.
5. Damp points and roll up loosely from broad end, having the point turned upwards. Place on a greased tin.
6. Brush over with beaten egg and milk. Bake in a fairly hot oven for about 20 minutes.

DROPPED SCONES

½ lb. flour	¼ teaspoonful salt
¼ teaspoonful bread soda	1 oz. sugar
1 egg	About ½ pt. buttermilk

(½ teaspoonful of Baking Powder and sweet milk may be used)

To serve:—Butter, golden syrup.

1. Sieve flour and salt into a bowl. Add bread soda, free from lumps, and sugar.

2. Make a well in the centre of the flour, drop in the egg and add sufficient buttermilk to mix to a stiff batter of dropping consistency.

3. Heat and grease a heavy iron pan. Drop batter in dessert-spoonfuls on to it.

4. Cook steadily until set, well risen, and nicely browned underneath.

5. Turn carefully and cook on the other side until nicely browned. Keep on a plate over boiling water while the others are being cooked.

6. Dredge with castor sugar, and serve.

STRAWBERRY SHORT CAKE

8 ozs. flour	¼ teaspoonful salt
3 ozs. butter or margarine	1 teaspoonful baking powder
2 ozs. castor sugar	1 egg

A little milk

Filling: ½ lb. strawberries, butter, sugar.

1. Sieve flour, baking powder and salt into a bowl.

2. Rub in the butter, add the sugar and mix well.

3. Make to a loose dough with the beaten egg (keeping back a little) and a little milk.

4. Turn on to a floured board, divide in two, knead each piece and flatten out into a round shape with the hand.

5. Put one piece into a greased 8-inch sandwich tin, brush over with melted butter, put the second piece of dough on top and brush over with beaten egg.

6. Bake in a fairly hot oven for about 30 minutes.

7. Split, butter, spread with mashed sweetened strawberries, sandwich together and serve hot.

RASPBERRY BUNS

½ lb. flour	2 ozs. butter or margarine
Pinch of salt	1 teaspoonful baking powder
2 ozs. sugar	1 egg
Raspberry jam	A little milk

1. Sieve flour, salt and baking powder into a bowl. Rub in the butter. Add sugar, mix thoroughly.
2. Mix to a loose dough with beaten egg (keeping back a little) and sufficient milk.
3. Turn on to a lightly-floured board. Form into a roll, divide into 10 pieces.
4. With floured finger make a hole in the centre of the cut side of each piece. Drop about ¼ teaspoonful jam into the centre and draw the edges of the dough over, completely covering the jam. Place on a greased tin.
5. Brush over lightly with beaten egg. Sprinkle a little coarse sugar on top of each. Bake in a fairly hot oven for about 20 minutes.

OAT-CAKES

4 ozs. fine oatmeal	Pinch of salt
Pinch of bread soda	1½ tablespoonfuls boiling water
½ oz. lard or butter	

1. Mix oatmeal, salt and soda together in a bowl.
2. Melt the lard in the boiling water, pour over the oatmeal, stir quickly, mixing well.
3. Turn on to a board which has been dredged lightly with some fine oatmeal. Knead until free from cracks. Roll out very thinly.
4. Dust a little oatmeal over the surface. Even off the edges by cutting into a round with a large saucepan lid. Divide into eight pieces, triangular in shape.
5. Cook on a heated greased heavy pan until the edges begin to curl up. The surface should not become browned.
6. Place in a cool oven until crisp and quite dry.

CRUMPETS

½ lb. flour	¼ teaspoonful salt
1 teaspoonful baking powder	1 egg
2 ozs. castor sugar	2 ozs. butter or margarine
About ¼ pt. milk	

1. Sieve flour, salt and baking powder into a bowl. Add sugar.
2. Melt the butter. Make a well in the centre of the flour, and drop in the egg, melted butter and sufficient milk to mix to a fairly thick batter,

3. Grease some crumpet rings, place them on a hot greased heavy pan. Pour a little batter into each ring, and cook slowly until the air bubbles appear in the crumpets.

4. Remove the rings, turn the crumpets and cook until nicely browned on the other side—about 8-10 minutes to cook. Keep hot on a plate over boiling water while the others are being cooked. Repeat with the remainder of the batter.

5. Split, butter and serve at once, or toast and butter, if liked.

SODA APPLE CAKE

5 ozs. flour	$\frac{1}{4}$ teaspoonful bread soda
Pinch of salt	1 oz. castor sugar

Sour milk

Filling: $\frac{3}{4}$ lb. apples.   Sugar to sweeten.
Pinch ground cloves.

1. Sieve the flour, salt and bread soda. Add the castor sugar and mix to a fairly stiff dough with the sour milk.

2. Divide the dough in two, knead each piece lightly, flatten out with the floured hand. Press one piece into a greased sandwich tin. Put in the peeled and sliced apples, sugar and cloves. Brush the edges with water and place the second piece of dough on top. Press the edges together.

3. Brush the top with sour milk and dust with a mixture of castor sugar and ground cloves. Bake in a fairly hot oven for about 40 minutes.

POTATO CAKES

$\frac{1}{2}$ lb. cooked potatoes	2 ozs. flour
$\frac{1}{4}$ teaspoonful salt	$\frac{1}{4}$ teaspoonful baking powder
$\frac{1}{2}$ oz. butter or margarine	A little milk

1. Sieve flour, salt and baking powder into a bowl. Add sieved potatoes, and melted butter.

2. Mix to a smooth dough, adding a little milk if necessary.

3. Turn on to a floured board, knead until smooth. Divide in two.

4. Roll out each piece to a circle $\frac{1}{4}$ inch in thickness. Cut into 6 or 8 triangles.

5. Cook on a heated greased heavy pan until nicely browned on both sides.

HOT CROSS BUNS

8 ozs. flour	Pinch of salt
1½ ozs. butter or margarine	½ teaspoonful mixed spice
1 oz. sugar	1 egg
¼ teaspoonful bread soda	About ¼ pint sour milk

1 oz. short pastry (page 174)

1. Sieve flour, salt and bread soda, free from lumps, into a bowl.
2. Rub in the butter, add sugar, spice, and mix well.
3. Mix to a loose dough with beaten egg (keeping back a little) and sufficient milk.
4. Turn on to a floured board, knead lightly. Form into a roll. Cut into even-sized pieces and form each piece into a round bun.
5. Place on a greased tin, brush with beaten egg, cross two ¼-inch wide strips of pastry on top of each bun.
6. Bake in a fairly hot oven for about 20 minutes.

NOTE.—Baking powder and sweet milk may be used instead of bread soda and sour milk ; 2 ozs. prepared currants (page 178) may be added, if liked.

ROCK BUNS

½ lb. flour	Pinch of salt
1 teaspoonful baking powder	3 ozs. butter or margarine
¼ teaspoonful mixed spice	A little nutmeg
3 ozs. sugar	1 egg
1 oz. mixed peel	A little milk

3 ozs. currants

1. Prepare fruit (page 178). Chop peel.
2. Sieve the flour, salt and baking powder into a bowl.
3. Rub in the butter. Add sugar, chopped peel, mixed spice, grated nutmeg and currants. Mix well.
4. Mix to a fairly stiff consistency with a beaten egg, using a little milk if required.
5. Take a piece of the mixture between two forks and pile on a greased tin. Continue until all the mixture is used.
6. Bake in a fairly hot oven for about 20 minutes.

PARIS BUNS

8 ozs. flour	1 teaspoonful baking powder
2 ozs. butter or margarine	1 egg
Pinch of salt	About ¼ pint milk

2 ozs. sugar

1. Sieve flour, baking powder and salt into a bowl.
2. Rub in the butter ; add sugar, mix well.
3. Mix to a loose dough with beaten egg (keeping back a little) and sufficient milk.

4. Turn on to a floured board. Knead lightly. Form into a roll. Cut into even-sized pieces. Knead each piece into a bun.

5. Place on a greased tin, brush over with beaten egg and sprinkle a little coarse sugar on top of each.

6. Bake in a fairly hot oven for about 20 minutes.

COCONUT BUNS

8 ozs. flour	1 teaspoonful baking powder
Pinch of salt	1 egg
3 ozs. butter or margarine	A little milk
3 ozs. sugar	2 ozs. dessicated coconut

1 tablespoonful jam

1. Sieve flour, baking powder and salt into a bowl.

2. Rub in the butter ; add sugar and coconut (keeping back a little) and mix well.

3. Mix to a fairly stiff consistency with well-beaten egg and a little milk.

4. Take a piece of the mixture between two forks and pile on a greased tin. Continue until all the mixture is used.

5. Bake in a fairly hot oven for about 20 minutes.

6. Brush over with jam, dip in coconut.

DOUGHNUTS

$\frac{1}{2}$ lb. flour	1 oz. castor sugar
Pinch of salt	1 teaspoonful baking powder
2 ozs. butter or margarine	A little milk

1 egg

To fry:—Bath of fat.
To coat:—Castor sugar and cinnamon.

1. Sieve flour, baking powder and salt into a bowl.

2. Rub in the butter. Add sugar and mix well.

3. Add beaten egg and sufficient milk to mix to a loose dough.

4. Turn on to a floured board, knead lightly. Roll out to $\frac{1}{2}$ inch in thickness.

5. Stamp into 3-inch rounds. Cut out centre of each with a small cutter.

6. Fry in hot fat 10–12 minutes and drain on kitchen paper.

7. Toss in sugar and cinnamon and serve with the centre piece in each ring.

NOTE.—If jam is required in the doughnuts : Roll out the dough to $\frac{1}{4}$ inch in thickness, stamp into rounds $1\frac{1}{2}$ inches in diameter. Put $\frac{1}{2}$ teaspoonful of jam in the centre of the round of dough, damp around the edges, place another round on top and press the edges together. Cook as above.

GRIZANI ROLLS

1 lb. flour	2 ozs. margarine
2 teaspoonfuls sugar	$\frac{3}{4}$ oz. fresh yeast or
$\frac{1}{2}$ teaspoonful salt	$\frac{1}{2}$ oz. dried yeast (page 179)
3 tablespoonfuls hot water	1 egg
$\frac{1}{4}$ pt. milk	

1. Dissolve the sugar and salt in the hot water. Add the margarine and stir until melted. When lukewarm, mix with the yeast (page 179). Scald the milk (190° F.), cool.

2. Sieve the flour into the bowl. Make a well in the centre and pour in the yeast mixture, beaten egg (keeping back a little to brush over the rolls) and the lukewarm milk. Mix to a loose dough.

3. Relax the dough for about 10 minutes. Knead until smooth. Scale off according to size required, e.g. for Bread Rolls—18–20 pieces. Shape and put on to a greased baking tin.

4. Cover and leave to rise until about double in size. Egg wash and bake in a fairly hot oven for about 20 minutes.

SODA FRUIT CAKE

8 ozs. flour	4 ozs. prepared fruit—
$\frac{1}{4}$ teaspoonful salt	currants and sultanas (page 178)
2 ozs. butter or margarine	About $\frac{1}{4}$ pt. sour milk
2 ozs. sugar	1 teaspoonful treacle
$\frac{1}{8}$ teaspoonful bread soda	

1. Sieve the flour, salt and bread soda, free from lumps, into a bowl.

2. Rub in the butter. Add the sugar and fruit and mix well.

3. Heat milk and treacle, add to the dry ingredients, and mix to a stiff batter.

4. Put into a greased 6″ square tin and bake in a moderate oven for about 45 minutes.

RICHMOND CAKE

$\frac{1}{2}$ lb. flour	$\frac{1}{2}$ teaspoonful baking powder
Pinch of salt	4 ozs. currants
3 ozs. butter or margarine	2 eggs
4 ozs. sugar	A little milk

1. Rub butter into the sieved flour and salt.

2. Add the other dry ingredients and prepared currants (page 178) ; mix well.

3. Add well-beaten eggs and sufficient milk to mix to a stiff batter.

4. Turn into a greased 6″ round tin. Bake in a moderate oven for about three-quarters of an hour.

DINNER BUNS I

1 lb. flour	$\frac{1}{2}$ oz. fresh yeast or
$\frac{1}{2}$ teaspoonful salt	$\frac{1}{4}$ oz. dried yeast (page 179)
$\frac{1}{2}$ oz. margarine	$\frac{1}{2}$ oz. sugar
$\frac{1}{2}$ pt. hot water (a little less)	

1. Dissolve the sugar and salt in the hot water. Add the margarine and stir until melted. When lukewarm mix with the yeast (page 179).
2. Sieve the flour into a bowl. Make a well in the centre and pour in the liquid. Mix to a loose dough. Cover and leave to relax for about 10 minutes.
3. Knead for about 7 minutes. Dredge a little flour under the dough in the bowl, cover with greased polythene or a damp cloth and set to rise in a warm place until double in size. Time 1–1½ hours.
4. Turn the dough on to a lightly floured board, knock-back and leave to relax for 10 minutes.
5. Scale off to required size—about 18–20 pieces. Mould into buns or rolls. Place on a greased tin. Prove for about ½ hour until about double in size.
6. Brush over with beaten egg or milk and bake in a fairly hot oven for about 20 minutes.

DINNER BUNS II

1 lb. flour	About $\frac{1}{2}$ pt. hot water (a little less)
$\frac{1}{2}$ teaspoonful salt	$\frac{1}{2}$ oz. margarine
$\frac{1}{2}$ oz. sugar	1 oz. fresh yeast or
	$\frac{1}{2}$ oz. dried yeast (p. 179)

1. Dissolve the salt and sugar in the hot water. Add the margarine and stir until melted. When lukewarm add the yeast and mix well together.
2. Sieve the flour into a bowl. Make a well in the centre and pour in the yeast mixture. Mix to a fairly loose dough. Cover and leave to relax for about 10 minutes.
3. Knead until smooth. Scale off to required size—about 20 one-ounce pieces. Form into buns or rolls.
4. Place on a greased tin. Prove for about 30 minutes until about double in size.
5. Brush over with beaten egg or milk and bake in a fairly hot oven for about 20 minutes.

YORKSHIRE TEA CAKES

³/₄ lb. flour	About ¼ pt. tepid milk
2 ozs. margarine	½ teaspoonful salt
½ oz. fresh yeast or	1½ ozs. castor sugar
¼ oz. dried yeast (p. 179)	1 egg
⅛ pt. hot water.	2 ozs. cleaned currants

1. Dissolve the salt and sugar in the hot water. When luke-warm mix with the yeast (page 179). ᐟ Scald the milk and cool.

2. Sieve the flour, rub in the margarine. Make a well in the centre of the flour and pour in the yeast mixture, beaten egg and sufficient tepid milk to mix to a loose dough. Cover and leave to relax for about 10 minutes.

3. Knead for about 5 minutes, grease the bowl, put back the dough, cover and set to rise in a warm place until double in size 1–1½ hours.

4. Turn risen dough on to a floured board, knead lightly, then knead in currants. Knead again lightly.

5. Divide into four pieces. Form each into a round flat cake. Place on a greased baking shelf.

6. Leave to prove in a warm place for about 15 minutes. Brush with beaten egg. Bake in a fairly hot oven for about 20 minutes.

7. Serve hot and buttered.

BARM BRACK

1 lb. flour	2 ozs. margarine
½ teaspoonful salt	About ½ pt. milk
2½ ozs. castor sugar	1 egg
3 tablespoonfuls hot water	½ lb. sultanas
³/₄ oz. fresh yeast or	2 ozs. mixed peel
½ oz. dried yeast	

1. Dissolve the salt and sugar in the hot water. When luke-warm mix with the yeast (page 179). Scald the milk and cool.

2. Sieve the flour into a bowl, rub in the margarine. Make a well in the centre of the flour, pour in the yeast mixture, beaten egg and sufficient tepid milk to mix to a stiff batter.

3. Beat for 7 minutes with a wooden spoon, until the mixture is smooth and elastic. Mix in the prepared fruit.

4. Turn into a warm greased tin. Cover with a cloth, place in a warm place to rise until double in size—about 1 hour.

5. Bake in a hot oven for the first 5 minutes. Reduce the heat and cook for about three-quarters of an hour.

6. Put a teaspoonful of sugar and a dessertspoonful of water into a saucepan. Heat until the sugar is melted, and brush the brack over with this syrup. Return to the oven for a few seconds.

VIENNA BREAD

1 lb. flour	½ oz. fresh yeast or
1 teaspoonful sugar	¼ oz. dried yeast (page 179)
½ teaspoonful salt	¼ pt. hot water
1 oz. margarine	¼ pt. milk
	1 egg

1. Dissolve the sugar and salt in the hot water. Add the margarine and stir until melted. Cool. Add the yeast and mix well together. Scald the milk and cool.

2. Sieve the flour into a bowl, make a well in the centre and pour in the yeast mixture, the beaten egg (keeping back a little to brush over the rolls) and the milk. Mix to a loose dough.

3. Beat until the dough leaves the sides of the bowl clean.

4. Cover and leave in a warm place to rise until double in size 1–1½ hours.

5. Turn on to a floured board, knead lightly, leave to relax for 10 minutes. Cut in two, form into long rolls, place on a greased baking sheet. Prove at room temperature for about ½ hour.

6. Brush over with egg wash. Bake in a fairly hot oven for about 20 minutes.

BASIC MADEIRA MIXTURE

I. PLAIN:

4 ozs. castor sugar	2 eggs
4 ozs. butter or margarine	½ teaspoonful baking powder
6 ozs. flour	Flavouring
	About 1 tablespoonful water

II. RICH:

4 ozs. castor sugar	2 eggs
4 ozs. butter or margarine	¼ teaspoonful baking powder
5 ozs. flour	Flavouring
	About 1 tablespoonful water

1. Have the butter or margarine at room temperature. Put it with the sugar into a bowl and beat until white and creamy using a wooden spoon or electric mixer. When using an electric mixer use no raising agent and follow the instructions supplied by the manufacturer because there is danger of overbeating.

2. Beat the eggs and flavouring and add gradually to the creamed butter and sugar. Beat well. If preferred the eggs may be broken and beaten into the mixture one at a time. A little sieved flour may be added between each addition of egg if liked.

3. Fold in the remainder of the flour with a metal spoon, adding a little water if necessary to make to a dropping consistency. Add the baking powder mixed with the last addition of flour.

JAM TARTS

4 ozs. short pastry (page 174)

Filling: Jam.

1. Roll out pastry to ¼ inch in thickness on a floured board. Cut into rounds with a large cutter.

2. Spread a little jam on one half. Brush edge with cold water, fold pastry in two. Press edges together, flake and decorate.

3. Place on a greased tin, bake in a hot oven until lightly browned. Reduce heat and bake for 20 minutes.

QUEEN CAKES

Ingredients and method as for Basic Madeira Mixture. Put the mixture in spoonfuls into well-greased patty tins and bake in a fairly hot oven for about 20 minutes.

FAIRY CAKES

As for Queen Cakes, with the addition of 2 ozs. prepared sultanas (page 178).

CHERRY CAKES

As for Queen Cakes, with the addition of 2 ozs. chopped glacé cherries.

EXCELSIOR CAKES

3 ozs. castor sugar	1 oz. dessicated coconut
3 ozs. butter or margarine	½ teaspoonful Vanilla essence
8 ozs. flour	½ teaspoonful baking powder
1 egg	A little water
A few glacé cherries	

Make and bake as for Queen Cakes, adding flavouring and coconut. Place half a cherry on top of each cake before putting into the oven

CHOCOLATE CAKES

5 ozs. castor sugar	2 eggs
4 ozs. butter or margarine	½ teaspoonful Vanilla essence
6 ozs. flour	½ teaspoonful baking powder
½ oz. cocoa	A little water

Make and bake as for Queen Cakes, sifting the cocoa with the flour.

MADEIRA CAKE

4 ozs. castor sugar	2 eggs
4 ozs. butter or margarine	$\frac{1}{4}$ teaspoonful baking powder
5 ozs. flour	Flavouring
About 1 tablespoonful water	

Make as for Basic Madeira Mixture (page 193). Put into a greased and lined 6-inch round or 8-inch loaf tin (page 216). Bake in a fairly moderate oven for about 1 hour.

SEED CAKE

Make and bake as for Madeira Cake as above, adding $1\frac{1}{2}$ teasp. of carraway seeds.

SULTANA CAKE

4 ozs. castor sugar	2 eggs
4 ozs. butter or margarine	4 ozs. sultanas
6 ozs. flour	Grated rind of half a lemon
$\frac{1}{2}$ teaspoonful baking powder	2 ozs. mixed peel
About 1 tablespoonful water	

Make and bake as for Madeira Cake as above, adding the prepared sultanas, peel and lemon rind. Bake about $1\frac{1}{4}$ hours.

CHERRY CAKE

4 ozs. castor sugar	2 eggs
4 ozs. butter or margarine	$\frac{1}{2}$ teaspoonful baking powder
6 ozs. flour	4 ozs. glacé cherries
About 1 tablespoonful water	

Make and bake as for Madeira Cake as above, adding the cherries cut in halves or quarters. Bake about $1\frac{1}{4}$ hours.

JAM SANDWICH

6 ozs. butter or margarine	6 ozs. castor sugar
3 eggs	7 ozs. flour
Flavouring	$\frac{1}{2}$ teaspoonful baking powder
About 1 tablespoonful water	

Filling: 2 tablespoonfuls jam.

Make as for Basic Madeira Mixture (page 193). Divide equally between two greased 8-inch sandwich tins and bake in a fairly moderate oven for about 20 minutes. When cool, spread each half with jam and sandwich together. Dust the top with castor or icing sugar.

DREAM CAKE

Make and bake as for Madeira Cake (page 195), with the
addition of 2 ozs. chopped walnuts and 4 ozs. glacé cherries.

BIRTHDAY CAKE

8 ozs. castor sugar	6 eggs
8 ozs. butter or margarine	1½ lb. sultanas
14 ozs. flour	4 ozs. mixed peel
¼ teaspoonful baking powder	4 ozs. cherries

About 2 tablespoonfuls sherry

Make as for Madeira Cake (page 195), adding prepared sultanas,
chopped peel and cherries cut in quarters. Bake in a 9-inch round
cake tin for about 3 hours in a slow oven. Ice and decorate as
required.

ATHASSEL CAKE

3 ozs. butter or margarine	¼ teasp. baking powder
3 ozs. castor sugar	½ oz. chocolate powder
2 eggs	¼ teasp. vanilla essence
4 ozs. flour	¼ teasp. almond essence

Few drops of carmine

Raspberry jam

Almond Paste :

2 ozs. ground almonds	1 teasp. sherry
2 ozs. castor sugar	A few drops almond essence

1. Make as for Basic Madeira Mixture (page 193), keeping back
a little of the egg for the almond paste.

2. Divide into three parts. Flavour one part with almond
essence, colour the second part a faint pink with carmine, and add
prepared chocolate (page 177) and vanilla essence to the third part.
Add a little water if necessary to make to a dropping consistency.

3. Put in spoonfuls, varying the colours, into a greased 7-inch
sandwich tin, and bake in a moderate oven for about 25 mins. Cool.

4. When cold, split and spread jam on each cut surface, put the
cake together again.

5. Mix the ground almonds and castor sugar together and
make into a fairly stiff paste with the beaten egg and flavourings.

6. Turn on to a sugared board, knead well and roll out to the
size of the cake.

7. Spread a little jam on the top of the cake, place the almond
paste on top and mark it with a trellis pattern, using the back of
a knife. Decorate the edge.

CHRISTMAS CAKE

½ lb. butter	½ lb. raisins
½ lb. brown or castor sugar	½ lb. sultanas
6 eggs	½ lb. currants
12 ozs. flour	2 ozs. whole almonds
¼ teaspoonful baking powder	¼ lb. mixed peel
½ glass whiskey	2 ozs. cherries
Grated rind of 1 lemon	½ teaspoonful spice
2 ozs. ground almonds	1 chopped apple

1. Prepare fruit (page 178), blanch almonds (page 178), chop and mix well with fruit in a bowl, add spice, ground almonds, lemon rind and chopped peel (page 178) ; mix all thoroughly.

2. Put butter and sugar into a bowl and beat until white and creamy, using a wooden spoon or electric mixer. Beat eggs and add gradually to the creamed butter and sugar. Beat well. Mix in a little flour between each addition of egg if liked.

3. Fold in the remainder of the sieved flour and baking powder, using a metal spoon.

4. Mix in the prepared fruit and half of the whiskey.

5. Turn into a prepared 9-inch tin (page 216), spread with a knife, leaving a slight hollow in the centre.

6. Bake in a slow oven for about 3½ hours. Test with a warm skewer. Lift out of the oven and pour the remainder of the whiskey over.

7. Leave the cake in the tin until cold. Turn out, remove paper and wrap in cooking foil and store until required.

RICH CHRISTMAS CAKE

9 ozs. raisins	3 ozs. ground almonds
9 ozs. sultanas	¼ teaspoonful mixed spice
12 ozs. currants	Grated rind of ½ lemon
6 ozs. mixed peel	9 ozs. butter
3 ozs. prunes	9 ozs. castor sugar
3 ozs. dates	6 eggs
3 ozs. cherries	11 ozs. flour
½ apple	1 glass whiskey
3 ozs. chopped almonds	¼ teaspoonful baking powder

Almond Icing : 1 lb. (page 203).
Water Icing : 6 ozs. (page 204).
Royal Icing : To coat 1 lb. To decorate ½–¾ lb. (page 203).

Make as for Christmas Cake. Put into a prepared 9-inch round or 8-inch square tin. Bake in a slow oven for about 4 hours.

GINGER FRUIT CAKE

4 ozs. butter or margarine	1 tablespoonful golden syrup
3 ozs. sugar	1 teaspoonful ground ginger
6 ozs. flour	$\frac{1}{2}$ teaspoonful baking powder
2 eggs	6–8 ozs. sultanas

Make and bake as for Madeira Cake (page 195), adding golden syrup, ginger, prepared sultanas (page 178). Bake in a 6-inch round tin or an 8-inch loaf tin.

GENOA CAKE

4 ozs. castor sugar	2 eggs
4 ozs. butter or margarine	6 ozs. sultanas
6 ozs. flour	2 ozs. mixed peel
$\frac{1}{4}$ teaspoonful baking powder	2 ozs. cherries
1 oz. split almonds	

Make and bake as for Madeira Cake (page 195), adding prepared sultanas, chopped peel and cherries cut in quarters. Place almonds on top. Bake for about $1\frac{1}{2}$ hours.

GINGERBREAD

8 ozs. flour	1 egg
$\frac{1}{2}$ teaspoonful salt	3 ozs. brown sugar
$\frac{1}{4}$ teaspoonful bread soda	1 tablesp. treacle
1 teaspoonful ground ginger	1 tablesp. golden syrup
3 ozs. butter or margarine	A little sour milk

1. Sieve flour, salt, ginger and bread soda, free from lumps, into a bowl.

2. Melt the butter, treacle, syrup and sugar over a very low heat. Do not allow to become hot, only warm.

3. Add this mixture to the dry ingredients, mixing as for a batter, from the centre to the sides. Add the beaten egg and sufficient milk to make to a dropping consistency.

4. Pour into a well-greased 7-inch tin and bake in a moderate oven for about $\frac{3}{4}$–1 hour.

5. Allow to cool a little in the tin, then turn out and cut into squares.

NOTE.—For richer gingerbread, 2 ozs. sultanas (prepared as on page 178), 1 oz. preserved chopped ginger may be added to the dry ingredients.

SWISS ROLL

3 eggs
3 ozs. sugar
3 ozs. flour

Few drops of flavouring
1/4 teaspoonful baking powder
Jam (heated).

1. Line a Swiss Roll tin (page 216).
2. Whisk eggs and sugar until thick and creamy.
3. Fold in the sieved flour, baking powder and flavouring.
4. Pour into the prepared tin and bake in a moderate oven until set and lightly browned—about 10 minutes.
5. Turn on to a sheet of paper which has been lightly dredged over with castor sugar.
6. Spread with hot jam, and roll up quickly in paper. Place on a wire tray. Leave in the paper until it cools a little, then remove paper and leave to cool. Dust a little castor sugar over.

SPONGE SANDWICH

3 eggs
3 ozs. castor sugar
3 ozs. flour
1/4 teasp. baking powder

A few drops of vanilla essence
Filling:—2 tablespoonfuls jam, cream—whipped, flavoured and sweetened

1. Whisk eggs and sugar until thick and creamy.
2. Fold in the sieved flour, baking powder and flavouring.
3. Divide the mixture between two greased 7-inch sandwich tins. Bake in a moderate oven for about 15 minutes.
4. Turn out on a wire tray. Place another wire tray over and reverse. Leave until cold.
5. Spread each sandwich with jam. Spread whipped cream over one side. Place the other half of sandwich on top. Dredge a little castor sugar or icing sugar over the top.

TEA BRACK

1 lb. mixed dried fruit
1/2 pt. cold tea
6 ozs. brown sugar
2 teasps. baking powder

1 lb. flour
1 egg
1/4 teasp. mixed spice

1. Clean the fruit and put to steep in the cold tea with the brown sugar. Leave overnight.
2. Add the flour, beaten egg, mixed spice and baking powder. Mix well together.
3. Put into a greased lined 8-inch tin. Place a piece of tinfoil on top. Bake in a moderate oven for about 2 hours.

CHOCOLATE BISCUIT CAKE

½ lb. plain chocolate
½ lb. plain sweet biscuits
2 eggs
2 ozs. castor sugar

A few drops of Vanilla Essence
½ lb. margarine
½ oz. dessicated coconut
(or chopped walnuts)

2 ozs. glacé cherries

1. Line a 7-inch cake tin with cooking foil.
2. Break the chocolate into pieces, melt slowly in a cool oven or stand the bowl in warm water.
3. Break the biscuits into small pieces.
4. Beat the eggs, sugar and vanilla essence together. Add the melted tepid margarine in a slow steady stream beating continuously. Add to the chocolate and beat well. Fold in the biscuits and cut cherries.
5. Put into the tin and spread evenly. Sprinkle it with coconut. Cover and put in a refrigerator for about 1 hour or leave in a very cold place to set.

GOLDEN BISCUITS

3 ozs. flour
¼ teaspoonful bread soda
1½ ozs. castor sugar
2 ozs. coconut

2 ozs. flakemeal
3 ozs. margarine
1 tablespoonful golden syrup
1 teaspoonful water

1. Sieve the flour, bread soda and sugar, add the coconut, and flakemeal.
2. Put the margarine, golden syrup and water into a saucepan, heat until the margarine is melted. Pour on to the other ingredients and mix well together.
3. Cool, make into balls the size of a large marble, place on a greased tin, well apart. Flatten a little. Bake in a fairly moderate oven for about 15 minutes.

CHOCOLATE BISCUITS

3 ozs. margarine
3 ozs. castor sugar
1 oz. cocoa

¼ teaspoonful vanilla essence
6 ozs. flour
½ egg

Chocolate coverture

1. Cream the margarine and sugar. Add the cocoa mixed with 1 tablespoonful water and vanilla essence and beat well.
2. Mix in the flour and sufficient beaten egg to made a stiff dough. Knead well, roll out thinly.

3. Stamp into rounds with a 2½" floured cutter. Cut out the centre with a 1" cutter. Knead the pieces left over together, roll out and cut into biscuits as before.

4. Lift on to a greased tin ; bake in a fairly moderate oven for about 20 minutes. Leave to cool on the tin.

5. Cut the chocolate into pieces, put in to a bowl, place over hot water or in a cool oven until melted. Dip the top of each biscuit into the chocolate. Shake off surplus chocolate and leave to set.

WHEATMEAL BISCUITS

4 ozs. wheatmeal flour	4 ozs. margarine
2 ozs. flour	3 ozs. castor sugar
Pinch salt	¼ teaspoonful baking powder
½ egg	

1. Mix the wheatmeal, flour and salt. Rub in the margarine, add the sugar and baking powder and mix well together.

2. Mix to a stiff dough with the beaten egg. Knead well, roll out thinly.

3. Stamp into rounds with a floured cutter. Place on a greased tin and bake in a fairly moderate oven for about 20 minutes.

GINGER BISCUITS

6 ozs. flour	¼ teaspoonful bread soda
4 ozs. castor sugar	2 ozs. margarine
1 teaspoonful ground ginger	1 dessertspoonful golden syrup
½ egg	

1. Put the margarine and golden syrup into a saucepan, heat until the margarine is melted.

2. Sieve the flour, sugar, ginger and bread soda, mix well together. Add the margarine, golden syrup and sufficient beaten egg to form a stiff dough.

3. Cool, make into about twenty balls. Place on a greased tin, well apart. Bake in a fairly moderate oven for about 15 minutes.

FLAKEMEAL CRISPIES

3 ozs. castor sugar	9 ozs. flakemeal
6 ozs. butter or margarine	2 teaspoonfuls golden syrup or honey

1. Cream butter and sugar.
2. Work in the flakemeal, add syrup or honey, and mix well.
3. Spread on a greased tin to ¼ inch in thickness
4. Bake in a fairly moderate oven for about half an hour.
5. Cut into fingers. Allow to cool on tin.

SHORTBREAD

7 ozs. flour
4 ozs. butter

1 oz. rice flour
2 ozs. castor sugar

1. Cream butter and sugar.

2. Work in sieved flour and rice flour. Turn on to a floured board and knead well until free from cracks.

3. Roll out into a round shape about 6 inches in diameter. Pinch the edge. Cut into eight pieces.

4. Place on a greased tin. Prick with a fork.

5. Bake in a fairly moderate oven for about 20 minutes until a pale biscuit colour. Dust a little castor sugar over.

ICINGS

ALMOND PASTE OR ICING

1 lb. ground almonds	2 tablesps. whiskey
1 lb. castor sugar	2 eggs
1/4 teasp. almond essence	1/4 teasp. ratafia essence

1. Crush all the lumps out of the almonds and sieve the castor sugar, mix both well together.

2. Beat the eggs (keeping back a little white of egg), add flavourings and whiskey to them. Pour into the almonds and sugar and mix to a fairly stiff paste.

3. Turn on to a sugared board, knead and roll out. Brush the cake with white of egg and put on the almond paste.

ROYAL ICING—I

1 lb. icing sugar	2 whites of eggs
Juice 1/2 lemon	1/2 teaspoonful glycerine

Sieve the icing sugar. Beat the whites of eggs a little, add half the sugar and beat for about 10 minutes. Cover with a wet cloth and leave to rest. Mix in the remainder of the sugar, strained lemon juice and glycerine. A few drops of water coloured with blue colouring may be added to the icing to improve the colour.

ROYAL ICING—II

1 lb. icing sugar	3 level teaspoonfuls powdered albumen
	3 tablespoonfuls water

Sieve the icing sugar. Put the water into a bowl, sprinkle in the powdered albumen and beat with a fork until frothy. Add half the sugar, beat for about 10 minutes. Cover with a wet cloth and leave to rest. Mix in the remainder of the sugar, adding a little cold water if necessary to obtain the required consistency. A few drops of water coloured with blue colouring may be added to the icing to improve the colour.

WATER ICING

6 ozs. icing sugar   Boiling water

Sieve the icing sugar. Add boiling water slowly until it is of the consistency of thick cream. Put on top of the almond icing and spread over the top and sides. This icing is also used to coat light cakes when suitable flavouring or colouring may be added.

INVALID COOKERY

INVALID and convalescent dishes form a section in cookery which demands careful thought and consideration.

Rules

1. The doctor's orders should be strictly adhered to.

2. The greatest amount of nutriment should be supplied in a relatively small bulk. This aids digestion, which is considerably impaired by illness and confinement to bed.

3. Glass, china and silver should be sparkling.

4. Food for an invalid or convalescent should be prepared in an attractive manner and in small quantities.

5. Vary the diet as much as possible—the same food may be prepared in several ways.

6. Seasoning and flavouring should only be a suggestion in the invalid's food.

7. Greasy foods should never be served ; they are unpalatable, unsightly and indigestible.

8. Serve food punctually.

9. Hot foods should be served hot, cold foods should be cold.

10. The diet should not be discussed with the patient—his likes or dislikes may be ascertained unobtrusively ; an occasional surprise stimulates the appetite.

11. The invalid's tray should contain all the necessary articles but nothing superfluous.

12. On no account should any food be prepared in the sick room ; untouched or left-over food should be removed from the room immediately and put aside in a cool place.

13. In cases of severe illness some nourishing food or beverage should be in readiness, *e.g.*, broth, beef-tea, jelly, barley water, lemonade.

CHICKEN BROTH

1 chicken	1 teasp. pearl barley
2 pints cold water	1 teasp. finely-chopped parsley
Salt	

1. Prepare chicken as on page 86.
2. Remove breasts as for Steamed Breast of Chicken (page 208), and keep for that purpose.
3. Cut remainder of chicken up into joints. Cut each leg into two pieces.
4. Put prepared pieces of chicken, neck, gizzard and heart into a saucepan—cover completely with cold water. Season, if allowed.
5. Cover saucepan with tightly-fitting lid, bring slowly to the boil, skim, simmer gently for about 2 hours. Skim occasionally.
6. Strain, when cold, remove fat from top of broth.
7. Put broth back into saucepan, boil and add blanched barley, simmer until the cereal is cooked.
8. Serve hot, with finely-chopped parsley sprinkled on top.

NOTE.

A.—A yolk of egg may be added to enrich the broth ; pour the broth slowly over the well-beaten egg, whisking all the time.

B.—Vegetables may be added during first cooking of broth.

C.—As a garnish—small dice of chicken flesh may be served in the broth.

BAKED FISH

1 fillet of white fish—about 3 ozs.
Seasoning and lemon juice, if allowed.
A piece of butter.

To serve:—Maître d'Hôtel Butter (page 157).

1. Wash and dry fish. Place on a fireproof dish or plate greased lightly with butter, cover with greased paper.
2. Bake in a moderate oven for 20 minutes, or until fish is tender.
3. Serve on a hot plate with a pat of Maître d'Hôtel Butter on top.

FISH CUSTARD

1 oz. boned and flaked cooked fish	1 egg
Pepper and salt, if allowed	3 tablespoonfuls milk

1. Prepare fish and season it. A few drops of lemon juice may also be sprinkled over, if allowed.
2. Beat egg and add the milk. Add prepared fish to raw custard, mix well. Pour into a small greased bowl. Cover with greased paper and place in a deep tin with hot water coming half-way up the bowl. Cook in a very moderate oven until set, about 25 minutes.
3. Turn on to a hot plate, garnish with a small piece of parsley and serve at once.

STEAMED FISH

A fillet or cutlet of white fish   Lemon juice, if allowed
Pepper and salt

To garnish:—Parsley.

1. Remove skin and bone from the fish. Wash and dry, sprinkle with lemon juice, pepper and salt. Place on a buttered plate, cover with a piece of buttered paper.
2. Cover with another plate, put plates on top of a saucepan of boiling water and cook until the fish loses its transparent appearance and looks white and creamy. Time varies according to thickness of fish—about 15 minutes.
3. Serve fish on a hot plate. Pour over it the liquor which comes from it in cooking. Garnish with parsley.

STEWED FISH

1 fillet plaice or sole—about 3 ozs.   ¼ oz. butter
¼ pint of milk   1 teasp. blended cornflour
                Lemon juice

1. Wash and dry fish. Sprinkle a little lemon juice over, if allowed, and season. Roll up and place in a greased bowl, pie-dish, or fireproof dish, cover with milk, add butter.
2. Cover the bowl with greased paper or put lid on fireproof dish. Cook in a moderate oven until fish is tender—about 15 minutes.
3. Serve the piece of fish on a hot plate ; thicken the liquid with 1 teaspoonful blended cornflour. Boil for about 5 minutes and pour over fish.

CHICKEN CREAM

3–4 ozs. breast of uncooked chicken   Seasoning, if allowed
2 tablespoonfuls cream

1. Remove skin and bone from chicken. Shred finely with a knife. Add seasonings, if allowed.
2. Slightly beat the cream, add chicken, mix well. Put mixture into a well-greased, very small bowl, cover with greased paper and place in a deep tin with hot water coming half-way up the bowl. Cook in a very moderate oven until set, about 25 minutes.
3. Turn on to a hot plate, garnish with a small piece of parsley, and two diamond-shaped pieces of toast.
Veal may be used instead of chicken for this dish.

CHICKEN CUSTARD

Chicken Custard may be prepared in the same way as Fish Custard.—Use 1 oz. of shredded cooked chicken instead of fish. Serve with small fingers of toast.

(See Fish Custard, page 206.)

STEAMED BREAST OF CHICKEN

Breast of chicken	1 tablespoonful milk
Lemon juice	1 tablespoonful water

1. Slit skin along breast bone, and remove flesh from one side. Skin it.

2. Rub over with a little lemon juice, if it is allowed by doctor.

3. Place on a lightly-greased soup plate, add the milk and water ; this will prevent the chicken flesh from becoming dry while steaming.

4. Cover the plate with a saucer or bowl and place over a saucepan of boiling water, steam for about three-quarters of an hour. The water in the saucepan must be kept boiling all the time.

5. Lift on to a clean hot plate, pour liquid from soup plate over. Season with pepper and salt, if allowed.

STEWED SWEETBREAD

1 calf's sweetbread	1 teasp. chopped parsley
Cold water	1 teaspoonful cornflour
½ pint light stock	1 yolk of egg or 1 tablesp.
Seasoning, if allowed	cream

1. Use heart sweetbread if possible, and it must be fresh. Wash the sweetbread, blanch it, remove all skin and fat. Divide into small pieces.

2. Put the prepared sweetbread into a casserole or fireproof dish. Add stock and seasoning, if allowed. Cover.

3. Cook slowly in a moderate oven—1½ hours, until tender. Skim and remove pieces of sweetbread, place on a hot dish.

4. Thicken stock with blended cornflour. Boil 7 minutes. Cool slightly, add cream or yolk of egg and parsley.

5. Pour over the sweetbread, and serve at once. Serve fingers of toast with stewed sweetbread.

STEAMED CHOP

1 centre loin chop
Salt, if allowed
1 tablesp. stock or water

1. Trim, wipe and batten the chop.
2. Place on a greased plate, season if allowed, add stock or water, cover with a piece of greased paper and then with the saucepan lid.
3. Place over a saucepan of boiling water and steam for about 40 minutes.
4. Serve on a hot plate, pour juice over.

OTHER MEAT DISHES SUITABLE FOR INVALIDS

Stewed Tripe
Grilled Chop
Chicken
Boiled Rabbit

See " Meats " for these recipes. Avoid the use of strong stock, onions, turnips, carrots or strong flavourings when preparing these dishes for invalids.

APPLE CREAM

2 apples
2 tablesps. of cream

A squeeze of lemon juice
A little sugar to taste, if allowed

1. Core and bake apples (see page 137). Remove all the pulp and beat until smooth.
2. Add lemon juice and sugar. Mix and beat well. When cold, add cream. Serve in a small glass dish.

STEAMED CUSTARD

1 egg
1 teaspoonful sugar

$\frac{1}{4}$ pint milk
Flavouring

1. Heat the milk, add the sugar and flavouring. Pour on to the beaten egg.
2. Strain into a greased cup or small bowl. Cover with greased paper.
3. Place in a deep tin with hot water coming half-way up the cup or bowl. Cook in a moderate oven until set—about 30–40 mins.
4. Turn on to a hot plate and serve. Fruit, cream or jelly may be served with the custard.

CUP OF ARROWROOT

½ pint of milk   1 teaspoonful sugar
1 teaspoonful arrowroot

1. Blend arrowroot with a little of the milk. Bring the remainder of the milk to the boil, add blended arrowroot, stirring well all the time. Simmer for 10 minutes.

2. Add sugar, stir until dissolved, pour into a heated cup, and serve.

EGG JELLY

½ oz. powdered gelatine   ¾ pint cold water
Rind of 1 lemon   Juice of ½ lemon
2 ozs. sugar   1 tablespoonful sherry or brandy
2 eggs—yolk and whites   (if liked)
   separated from each other

1. Infuse lemon rind in the water, strain, add lemon juice.

2. Cream yolks of eggs and sugar, strain the hot liquid on to them, return to saucepan and cook until the mixture begins to thicken, but do not boil. Stir in the brandy or sherry, if used.

3. Add 2 tablespoonfuls of cold water to the gelatine, leave for a few minutes, until it has absorbed the water. Add to the hot liquid and stir until dissolved.

4. Leave aside until beginning to set. Whisk for a few minutes.

5. Beat whites of eggs until stiff, fold into the mixture.

6. Pour into a wet mould, leave until set. Turn on to a glass dish, and serve.

HONEYCOMB CREAM

1 egg   ¼ oz. powdered gelatine
1 teaspoonful sugar   ¼ pint milk
⅛ pt. cream   A strip of lemon rind
To serve:—Whipped cream.

1. Put milk and lemon rind into a saucepan and leave at the side of the stove to infuse. Lift out the lemon rind.

2. Beat sugar and egg yolk well together. Add slightly-cooled milk to beaten egg yolk, stirring all the time. Cook over a low heat until it coats the back of a wooden spoon.

3. Add 2 tablespoonfuls of cold water to the gelatine, leave for a few minutes until it has absorbed the water. Add to the hot custard and stir until dissolved.

4. Leave in a cold place until beginning to set. Whisk for a few minutes. Fold in the half-whipped cream and lastly the stiffly-beaten egg white.

5. Turn into a small, wet mould and leave until set. Turn on to a glass dish, decorate with whipped cream.

JUNKET

1 pint milk	2 teaspoonfuls sugar
1 teaspoonful rennet	Grated nutmeg

1. Put ½ pint of milk and sugar to heat until sugar is dissolved. Add the other ½ pint of milk and rennet.

2. Pour into a glass dish. Grate a little nutmeg on top and leave in a warm atmosphere until set. Serve with stewed fruit or cream.

NOTE.—If allowed by the doctor, 2 teaspoonfuls of rum or whiskey added to the milk before the rennet, is a great improvement to this dish. Milk must not be warmer than blood heat.

INVALID FRUIT TRIFLE

2 small sponge cakes	1 apple (stewed)

Custard Sauce (page 153)

¼ pt. milk	1 egg yolk
½ teasp. sugar	Flavouring

1 white of egg	1 tablesp. castor sugar

1. Split the sponge cakes. Spread the stewed apple on the bottom layer, replace the top and put them into a pie-dish.

2. Make the custard, when cool pour over the sponge cakes.

3. Beat the white of egg until stiff, fold in the castor sugar. Pile on top of the custard and bake in a cool oven for about ½ hour, until the meringue is crisp.

To serve cold: Make the custard using the whole egg. Prepare the pudding as above, do not bake. Instead of the meringue, decorate with whipped, sweetened and flavoured cream.

BARLEY WATER

1 oz. pearl barley	1 pint cold water
1 teaspoonful sugar	Rind and juice of ½ lemon

1. Wash the barley in cold water, and blanch it (page 217).

2. Put into a saucepan with required amount of water. Add thinly-pared rind of lemon. Bring to simmering point. Simmer 1½–2 hours

3. Strain, add sugar and lemon juice. Serve hot or cold.

NOTE.—If required for the dilution of milk, omit the sugar **and** lemon rind and juice.

If required for infants, use only half the quantity of barley.

ALBUMEN WATER

1 white of egg   Pinch of salt or sugar
1/4 pint cold water

1. Cut through the white of egg with a stainless knife to break up the membrane, allowing as little air as possible to get in. Add the water and sugar, and mix.

2. Strain through muslin. Leave for a few minutes to allow it to go through the muslin. Serve in a glass.

BEEF TEA

1/2 lb. lean beef   Pinch of salt, if allowed
1/2 pint cold water

To serve:—Fingers of toast.

1. Remove skin and fat from meat. Wipe with damp meat cloth. Shred finely with a knife and fork to separate the fibres from the connective tissue.

2. Put into a small bowl. Cover with cold water. Add a pinch of salt, if allowed, stir well ; stand in a cool place for half an hour. Occasionally press meat against side of bowl to extract juice.

3. Cover the bowl with greased paper (greased side up) and stand in a saucepan containing cold water, sufficient to come half way up the bowl.

4. Put a lid on the pan and bring slowly to simmering point. Simmer from 2–2½ hours, stirring the contents occasionally, to prevent meat from forming into a cake.

5. When ready, strain through a coarse strainer. Remove any fat from the surface by drawing a piece of kitchen paper over it. Serve in a hot soup cup with fingers of toast.

RAW BEEF TEA

4 ozs. lean beef   Pinch of salt, if allowed
1/4 pint of cold water

1. Use a knife and fork to shred meat finely. Put into a clean bowl, pour water over, add salt, if allowed. Leave steeping for 2½ or 3 hours. Stir occasionally.

2. Strain, pressing all juice well out of meat. If possible, serve in a red glass.

BLACKCURRANT TEA

½ pint freshly-boiled water   Sugar, if liked
1 tablespoonful blackcurrant jam

1. Put jam into a warm bowl, pour the boiling water over.
Leave at the side of the stove to infuse, or stand bowl with tea in a
saucepan of boiling water for 10 minutes.
2. Strain through fine muslin, and serve in a warm glass. Stand
glass on a small plate. Add sugar, if liked.

EGG FLIP

1 egg (whole or separated)   ¼ pint of milk
1 teaspoonful castor sugar   1 teaspoonful whiskey, brandy,
                                      or other flavouring

1. Heat the milk but do not boil.
2. Beat the egg, sugar and flavouring together.
3. Add the milk to beaten egg, whisking well all the time.
4. Pour into a heated glass, stand the glass on a plate and
serve immediately.
NOTE.—If separating the egg, proceed as above, using yolk only.
Lastly, mix in the stiffly-beaten white.

GRUEL

1 pt. water   1 oz. flakemeal or fine oatmeal
¼ teasp. salt   Sugar

To serve:—Milk.

Put the water and salt into a saucepan, bring to the boil.
Sprinkle in the meal, stirring well. Simmer for about 25 minutes
for flakemeal, and 1½ hours for oatmeal. Add sugar if liked. Strain
and serve in a heated cup.

LEMON DRINK

1 lemon   1½ ozs. sugar
                  ½ pint water

1. Roll lemon lightly on table. Wash or wipe it. Pare off
the rind thinly.
2. Put the water and rind into a saucepan, bring slowly to the
boil and infuse for about 10 minutes.
3. Add the sugar and lemon juice. Stir until dissolved.
4. Strain into a heated glass and serve immediately.

CARRAGEEN DRINK

Pinch of carrageen moss	Sugar
1 pint of milk	Flavouring

Make as for Carrageen Mould (page 123). Strain and serve in a warm glass.

WHEY

Equal parts of sweet and sour milk

Put sweet and sour milk into a saucepan. Bring to the boil. Strain through a very fine strainer or a piece of muslin. Serve in a warm glass.

PRUNE DRINK

$\frac{1}{4}$ lb. prunes	1 pint cold water
About $\frac{1}{2}$ oz. sugar	1 dessertspoonful port wine

1. Steep prunes in warm water for 10 minutes, wash well. Cut each prune into two pieces. Put into a small bowl. Add the pint of cold water, leave steeping for half an hour.
2. Pour into a saucepan, add sugar, stew 25–30 minutes.
3. Strain and add port wine. Serve hot or cold.

PUNCH

Put 2 teaspoonfuls of sugar, $\frac{1}{2}$ glass whiskey and 1 thin slice of lemon into a heated glass. Stir and fill glass up with boiling water. Serve at once.

MISCELLANEOUS

To Chop Suet

1. Remove the skin from the suet and shred finely on chopping board.
2. Sprinkle with some of the flour weighed for the pudding, to prevent the suet sticking to the knife or board.
3. Chop very finely, holding the point of the knife steady on the board and working the handle up and down.

To Chop Parsley

1. Remove the stalks, wash parsley well.
2. Put into a clean cloth and squeeze tightly.
3. Put on a chopping board, chop finely with a long pointed knife, keeping the point on the board with the left hand and working the handle up and down with the right hand. A parsley chopper may be used.
4. Put on to a plate and leave in a warm place to dry.

Butterfly Lemon Garnish

1. Cut off the end of the lemon, slice thinly.
2. Serrate the edge, if liked, with a small pointed knife.
3. Cut the slice of lemon in two, then cut each half again, leaving the centre pith to form a hinge.
4. Open into a butterfly shape.

Melba Toast

Use a sliced panloaf. Toast each slice quickly to a golden brown colour on both sides under a hot griller. Cut off the crusts and split the toast. Reduce the heat and toast the cut sides more slowly, to dry out and make golden brown. If liked they may be placed on a baking tray with the cut side up and put into a cool oven to dry out. The toast will curl, giving the characteristic shape of Melba Toast.

Fried Croûtons of Bread

1. Use sliced panloaf. Cut off the crusts from a few slices. Cut the slices into strips $\frac{1}{4}$ inch in thickness and the strips into $\frac{1}{4}$ inch dice.
2. Fry in hot fat until a golden brown colour. Drain well and serve.

To Make Dried Browned Crumbs

1. Put crusts of bread on to a tin and leave in a cool oven until dry and crisp.
2. Crush with a rolling pin.
3. Put through a fine sieve and store in an air-tight tin.

To Beat Whites of Eggs

Make sure that the bowl and whisk are absolutely free from grease. Any trace of yolk must be removed before beating because of the fat in the yolk. Beat until they are stiff and stand in points but are not dry. An electric mixer may be used, but be careful not to overbeat.

To Whip Cream

1. Put into a clean, dry bowl, whisk until fairly thick, then whip more slowly to prevent over-whipping, as the cream thickens very quickly when it reaches this stage.
2. Flavour and sweeten.
3. For piping purposes, the cream should stand in little points if the beater is raised out of it.

To Line a Round Tin

1. For light cakes line the tin with one layer of greaseproof paper. For rich fruit cakes, where they will be in the oven for some time, one layer of brown paper and one of greaseproof is generally used.
2. Mark out the circumference of the tin on the paper. Cut a round of paper inside this marking.
3. Next cut a strip of paper 1 inch deeper than depth of tin and 2 or 3 inches longer than the circumference.
4. Fold one edge of the strip over 1 inch, cut folded-in edge on the slant, having 1 inch between the cuts.
5. Grease the tin. Put in paper, having the cut edge lying flatly on the bottom of the tin, and the ends overlapping.
6. Place the round of paper into the bottom of the tin, and grease all over.

To Line a Flat Tin

Place tin on a sheet of greaseproof paper, and mark size of tin. Cut out, allowing sufficient paper to come up the side of the tin. Crease along line marking size of tin. Snip into the mark at corners. Put into the greased tin, overlapping corners, grease paper.

Seasoned Flour

| 1 oz. flour | ½ teaspoonful salt | Pinch of pepper |

Mix well together.

To Clarify Butter or Margarine

Put the butter or margarine and a little water into a saucepan and heat slowly until still. Strain through muslin or fine mesh strainer keeping back the sediment.

To Cook Macaroni

1. Break the macaroni into 1 inch pieces.
2. Put into a saucepan containing plenty of boiling salted water.
3. Boil until soft, about 15 minutes.

To Boil Spaghetti

Cook as for macaroni, but do not break into pieces.

To Boil Rice for Curry

1. Have a pot of boiling water ready, add salt (1 dessertsp. salt to 1 quart water).
2. Put in the rice and boil rapidly until the grains of rice are soft. Time—17 minutes.
3. Drain in a colander or hand sieve. Pour boiling water over the rice. Shake well and serve.

To Prepare a Pudding Cloth

1. Dip the cloth into boiling water and wring out as much water as possible. Grease.
2. Sprinkle lightly with flour to form a paste, which will prevent the water getting into the pudding.

To Blanch :—To put into cold water and bring to the boil. Place the saucepan under the cold tap and let the water run slowly into the saucepan until the contents are quite cold. Drain.

JULIENNE STRIPS

4 ozs. carrot   2 ozs. white turnip

Cut off the tops and roots from the vegetables. Wash well, using a vegetable brush. Scrape the carrot. Peel the white turnip thickly. Cut the vegetables into match-like strips. Cook in boiling salted water until tender. Drain.

CARVING
of Meat, Poultry, Game and Fish

GENERAL RULES

1. A general knowledge of the bone structure is necessary.

2. Before cooking, do as much preparation as possible without spoiling the appearance of the meat.

3. The dish on which the joint is served should be large enough to do the carving at ease, and to hold a certain amount of the slices.

4. If the carving is to be done at the table, the dish must be placed in the right position, and the carver's chair must be high enough to facilitate his doing the work with ease.

5. Meat is generally carved across the grain.

6. The carving must be neat, and the slices straight and uniform, not jagged. Bad carving is most wasteful.

7. In distributing the slices, the different cuts must be shared out fairly.

METHODS FOR CARVING

BEEF

When preparing sirloin or ribs of beef for roasting, the following will greatly facilitate carving :

(a) For sirloin—saw through the bone at either side of the back-bone cavity (see diagram page 219).

(b) For ribs of beef—saw through the back-bone cavity about 1 inch from the rib bone (see diagram page 219).

(c) Before dishing, remove the loosened bones from the joints.

Sirloin

Invert the joint. Carve the undercut (or fillet) in slices of medium thickness down to the bone. Slip the knife underneath and detach the slices from the bone. Now replace the joint as it was served, and slice the head and tailpiece down fairly thinly, starting at the near side. Insert the knife and run it along between the bone and meat to detach the slices.

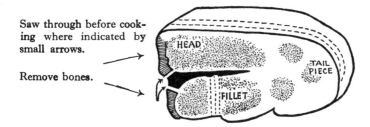

Saw through before cooking where indicated by small arrows.

Remove bones.

Ribs of Beef

First, insert the knife between the meat and the bone, and run it along from end to end of joint. Cut long fairly thin slices the whole length of the joint.

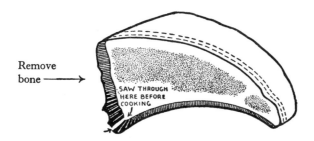

Remove bone

Rolled Ribs

First make the top surface even by removing a fairly thick slice with a well-sharpened knife. Then carve the remainder in fairly thin, even slices right across the joint.

Ox Tongue

About 4 inches from the top of the tongue make a deep cut. This is the choicest portion of the tongue. Then, cut slices from each side. Serve a small portion of the fat from the root end with each portion.

MUTTON AND LAMB

Leg of Mutton

Serve with the small end to the left side of the dish. Insert the fork in the thick part of the shank end, and, raising the joint towards you, remove a wedge-shaped slice, carve several medium-thick slices down to the bone, as in diagram from A to B. Detach the slices from the rest by slipping the knife underneath. Serve a small piece of fat, which lies under the thick part, with each portion.

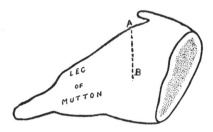

Loin of Mutton or Lamb

Have this cut disjointed beforehand by the butcher. Insert the knife between the bones and carve right through, separating the chops. All chops should be uniform and of moderate thickness. If the kidney is included in the joint, serve a piece with each chop.

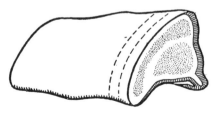

Saddle of Mutton

The saddle is the complete loin from both sides of the animal. This is one of the joints where the carving may be done with the grain of the meat. Firmly insert the fork into the centre of the joint, and carve slices parallel with the backbone. Detach the slices from the ribs. If the slices are too long, divide into two or three pieces. Cut the thin part or crisp in the opposite direction, and serve a piece with each helping.

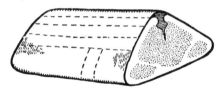

Shoulder of Mutton

Serve with the skin side uppermost on the dish. Insert the fork in the fleshy part, and raise up the joint slightly from the dish. Carve downwards right to the bone from A to B, and with the point of the knife detach the slices. Next, turn upwards the part that was resting on the dish, while the upper part was being carved, and slice downwards to the bone. Detach the slices. Now, invert the joint and carve off slices from the lean, juicy meat lying underneath.

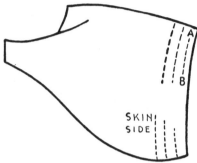

Forequarter of Lamb

In carving this joint, the shoulder must first be " raised " from the joint. This is done by inserting the fork in the fleshy part of the shoulder, and cutting round with the knife as in the diagram at A. Then the shoulder is raised up with the fork and cut away, leaving as much meat as possible underneath. This part of the joint is usually kept to be served cold, and is carved in the same manner as the foregoing joint—Shoulder of Mutton. Then, remainder is carved as follows : the breast part is separated from the ribs by cutting right through, as at B—C, and then slicing downwards. The ribs are carved by separating one from the other, as for loin of mutton (D—E in diagram). A piece of each should comprise each helping.

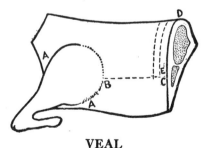

VEAL

Loin of Veal

If small, follow method for carving Loin of Mutton. If large, use method for Ribs of Beef.

Fillet of Veal

Carve in the same way as Leg of Mutton.

If boned and rolled, follow method for carving Rolled Ribs of Beef.

Knuckle of Veal

Same method as Leg of Mutton.

PORK

Loin of Pork

This is carved in the same way as Loin of Mutton. Serve a piece of " crackle " with each helping.

Leg of Pork

Carved in the same way as Leg of Mutton. Serve some of the ' crackle " or crisp, as well as some stuffing, with each portion.

Ham

Make a cut into the centre of the thick part right down to the bone, and carve thin slices from each side. Serve a piece of fat with each portion.

Or

A more economical method : With the fork firmly inserted into the thick part, cut off thin slices, starting at the shank end and working towards the thick end.

GAME AND POULTRY

A meat carver is of little use for carving game or poultry, as it is too long and pliable. There is a special knife for the purpose—a Game or Poultry carver. If you haven't one of these, use a sharp-pointed cook's knife, one with a short stiff blade.

To Carve a Chicken or Fowl

Keep to the following order :—

(*a*) *To remove the Wing.*—Judging the position of the wing joint, and holding the outer part of the wing with the fork, cut through the outer layer of the breast as in diagram. Gently, but firmly ease the wing away from the joint, and cut through the cartilage.

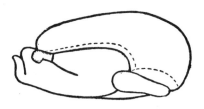

(b) *To remove the Leg.*—Hold the blade of the knife firmly against the bird above the leg, then using the fork, prise the leg outward, thereby exposing the thigh joint. Sever the leg with one clean cut of the knife, using the point.

(c) *To disjoint the Leg.*—Cut through the joint of the leg. If the bird is large the meat on the thigh may be carved.

(d) *To carve the Breast.*—Carve this parallel to the breastbone in thin uniform slices, carving a piece of stuffing with each slice.

(e) Repeat with the other half of the chicken. Serve the remainder of the stuffing with a spoon. Then remove the wishbone, and carve away the piece of the breast thus exposed.

(f) Turn the carcase over, and using the point of the knife, detach the oyster pieces which lie near the centre of the backbone.

Turkey

Follow method for carving fowl. If the whole bird is not required, first carve some slices from the breast. Then remove wing and leg from the same side as in previous method. Disjoint the thigh from the drumstick in the same way, and carve slices from the thigh, as this would make too large a portion by itself. Serve a small quantity of stuffing to each person.

Goose

First, carve the breast, beginning at the wing end, carving thin parallel slices, and continue to the breast-bone. Detach slices from bone altogether by slipping the knife underneath. Then remove the legs and wings by method given in carving a fowl.

Duck

Follow method given for Roast Goose.

Pigeon

Divide the bird right down the middle, lengthwise, and if these portions are too large, they may be cut across in halves again.

Partridge and Grouse

These may be divided in the same way as pigeon, or by this method :—Sever the legs and wings from the bird with some of the breast adhering, then detach the breast neatly, from the carcase. Each bird usually gives two or three portions.

Small Game Birds—*e.g.*, snipe, are served whole.

FISH

A steel knife should not be used to divide fish, as it is apt to spoil the flavour. Silver or plated fish servers are sold for the purpose, but a fish knife and fork may be used if the carvers are not available. In serving fish, care must be exercised to avoid breaking up the portions.

Salmon or Cod

Remove all the skin from one side. Make an incision from head to tail of fish, as in diagram, and carve rather thick slices from each side of incision right down to centre bone. Detach from bone by slipping the knife underneath. When this side is finished, remove the bone, and divide the lower portion in the same way.

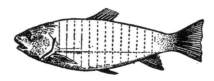

Turbot and Brill

Make an incision right down to the bone from head to tail as indicated in diagram. Now slice across from the centre to each side of the fish in fairly thick pieces, and then slip the knife underneath to detach them from the bone. Remove the bone, and divide the second side in the same manner.

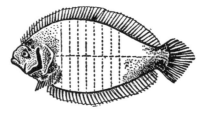

Sole

Make an incision down centre from head to tail. Carefully detach the fillet from each side. Remove the bone, and divide the other side into two fillets.

Plaice

If small, follow method given for division of sole ; if large, divide as for Turbot and Brill.

Small Fish

Serve whole, or simply cut in two pieces.

What we should eat, and why

FOOD is essential to the body :—
1. For the growth, maintenance and repair of the body tissue,
2. To supply energy.

Food is divided into the following classes :—
1. Proteins.
2. Carbohydrates and Vegetable Fibre.
3. Fats.
4. Minerals.
5. Vitamins.
6. Water.

1.—Proteins

Proteins are the most important constituents of food, because not only do they provide heat and energy but they alone can supply the material necessary for the repair of the body's framework, therefore protein foods are irreplaceable.

Since human protein differs from animal protein, and even more so from plant protein, it is recommended that we should take at least 50% of the daily intake in animal protein or, as it is usually called, first-class protein. If, however, for reasons of economy, one wishes to cut down the expenditure on protein food, one must always remember that this amount of animal protein is essential and must be included in the daily diet.

Sources of Protein :—

First Class Protein :—meat, fish, milk, eggs, cheese.
Second Class Protein :—peas, beans, lentils, potato and cereals.

2.—Carbohydrates

These are the most abundant and cheapest constituents of any diet. A certain amount of carbohydrate is essential for the health of the body, and excess is stored as fat.

Sources of Carbohydrate:—All sugar foods, *e.g.*, sugar, jam, sweets of all kinds, honey, etc. Starches, *e.g.*, cereals, bread, potatoes, pulses and other vegetable foods.

Vegetable Fibre or Cellulose

Cellulose is the name given to the indigestible fibre of fruits and vegetables. A certain amount is necessary to form bulk in the intestine and so help to stimulate the gut movements, which propel the food through the intestinal canal. Many modern foods, *e.g.*, white flour, have this roughage removed by fractionation.

3.—Fats

These are highly valuable fuel foods, as weight for weight, fat has more than double the fuel value of starch or sugar. Any reserve of fat is stored in the body in the form of adipose tissue, which helps to protect the delicate internal organs, and to insulate the body against heat loss.

Sources of Fat:—Butter, cream, meat (particularly pork and bacon), oily fish, cheese and oils.

4.—Minerals

These act as regulators of the various body processes. They are present in all foods of animal and plant origin, but vary greatly in amount—some foods being deficient in one or more, *e.g.*, no iron in milk. Their presence in the diet must always be ensured by careful planning and including daily some mineral-rich foods. Calcium, iron and iodine are the minerals which are most often deficient in the diet.

Sources of Iron:—Organ meats, muscle meats, eggs and wholegrain cereals.

Sources of Calcium:—Milk, cheese, green vegetables.

Iodine:—In areas where there is deficiency of iodine, iodised salt should be used.

5.—Vitamins

These are organic substances found in very small quantities in foods, which, though not contributing any appreciable energy, are vital for growth and normal metabolism. A diet which is lacking or deficient in vitamins causes disorders affecting the general development of the body, especially growth, development of teeth and bone, mucous membrane, joints and nervous system. All are essential, but some are often lacking in the diet, and these only, therefore, are considered here.

They are divided into two classes :—

    (1) Fat-Soluble Vitamins—A, D, E, K.

    (2) Water-Soluble—Aneurin or Thiamine, Riboflavin, Nicotinic Acid and Ascorbic Acid, or as it is more commonly known, Vitamin C.

Vitamin A

This vitamin is closely related to carotene—the yellow colouring in carrots and oranges—sunlight is necessary for its formation in the plant. It is stored in the liver of animals, especially of certain fishes. It is not impaired by ordinary cooking (since it is insoluble in water), nor is there any great loss if the food is canned or tinned.

Vitamin A is necessary for growth and general development especially of skin, mucous membrane and central nervous system. A deficiency of Vitamin A leads to night blindness, and lessens the resistance to infection, *e.g.*, infection of nose, throat, etc.

Sources of Vitamin A :—Liver, cod liver oil, halibut liver oil, butter, vitaminized margarine, cheese, eggs, milk, tomatoes, carrots, spinach, cabbage, peas and beans.

Vitamin D

This vitamin is usually found in association with Vitamin A, and like it, it is not impaired by ordinary cooking since it is not soluble in water. Deficiency causes rickets in children, osteomalacia in adults.

Sources of Vitamin D :—Cod liver oil, herrings, mackerel, sardines, tinned salmon, eggs, butter, cheese and milk.

Aneurin

This Vitamin is stable to ordinary boiling temperatures. A minor deficiency gives rise to neuritis, loss of appetite, nervous depression and constipation.

Sources of Aneurin :—Widely distributed in animal and plant worlds. It is present in yeast, whole grain cereals, liver, pork and pulses.

Riboflavin

This vitamin is resistant to the ordinary heat of cooking. Deficiency causes eye sensitivity and cracking round the corners of the mouth and nose.

Sources of Riboflavin :—Present in liver, dairy produce except butter, fresh fruit and vegetables.

Nicotinic Acid

Like Riboflavin, this vitamin is resistant to the ordinary heat of cooking. Mild forms of deficiency result in sores on skin and tongue, diarrhoea and other digestive disorders.

Sources of Nicotinic Acid :—Yeast, liver, whole cereals, green vegetables and meat.

Ascorbic Acid or Vitamin C

This vitamin is not stable to heat and is very soluble in water. The amount destroyed depends on the rapidity of the cooking, and on the amount of water used. The usual time for boiling destroys 40–50% of the vitamin, but even more—sometimes 90%— is lost through dissolving out into the cooking water. This loss is much increased if the solution is alkaline, it is not so easily lost if the solution is acid. There is considerable loss on slicing food. Any metal except aluminium, and especially copper, accelerates the destruction.

A marked deficiency of Ascorbic Acid leads to scurvy. A minor deficiency gives rise to susceptibility to infection and a condition in which there is a tendency to bleeding.

Sources of Ascorbic Acid :—Potatoes and greens, citrous fruits, blackcurrants and rose-hips.

6.—Water

Water is absolutely essential to the health of the body. A human being can live for a considerable time—about 70 days, on water alone, without any food ; but he cannot exist for long without water—not more than 3 days. Water is necessary for the various physiological activities of the body, and it assists in regulating the body temperature.

Water is present in all solid foods, the actual water content of some foods is very high, *e.g.*, most fruits and vegetables contain 90% water. In addition to this water obtained from his food, the adult requires from 2½–3 pints of water or other beverage daily.

Calories and the Diet

We have said that food provides heat and energy. This heat can easily be measured by burning the food and measuring the quantity of heat evolved. The unit used is called the Calorie. In this way it is found that

1 gram of Protein when burned yielded 4 Calories.

1 gram of Carbohydrate when burned yielded 4 Calories.

1 gram of Fat when burned yielded 9 Calories.

Water, vegetable fibre and vitamins were found to provide no Calories when burned.

A Calorie is the amount of heat required to raise the temperature of 1,000 grams (2¼ lbs.) of water 1° Centigrade, *e.g.*, one would require 1 Calorie to raise the temperature of 2¼ lbs. of water from 10° Centigrade to 11° Centigrade.

1 gram of Protein when burned raises the temperature of 2¼ lbs. of water 4° Centigrade, but 1 gram of Fat when burned raises the

temperature of the same quantity of water 9° Centigrade, showing, as mentioned already, that fat provides $2\frac{1}{4}$ times as much heat as protein or carbohydrate.

The contents of the cells of the human body are continually burning away. The heat produced during their combustion is used by the body to keep itself warm and also to provide energy for its work. This heat is measured in Calories. It is obvious, therefore, that if the body is to keep going it must get a continual supply of calories, just as a motor car requires petrol. It is clear also that:

(i) the amount of Calories required varies with the temperature of the body's surroundings.

(ii) that the amount depends also on the body's activity.

A man of average size lying in bed needs far less Calories than when he is at work. If he is a manual labourer the difference will be very great. It has been calculated experimentally that such a man, *e.g.*, a stone-mason, would require 1,800 Calories daily, when lying in bed, but if at work he would require 4,000 Calories daily.

Similarly, a very active schoolboy requires more than a lazy schoolboy.

Since Calories are got from our food, the individual should only consume the amount which provides his Calorie requirement. If he consumes more he will store it as fat, if less he will get thin. In the case of the stone-mason he should take 4,000 Calories daily ; if he takes 5,000 daily he will get fat, and if he takes 3,000 he will waste away.

In planning a diet the first thing that must be done is to determine the daily Calorie requirement of the individual, and then supply the equivalent in food. Since the composition of each common food has been determined, if we know the amount of food consumed we can easily determine the number of Calories supplied, *e.g.*, 1 oz. of white bread contains 16·2 grams of Carbohydrate, 2·4 grams of Protein and 0 grams of Fat.

$$16\cdot2 \text{ grams of Carbohydrate provide} \quad 16\cdot2 \times 4 = 64\cdot8 \text{ Calories.}$$
$$2\cdot4 \text{ grams of Protein provide} \quad 2\cdot4 \times 4 = 9\cdot6 \quad \text{,,}$$
$$\text{therefore 1 oz. of bread provides } 56\cdot8 + 9\cdot6 = 66\cdot4 \quad \text{,,}$$

The Calorie requirements for different sexes, different ages, and different occupations are :—

An active man requires about	3,000 Calories.
A man leading a sedentary life requires about	2,500 ,,
An active woman requires about	2,500 ,,
A woman leading a sedentary life requires about	2,100 ,,
Youth 16–20 years of age requires about ..	3,800 ,,
Youth 12–16 years of age requires about ..	3,200 ,,
Girl 16–20 years of age requires about ..	2,400 ,,
Girl 12–16 years of age requires about ..	2,800 ,,
Child aged 10 years requires about ., ..	2,500 ,,

An Ideal Diet

A dietary to maintain a man in health and efficiency must fulfil the following requirements :—

1. It must have a sufficient calorific value.

2. It must contain proteins fats and carbohydrates. The quantity of each of the first two should be not less than 70 grams per day. The protein should contain a certain amount of animal protein.

3. It should contain a certain proportion of fresh foods such as green vegetables, meat and eggs, and in the case of children, milk, in order to supply the necessary accessory food substances.

4. It must contain a proper proportion of minerals, especially sodium, calcium, iron.

5. It must be palatable—appetite is an essential factor for the secretion of the digestive juices, and therefore for the digestion and assimilation of the food, so that good cooking becomes an important condition for the maintenance of health. The use of various flavouring agents and condiments is therefore physiologically justified.

Explanation of French Terms used in Cookery

à la :—according to the style of.

au gratin :—applied to a dish which has been covered with sauce, sprinkled with breadcrumbs or grated cheese, then browned in the oven or under a grill, and served in the dish in which it is cooked.

au naturel :—applied to food served uncooked, or very plainly and simply prepared.

Baba :—small yeast sponge cake soaked in syrup flavoured with rum or any other flavouring.

Bain-Marie :—a vessel containing about 3–4 inches hot water in which saucepans of food can be kept hot.

Bavaroise :—a rich cream mixture, usually half custard and half cream mixed.

Beignet :—type of fritter.

Bisque :—soup made from shell-fish.

Blanch :—Put into cold water and bring to boiling-point, then pour off this water. This is done to whiten, to cleanse, to remove skin from nuts or to remove strong flavour.

Bouquet garni :—bunch of herbs with other flavourings tied together (page 18).

Canapé :—rounds or fancy shapes of bread, toast, etc., on which small savouries are served.

Cassolette :—a small case made of potato purée for holding mince, etc.

Croissants :—crescents or horse-shoe shapes of rich yeast bread.

Croquette :—minced meat, game, potatoes, etc., coated with egg and crumbs and then fried.

Croustade :—a case of fried bread or pastry used for holding various savoury fillings.

Croûte :—thick slice of fried or toasted bread.

Croûtons :—fried dice or fancy shapes of bread.

Dartois :—a sandwich of a very light pastry with sweet or savoury filling inside.

En :—served in.

Entrée :—a meat dish which is complete in itself served after the fish course in a dinner.

Flan :—an open case of pastry.

Foie-gras :—preparation of goose liver.

Fricassée :—a white stew of chicken, rabbit or veal to which cream is often added.

Galantine :—a roll of meat or poultry without bone, pressed, glazed and decorated.

Gâteau :—a cake, or a dish made in the form of a cake.

Gelée :—jelly.

Hors d'oeuvre :—small tasty morsels of cold food served at the beginning of the meal as appetisers.

Kromeskis :—mixture of meat or any other savoury wrapped in bacon, dipped in batter and then fried.

Liaison :—binding or thickening used for soups and sauces.

Macédoine :—mixture of vegetables or fruit cut in dice or fancy shapes.

Marinade :—a mixture of vinegar or lemon juice, oil, flavourings and seasonings in which fish or meat is soaked before cooking to give additional flavour.

Menu :—bill of fare.

Mirepoix :—a mixture of vegetables and seasonings used as foundation for braising.

Mousse :—a very light and spongy sweet or savoury dish.

Mousseline :—a sauce of froth-like lightness.

Panada :—mixture of butter, flour and a liquid used for binding, or as a foundation for soufflé mixtures.

Purée :—smooth mixture of meat, fish, vegetables, or fruit, which has been reduced to a pulp and then sieved.

Quenelle :—a smooth mixture of fish, meat or poultry shaped with a spoon and poached.

Ragoût :—a rich type of stew.

Rechauffé :—re-heat of fish, meat, or vegetables.

Rissole :—mince of cooked fish or meat coated with egg and bread-crumbs and then fried.

Roux :—equal quantities of butter and flour cooked over the fire for 3 minutes, and not allowed to colour unless wanted for a brown mixture. It is used for thickening soups and sauces.

Sauté-pan :—a shallow stewpan.

Sauté :—toss over the fire in a small quantity of fat, until nicely browned.

Savarin :—a light yeast pudding.

Soufflé :—a very light mixture which is generally obtained by the addition of stiffly-beaten whites of eggs.

Dinner Menus
for Special Occasions

Recipes which are not found in this book are available in
ALL IN THE COOKING, Book II.

Consommé à l'Italienne	Cream of Mushroom
Saute of chicken with mushrooms Boiled Rice Buttered Peas	Baked Ham with Pineapple Baked Potatoes Sweet Corn
Trifle	Cream Caramel
Cream of Artichoke	Cream of Celery
Escalope of Veal Viennoise Maitre d'hotel Potatoes Creamed Spinach	Roast Duck, Apple Sauce Delmonico Potatoes Green Salad
Lemon Chiffon Pie	Strawberry Mousse
Prawn Cocktail	Chilled Melon
Cream of Asparagus	Salmon Mayonnaise
Boiled Salmon, Parsley Sauce New Potatoes Buttered French Beans	Roast Lamb, Mint Sauce New Potatoes Buttered Peas
Vanilla Bavarois	Pineapple Souffle
Grapefruit Cocktail	Smoked Salmon
Almond Cream Soup	Clear Soup
Roast Turkey, Baked Ham Potato Croquettes Buttered Sprouts Stewed Celery	Chicken Maryland Scalloped Potatoes Buttered Peas
Plum Pudding, Brandy Sauce Fresh Fruit Salad	Banana Chartreuse

233

Everyday Dinner Menus

Mixed Vegetable Soup	Lentil Soup
——	——
Mock Duck, Apple Sauce Roast Potatoes Buttered Leaf Spinach	Whiting in Batter, Dutch Sauce Potato Chips Cauliflower au gratin
——	——
Caramel Semolina	Sago Plum Pudding, Whiskey Sauce
Fresh Grapefruit	Mutton Broth
——	——
Brown Stew with Carrots Creamed Potatoes	Boiled Bacon, Parsley Sauce Boiled Potatoes Buttered Cabbage
——	——
Queen of Puddings	Eve's Pudding, Cream or Custard Sauce
Potato Soup	Green Pea Soup
——	——
Roast Beef, Horseradish Sauce Yorkshire Pudding Roast Potatoes Buttered Sprouts	Boiled Mutton, Caper Sauce Steamed Potatoes Mixed Root Vegetables
——	——
Moss Creams	Apple and Rice Meringue
Cauliflower Soup	Leek and Potato Soup
——	——
Beefsteak and Kidney Pie Baked Potatoes Buttered Turnips	Fried Fish, Parsley Sauce Potato Croquettes Buttered Mushrooms
——	——
Stewed Fruit, Baked Custard	Steamed Marmalade Pudding Marmalade Sauce

Florida Cocktail	Tomato Soup
—	—
Irish Stew	Cod au gratin Duchesse Potatoes Buttered Peas
—	—
Apple Pie, Custard Sauce	Lemon Meringue Pie

French Onion Soup	Tomato Soup
—	—
Blanquette of Lamb Duchesse Potatoes or Boiled Rice Buttered French Beans	Roast Chicken, Bread Sauce Creamed Potatoes Buttered Greens
—	—
Fruit Flan	Apple Snow

ALPHABETICAL INDEX

CLASSIFIED INDEX

THEORY INDEX

NOTES

NOTES

NOTES

NOTES

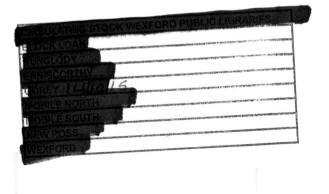